This book is dedicated to my friends from across the years, and to the Readers who would appreciate a little help.

Copyright 2021 by George Gilmore
The Bullsheet LLC

All rights reserved in the
United States of America and World-wide

The cover design is by George Gilmore from a drawing by his daughter.

Registered Trademark: The Bullsheet

THE BULLSHEET™

Building Great Relationships in the New Age

Chapter 1	The 3 Questions	5
Chapter 2	My Friend - Our Typical Guy	11
Chapter 3	Introduce Myself	19
Chapter 4	The Generations	29
Chapter 5	Women	39
Chapter 6	The New Age	51
Chapter 7	An Ideal Partner	63
Chapter 8	Be a Complete Person	74
Chapter 9	Are You Indoctrinated For Marriage?	86
Chapter 10	Starting Out	93
Chapter 11	A Good Attitude	104
Chapter 12	Meeting Someone You Like That Likes You	117
Chapter 13	Make Yourself More Interesting	126
Chapter 14	Different Creations	138
Chapter 15	The Art of Dating	149
Chapter 16	Sex	164
Chapter 17	Attachment	176
Chapter 18	Warning Signs	185

Chapter 19	Don't Lose Your Money	193
Chapter 20	Everyone's Emotional	204
Chapter 21	Danger	224
Chapter 22	The Green-Eyed Monster	238
Chapter 23	Lying	248
Chapter 24	It's Over	259
Chapter 25	Letting Go	267
Chapter 26	The House Party	276
Chapter 27	Should You Get Married, and When?	285
Chapter 28	Meditation	298
Chapter 29	A Happy Marriage	310
Chapter 30	Today and Tomorrow	327

THE 3 QUESTIONS

Chapter 1

The Bullsheet is about enjoying life, building great relationships, and learning to trust your intuition. It is a book for Women and Men of all ages, but the 3 Questions are from a young man looking for love. All of us have questions about relationships and the Modern World.

It has taken a lot longer than I thought to write this book. What at first seemed straightforward is not. People, life, and relationships are complicated.

The past 7 years has allowed us see the rise of new Movements, Coronaviris, greater awareness of Respect, and that many people are far removed from Nature. The World keeps presenting new events and new outlooks, but human nature remains the same.

Each person needs to adjust to their current situation. We have hope, but we might need to change the way we do things.

"Hope is not the conviction that something will turn out well. Hope is the certainty that something is worth doing no matter how it turns out."
Vaclav Havel, former President of Czech Republic

THE TYPE
BOLD – The bold is The Bullsheet. It is a combination of my experience, things learned, Real Talk, an attempt at the Truth, what might happen to a person, and what does happen

to some people. Some words are capitalized for emphasis, or it is the topic of a chapter.

ITALICS – Quotations and Definitions – When a quote provides greater expertise, we will learn from it. The definitions provide surprising meaning.

PLAIN TYPE - Stories from my life, or my opinion. Many statements in **bold** are probably just my opinion, but when that is clearly the case, it is in plain type. I will share stories from my life that fit the topic we are discussing.

"Scientists say we are made of atoms, but a little bird told me that we are made of stories."
Eduardo Galeano, Author

BACK FROM COLOMBIA
I returned from Colombia in 2019 after my 2nd attempt at retirement. While there, I asked my driver and friend about relationships. He told me, "Colombia is Very Open."

Different countries are more Open than others, but World-wide things are Opening Up. Women are on the rise. The Bullsheet helps you to open your mind and adjust to the New Age.

**YOU ARE GOING ON THE ADVENTURE
THAT IS THE REST OF YOUR LIFE**

THE TIPS
The Bullsheet doesn't present a plan, but it does show pathways for your life and relationships. It is a book of tips, suggestions, and ideas that can help a person find romance, get a better job, self-improvement, or whatever purpose you want to achieve.

In building great relationships, we know that we must first get along with ourselves before we can get along with anyone else.

The Lady Reader might think she doesn't understand men, but she will quickly realize she is over thinking the situation. In fact, she might already know the contents of this book, but she could enjoy the stories and quotes and still give a copy to her man.

The Male Reader might know 70%, but the 30% he learns (or is reminded of) could result in major life improvements.

If the Reader is married, <u>The Bullsheet</u> is encouraging you to make your marriage a lasting, loving relationship. Married readers can skip Chapter 12 - Meeting Someone You Like That Likes You.

GOING FORWARD

Many of us have had setbacks in our relationships. We feel like our progress is too slow, but we don't want to be doubtful or negative, "Love won't happen for me because _____."

The Reader needs to be empowered and intelligent in relationships. The wrong people will take your energy. The right people will be worth the wait. Be wise and don't make the mistakes I have made. Great Relationships are about Mutual Respect, Love, Patience, Friendship, and Mutual Attraction (chemistry), or is it Magic?

"Magic: any power or force that seems mysterious or hard to explain."

Webster's Dictionary

NOTE TO WOMEN READERS: The conversation is answering questions from my young male friend who will be dating a woman. He will be told: "If she does or says........." etc. Women Readers can simply change the gender to fit your situation.

ASKING THE QUESTIONS

Our Typical Guy wonders about his actions, and he wonders about women and relationships.

My friend is asking for help in approaching women he finds attractive. He is not having much "luck" with dating or relationships. Hopefully, he has learned to be discerning in the women he chooses to date.

He is a nice guy looking for a nice woman, so we will be helping him search for his version of his Ideal Woman. He is currently thinking that he would like to get married someday, but he accepts that marriage might not happen for him.

We answer the 3 Questions knowing it is impossible to generalize in the Modern World of 8 billion people (or 330 million in the U.S.). However, <u>The Bullsheet</u> cannot be told without generalizing. We acknowledge everyone is an Individual with their own likes, dislikes, morals, strengths, weaknesses, age, personality and perspective.

This conversation differs from other conversations of today in that we are not in a hurry, there are no time constraints, no one is interrupting, and we are never distracted. My friend is much younger, but we are good friends. We are here to focus on answering the questions.

"HOW CAN I HAVE GREAT SEX?"

"HOW CAN I HAVE GREAT RELATIONSHIPS?"

"SHOULD I GET MARRIED, AND WHEN?"

The 3 Questions might be difficult to answer, but we are going to try to help. The process of meeting someone, dating, and romance become our topics for conversation.

<u>The Bullsheet</u> is an invitation to take action for change. Without self-reflection, we will repeat past mistakes or hold misconceptions.

**WE TAKE A LOOK AT OURSELVES
AND MAKE ADJUSTMENTS
THAT LEAVE US FEELING GOOD
ABOUT WHO WE ARE**

INCLUDING OLDER MEN

Older men, ages 45+, are included in the conversation. Situations vary for their age, income level, relationship experiences, where they live, and personal factors. Many are looking to marry while many are not. Older men might think they know women, but times and women are changing along with rapidly evolving technology and social dynamics. <u>The Older Men are asking the same 3 Questions.</u>

WOMEN ARE INCLUDED TOO

Women are also in the conversation - they are half the equation. We have women of all ages, races, single and married.

<u>The Bullsheet</u> is based on Maximum Respect for women. Nothing is said that a woman cannot hear and comment. However, my young friend was jumping the gun when asking first about sex, but it's understandable when an attractive woman is involved.

Women will be quick to point out the questions need to be re-arranged to more accurately reflect Real Life:

"HOW CAN I HAVE GREAT RELATIONSHIPS?"

"HOW CAN I HAVE GREAT SEX?"

"SHOULD I GET MARRIED, AND WHEN?"

A Woman knows this is the correct order for the questions to be answered if a great relationship with great sex is to evolve. However, this order is not always true as there can be spontaneous moments of passion which arise. Good luck with having those magic moments.

KEEP TRYING

You will see that with patience and cheerful perseverance – good things will happen. You learn to go with the flow of life to avoid making big mistakes. We know that no one should rush into marriage, but some people do. We know that no one wants to ruin their relationships, but some people do.

If you do marry someday, you want a Happy Marriage. <u>The Bullsheet</u> will help you to expand your horizons, and where the light shines - you will see new ways to grow.

MY FRIEND – OUR TYPICAL GUY

Chapter 2

I was telling a friend this book is a conversation with The Typical Guy. Before I could describe him, my friend got huffy and stopped me, "That's your opinion - I am not like that at all!"

Maybe the description is only my opinion, my observations, my re-collection from when I was young, or the mistakes I have had to overcome. However, I need someone for our conversation. As respect for my friend, and the fact that No One is The Typical Guy, my conversation is now with Our Typical Guy. We know that many do not fit the description.

INTRODUCING MY FRIEND

Our Typical Guy is an imaginary friend who is asking the 3 Questions. He has found it difficult to build great relationships, so he is asking for help. We could say he is relationship challenged.

I haven't known him for long, but we made friends quickly. He is a younger man between 21 and 42 described from a combination of my experience; how I picture a young man today; what I hear men say; what I see men do; what I think people want in life, and the obstacles they might face. He is past High School, and realizes the Modern World requires earning money to build a life. Our Typical Guy is friendly, fun, clean, kind, and honest (sincere), but he doesn't know much about women or relationships.

He also lacks confidence, and is currently on 0 with the ladies (we know there is a lot bigger difference from 0 to 1 than there is from 1 to 2). When a man has had little success, or is

new to the Dating Game and Single World, it is difficult to be confident.

Our Typical Guy does not have a strong support group. If he does, he does not discuss his feelings or intimate details of his relationships. Otherwise, he would not be here talking to me.

He is trying for love and a great relationship, but he knows pursuing pleasure can lead to temptation and pain. He has figured out that "experience is the best teacher" to the extent that he would like to avoid bad experiences. He knows it is better to learn from talking with friends, seeing other's mistakes, and confiding in me. In other words, he no longer wants to rationalize ineffective behavior, or receive painful and expensive lessons.

There are more things I know about him from mutual friends. I think they might have sent him to me. He is not saving himself for marriage as he has told friends, "I'm looking for true love, but I need (want) a little help along the way." He understands he must go with the flow for good things to happen, so he is learning to see if she enjoys spending time with him.

He likes to party at times, and he has other interests, like playing sports, music, bands, cars, outdoor adventure, travel, reading, animals, running or something.

He wants to start at the top. Don't we all? This is an unrealistic expectation. He will probably need to practice being with women as he looks for dates and his Ideal Woman. It takes practice and patience to achieve optimum results with any endeavor. There is a saying, *"Luck Beats Skill"*, but we are trying for both.

The most difficult part of describing Our Typical Guy is generalizing when money is involved. Each Reader has a different financial situation, and income is an important factor. However, he is willing to spend money to date a woman. (If not, he might as well forget it.)

A friend, his wife, and boys came out to fish. I commented that a man needs to be willing to spend money on a woman to have a relationship.

I asked her for confirmation, and she summed it up for women: "If going on a date, we want to 'do something.' Women like it if the guy pays, especially on a date. She is going to be more impressed. If he does not pay for the date, the rest of the evening is probably not going to go the way he has in mind."

HIS CURRENT SITUATION

There is not the social pressure to marry as in the 1970s, and many women are reluctant. Our Typical Guy knows that some women do not want a serious romantic relationship, but some do. He thinks he would like to marry, so he is asking about marriage. (He doesn't realize marriage is a life-long learning experience.)

No one knows how relationships will evolve, but Our Typical Guy wants to get started and make progress.

I told my daughter that the people who write relationship books are Psychologists, Psychiatrists, Sociologists, Social Workers, and people with formal training in relationships and human nature. I told her I learned from experience, and didn't have the academic experience.

She replied, "Well, it's not difficult. All that is required is for a man to be responsible and accountable for his actions. A man has to realize if he keeps doing the same things, he will get the same results."

Being "responsible and accountable" can be difficult for some men. To women, it sounds like a No-Brainer as women are natural Planners. But for a man, it is going to take self-reflection and self-discipline. MEN DO WHAT WE WANT is a mindset that can jump up and bite us in the ass. I can testify, IT'S DIFFICULT TO LIVE WITH THE CONSEQUENCES OF BAD DECISIONS

Our Typical Guy doesn't take things seriously until he feels an impact in <u>his life</u>. When things go wrong, he usually has no one to blame but himself. Make good choices so you don't do things that bring you down.

WE CAN CHANGE OUR CHOICES AND BEHAVIORS TO GET GREAT RESULTS

PROBLEMS
Our Typical Guy has problems with relationships that he will need to face:
- **He has little awareness of his emotions except for desire, love, anger, or jealousy (discussed in Everyone's Emotional, D<u>anger</u>, The Green-Eyed Monster, and Attachment).**
- **He doesn't realize he needs boundaries (discussed in Don't Lose Your Money).**

- Our Typical Guy is vulnerable to manipulation, especially by an attractive woman. He needs to be able to identify and avoid Manipulators (discussed in An Ideal Partner).
- When he has a woman who will help him, <u>The Bullsheet</u> refers to her as his Scout (discussed in Different Creations).
- He is learning to "lighten up" (discussed in Meeting Someone You Like That Likes You).
- Dating has not given Our Typical Guy the experiences he would like to enjoy. He realizes that 'failure' is part of how he will learn, but he would like to speed up the process (discussed in The Art of Dating).
- Our Typical Guy often thinks about women or sex. Therefore, <u>The Bullsheet</u> calls the man's D*** his Big Brain, and his brain the Little Brain.

THE BIG BRAIN CAN <u>OVERPOWER</u> THE LITTLE BRAIN WITH DESIRE OR EXPECTATIONS
THE BIG BRAIN CAN <u>OVERPOWER</u> THE LITTLE BRAIN WITH FRUSTRATION AND RESENTMENT

- Our Typical Guy bases many of his decisions on the advice of his Big Brain. He can raise his awareness (discussed throughout this book).

SOME OF HIS POSITIVE ATTRIBUTES

Our Typical Guy has more going for him than being fun, friendly, kind and sincere. For example:
- He accepts that optimism (being cheerful and hopeful even when setbacks) leads to success in relationships and everything else in life.

- He is learning to let the Past be *"water under the bridge"*, a learning experience, someone to forgive, or an understanding for his peace of mind.
- He has a healthy sex drive.
- Our Typical Guy has been trying, but not having much luck with women. It might be difficult for him to get dates, or to be with the type of woman to which he is attracted. He understands he must go into action.
- He is willing to discover where he has unrealistic hopes or expectations.
- He is <u>not</u> a misogynist, and he understands what the term means.

"Misogyny: conscious or unconscious contempt against women manifested as social exclusion, sex discrimination, male privilege, belittling of women, hostility or violence against women..... Actually, it could be fear of women rather than hatred."

Wikipedia

- Our Typical Guy might be very intelligent, but women remain a mystery. He might not have had sisters or female friends to clue him in about women i.e. women's emotions, moods, motives, concerns, and thinking. Women are complicated, but he understands:

IT'S IMPORTANT FOR A WOMAN TO FEEL FREE
IF SHE WANTS TO SAY "NO", THEN "NO"
IF SHE SAYS "YES", BE THANKFUL

HE HAS WEAKNESSES

We all have weaknesses, but these describe Our Typical Guy:

- Because of his lack of confidence or awareness, he has <u>not</u> learned to rely on his intuition. An honest evaluation of reality, and trusting in his intuition could help prevent manipulation and emotion-based bad decisions.
- He might have a tendency to say, text, or do stupid things. In other words, he has a tendency to sabotage his own relationships because of expectations, assumptions, suspicions, frustration, anger, or jealousy.
- He is <u>not</u> a Good Listener. We can develop listening skills to improve our relationships.
- He has inhibitions. Hopefully not sexual hang-ups, but he might be self-conscious about his dancing, approaching women, or other inhibitions that hold him back.
- Our Typical Guy doesn't realize:
  WE CAN SEE OTHER PEOPLE'S
  SITUATIONS OR RELATIONSHIPS
  BUT IT'S DIFFICULT TO SEE OUR OWN

- He tends to be a *"Shallow Hal"* (sucker for looks). It is necessary to have attraction and desire, but a man needs to fully comprehended:

WE ALL NEED
TO MANAGE OUR EXPECTATIONS

WE GET STARTED

It is time we join him for our test of Strength, Love, and Resilience. We end all doubt, self-pity, and negativity such as, "It can't happen for me" or "I am too _____ (old, ugly, broke, shy, etc)."

We can't change the past no matter how much we would like to, *but* we can find the power to keep growing. We heed the saying, *"Lessons repeat themselves until we learn them."*

Through self-reflection, we will see through past difficulties and build on what we have learned. We are moving from struggle to insight.

WITH SELF-REFLECTION
YOU TAKE AN HONEST LOOK AT YOURSELF
TO KEEP MAKING ADJUSTMENTS THAT LEAVE YOU
FEELING GOOD ABOUT WHO YOU ARE

We summon hope, energy, and awareness to not give up on our dreams. We resolve to go easy on ourselves, to do our best, and to enjoy life. We know that we are responsible for our own happiness. Confidence and Respect are not a gift, but are how we build strength and love.

ON THE ROAD OF LIFE
THERE IS NO TURNING BACK

Regardless of how much the description of Our Typical Guy fits you: Look in the mirror – meet the person responsible for your actions. You are trying for the wisdom to choose what is right for you.

"You can ignore reality, but you can't ignore the consequences of ignoring reality."

Helen Keller

INTRODUCE MYSELF

Chapter 3

For us to be friends, it feels like I should introduce myself. My name is George, age 73 in 2021. I learned the lessons in this book by the hard and often dumb way of experience. Actually, I don't like revealing all these things about myself, but I am trying to help.

When I re-entered the Single World at age 50, I was terrible with women. It is because I had to learn that I know the difficulties, and how they can be overcome. However, I am probably a Hopeless Romantic.

"Hopeless Romantic; a person who holds sentimental and idealistic views on love, especially in spite of experience, evidence, or exhortations otherwise."

Dictionary.com

A quick life story brings us up to 1998, the year I re-entered the Single World.

I was born in Norman, Oklahoma in 1947. My Great-Grandparents rode in the Land Run of 1889 to claim 160 acres 5 miles from Norman. They didn't start out in a sod house, but in a dug-out with no electricity or running water. We can't imagine the difficulties. For example, besides living in a dug-out, there was hand digging the water well, no electricity, and my Great-Grandfather was President of the Oklahoma Anti-Horse Rustlers Association. My Grandparents built the land into a family farm with livestock, chickens, gardening, and fruit trees until their passing in 1977. This is where I live today with my dog Flash, and cat Rosie Rocks (there are rose rocks where I live).

The rest of a typical description is to say I am white, grew up in Southern Oklahoma and Northern Texas in a segregated society. My Dad worked as a geologist and my Mom a homemaker. I always had good teachers and loved sports. The family TV in 1957 looked cardboard, and had 4 black and white channels. Kids played outside until dark every day, and still did their homework.

A difference for me from my friends was the family was transferred every 4 years. When I would get to know classmates, the family would move. Getting transferred made it harder to get to know girls. I grew up in Ardmore, Oklahoma and Wichita Falls, Texas until the 9th grade. The Twist and Rock and Roll started while I was in Jr. High. I found the larger the town (Ft. Worth, Texas) the less friendly the people, so I was thankful to get back to Ardmore as a junior in High School. That move gave me my freedom back.

My senior year in High School was 1965. There were only land line telephones, no computers, total segregation, all the guys got a burr haircut, guys knew little about girls/women, few people divorced, no one was known gay, and there were good jobs with benefits and wage increases every year for anyone willing to work.

I never liked segregation, but people were separated. I did not have a Black friend until a summer job in 1967. I was 20. I had American Indian friends at Ardmore High, and a few Indian friends all my life. In those days in Ardmore, there were only Blacks, Indians, Whites and a few Mexican-Americans. The only people from a different country were foreign exchange students.

In 1960s and 70s Ardmore, it was easy to find a better job. Men would actually say: "I was looking for a job when I found this one" and "You can take this job and shove it." Almost everything manufactured said "Made in USA."

You were "old" if a man and not married by 28. Women tried to get married by the end of college. Most women who married didn't have to work, but many wanted a career and independence.

Everything was easy going and fairly innocent through High School. Things changed forever and the "Ozzie and Harriet Lifestyle" came crashing to an end with the Vietnam War. The burr turned into long hair, guitars went electric, and the rest is history. I remember my Dad saying in 1965 there were 3 lessons from the Vietnam War:
1. The United States cannot be the World Policeman.
2. The United States should not be sticking its nose into other country's business, especially on the other side of the world.
3. You (citizens) cannot trust the U.S. Government. I call Iraq, Afghanistan, Libya et al 'Vietnam Revisited'. From 1971 - 2021, the seemingly unheard refrain remains the same:

"All we are saying is 'Give Peace a Chance'."
John Lennon and the Plastic Ono Band

The Bullsheet is not a political or economics book, but people need to earn money. Economics, politics, and money permeate all of our lives.

I married at age 28, and we moved to Des Moines, New Mexico, a town of 550. My wife was a school teacher. It was there that I had my first Mexican-American friends from families that have lived there for 150+ years. I worked on a New Mexico State highway crew, handled race horses in the starting gate at La Mesa Park in Raton, and taught high school.

I have a Business Degree, Teaching Certificate and Law Degree. I coached football, won a State Championship, and moved on with a record of 24 - 0.

Some Readers might wonder, "How could 2 different teams (Blanchard Lions and Little Axe Indians) 2 years apart give me an undefeated record?" The answer is that I had good players, and Coaches Barry Switzer and Warren Harper allowed me to learn the techniques and drills from the OU team. Also, I never withheld a player from a game or kicked anyone off the team. One Coach asked, "Don't you have any Rules?" I told him, "Yes, I have Rules: 'Don't Piss-off the Coach'."

When I was thinking about moving out of coaching, a friend told me, "You have nothing to prove, and there is nothing like stopping while on top." I went back to Law School.

Later, I coached my kids for 5 years. Most of the Moms were great Football Moms, but there were 1 or 2 that were not. One of them said about a 5th Grade Tackle Team, "You try to have those little boys out there playing like Pros." I didn't say anything because I knew it was meant to be an insult, but it sounded like a compliment. I also coached my daughter's flag football team with 5 girls. My daughter said, "I didn't know the Coach could make such a difference." That was my best indirect compliment.

Also, I sold insurance on race horses for 18 years; worked in telecommunications with Nextel and American Tower; worked in the Oil & Gas business; and have practiced law at various times for 38 years. Some of these jobs overlapped, but there were gaps of unemployment (economic downturns) that would take my savings.

I believe in everything I do to concentrate on the fundamentals, pay attention to details, and be prepared.

Married Life was good for 24 years until close to the end. I am a Family Man and enjoyed my kids. My ex-wife is nice, but we did not have many shared interests outside of the kids. She told me I am a Dreamer. I didn't say anything because I thought it was a good thing, but later figured out it was an insult. I have a son 39, and a daughter 34.

A Chinese placemat showed a calendar with the year born to describe a person's basic nature. My description fit: *"Because you are Trusting and Loyal, you expect the same from others, and this makes you Naïve."* **The Bullsheet will help you to not be naïve.**

When I first entered the Single World, I was so out of practice after being married 24 years that I was awkward around women. Twenty years after the Divorce, what at one time seemed almost impossible with women has turned into something that is easy, even at 73. My son wonders how it is possible. To explain this change:

"It means we reach a level of awareness that makes inconceivable things available."
Juan Mateus, The Active Side of Infinity, Carlos Castaneda

MY MEMORABLE EVENTS

To further introduce myself, I am sharing conclusions from *"The Memorable Events"* of my past 22 years in the Single World.

"Every Warrior as a matter of duty, collects a special album that reveals the Warrior's personality, an album that attests to the circumstances of his life. I would say there are a few things

that I would consider likely to have changed things for you, to have illuminated your path - The Memorable Events. They will stand the test of time because they have nothing to do with him, and yet he is in the thick of them. The Memorable Events we are after have the dark touch of the impersonal that touch them. I don't know how else to explain this."

Juan Mateus, The Active Side of Infinity, Carlos Castaneda

In reflecting on the Warrior's duty to collect his/her *Memorable Events*, I feel the ones listed below qualify only as "Memorable Events for Relationships." The *Memorable Events* he is asking for might be more accurately found in the stories from my life.

MEMORABLE EVENT #1 – DIVORCE
A goal is to help you never get divorced. Discuss problems before they become big - talk it over with your partner, and with others.
MY MAIN MISTAKE
WAS KEEPING THINGS INSIDE

"Don't throw what's bothering you or the things that are of concern 'under the rug' because it just stays there and bugs you, and not anybody else. So get it out! Believe in yourself. Have a long range plan that will go into the future to provide yourself and others with security."

Greg Norman, The 'Shark', Pro Golfer

MEMORABLE EVENT #2 – A COMFORT ZONE
I saw people going back to people or situations which were easy or comfortable to them, but not in their best interest. During

the first 2 years after my divorce, I caught myself wanting to fall back into my Comfort Zone Trap of wanting to re-marry. I had to let that feeling go to live happy/content whether married or single, dating someone or not.

A relationship with easy sex is probably the #1 Comfort Zone Trap. (Our Typical Guy should know that being married does not necessarily mean easy sex.)
DON'T SETTLE IN A COMFORT ZONE

MEMORABLE EVENT #3 - DANCING
Although I was a terrible dancer, I gradually learned to dance. Dancing is an ice breaker, and a lot of fun. Dancing is a <u>must</u> for the Single World, and is great for marriage too.
LEARNING TO RELAX AND DANCE
WILL LEAD TO ROMANCE

MEMORABLE EVENT #4 - PROVERBS
I felt I was told:
"TAKE PROVERBS TO HEART
AND YOUR LIFE WILL CHANGE"

Proverbs highlights the battle between being Wise and being a Fool. There are many life lessons in Proverbs. I found that reading Proverbs 6-7 times is not the same as "Taking Proverbs to Heart."

I'm still working on this one.

MEMORABLE EVENT #5 - DO'S, DON'TS & PERSONAL LIST
In 2015, I found I had a serious neck injury. I tried to retire in Jamaica, but stayed only 6 months. In Jamaica, I was given

Do's, Don'ts, and Personal Areas for improvement. You are encouraged to use these, or change the list to fit your situation. Remember to create and live your lists.

DON'T

One day in Moore Town, a town hidden high in a mountain valley with lush vegetation and lots of birds, a man noticed me rubbing my forehead and said, "Don't do that."

Acting like I didn't know what he was talking about, "Do what?"

He replied, "Rub your forehead – Don't Worry, Don't Fret, and Don't Think Too Much." Then he added, "And try to not let things get to you."

I knew "trying" would not be enough for me, so it changed to "Don't let things get to you."

Don't Worry
Don't Fret   (Restlessness/Anxiety)
Don't Think Too Much
Don't Let Things Get to You

DO

Prior to my attempted retirement in 2015, I had visited Jamaica about 15 times over the previous 22 years. When I first started going there, Jamaicans had a relaxed attitude made famous by their saying, "No problem." They don't say "No problem" anymore because they have a lot of problems - few jobs, low pay, etc. I commented to a friend that with all these wars, the Earth in danger, what a terrible job he had, and little hope for his future, "I think I let it bother me more than it bothers you guys."

He replied, "Well George, here in Jamaica we say, 'Enjoy Life and Enjoy Yourself'."

Enjoy Life
Enjoy Yourself

Justice Ruth Bader Ginsberg replied when asked what she learned from 3 bouts with cancer: *"An enhanced appreciation of the joys of being alive."*

PERSONAL LIST
My Personal List started with going to hang my swimsuit on a clothesline in Jamaica. In typical American style, I walked right past the Housekeeper who said, "Good Morning George."
I replied, "Good Morning Ann."
She asked, "How is your day?"
I replied, "Fine, how is your day?"
This is a mundane conversation, but I would have walked past her and not said a word. This caused me to see that I need to Slow Down and Be Polite. It's embarrassing, but I don't think I ask anyone before in my whole life, "How is your day?" We can remember to be polite if we are patient with life. You are encouraged to make a Personal List of your most needed personal improvements. Mine are:

Slow Down
Be Polite
Be a Great Listener
Be Cheerful

Listen carefully to the people you are with to hear what is acceptable. If you take your time, you understand.

THE SINGLE WORLD

The Single World has been a learning experience. It was bumpy at the start, but most experiences have been opportunities to learn. Life is an adventure. However, it has been a Blessing that several relationships did not go the way I was promoting. Sometimes it is best we don't get what we want – we might have been going down a dead end road.

We start to see what it takes to build Great Relationships. It starts with ourselves. Be smart and wise to not make mistakes.

APPRECIATE YOUR BLESSINGS
TRY FOR GOOD DECISIONS

"Your visions will become clear only when you can look into your own heart. Who looks outside, dreams, who looks inside, awakes."

C.G. Jung

THE GENERATIONS

Chapter 4

I never did understand what Generation X, Y, or Z was supposed to mean, or what years were for each. I looked up "Generation" in the dictionary, and was surprised to find "X":

"Generation X: the generation born in the 1960's and 1970's, often thought of as lacking goals, and concern for others, caring only for material things, not having a sense of duty, etc."
Webster's Dictionary

It can be difficult to argue with the dictionary, so there must be a lot of people who fit this description. However, <u>The Bullsheet</u> does not agree this accurately describes such a large group of people. We will not be using the names X, Y, or Z. Let's name the Generations and their years of birth:

THE GENERATIONS
<u>Ages in 2021</u>

1930 – 1945 Greatest Generation (WWII & Depression)	75+
1946 – 1961 Baby Boom Generation	74-59
1962 – 1977 New Wave Generation	58-43
1978 – 1993 Plaid Shirt/Free Thinker Generation	42-27
1994 – 2009 Courageous or Millennial Generation	26-11
2010 – 2025 Creative Generation	10 - being born

We are designating Generations because the people of each one have differences in historical events, lifestyle experiences, social movements, music, movies, technological innovations, economic periods, sexual attitudes, evolution of feminism, etc. that influenced members thinking and behavior.

For discussion, a Generation is 15 years as siblings are seldom more than 15 years apart. Each Generation has unique characteristics, and members have a different perspective on relationships and the world.

Characteristics can overlap for those born near a generation timeline, but regardless of the dividing line dates between generations:

"Today's young adults are starting their lives on drastically different financial footing than their parents did decades ago. Necessities cost far more, and wages have flattened; as a result, many families (or individuals) have to dig through mountains of debt before they can even think about growing their wealth (homeownership). The current pressures facing would-be young adult home buyers aren't easing anytime soon."
Christopher Ingraham, The Washington Post, 2010

WE CAN'T PAINT AN ENTIRE GENERATION
WITH THE SAME STROKE
SO WE GENERALIZE

WORLD WAR TWO/DEPRESSION ERA GENERATION
BORN 1930-1945 AGES 75+
"THE GREATEST GENERATION"

The life of these people was dominated by the effects of the Great Depression and then World War Two. Members are currently ages 75-90, but many would like to enjoy a romantic relationship. People in America think older people don't want intimacy, but some do. Older people appreciate love, and there is the pharmacy.

Many are working to stay healthy and young at heart.

THE BABY BOOM GENERATION
BORN 1946-1961 AGES 74-59

The Baby Boom Generation has a 1946 starting point which gives the men returning from World War Two a little time to find a wife and 9 month gestation. Some features of this Generation were included when I introduced myself.

Men have not changed much over the Generations. The main difference is that those younger than Baby Boomers do not know of the days in America when jobs were plentiful, you could change jobs easily, move up within the company, receive a pay raise every year, retirement plans, good benefits, paid vacations, paid sick days, good health insurance, and have money left over to support a family and still save. The economy worked good for awhile. There was an upward trend with greater equality, labor unions, and social mobility. What happened? If you want to know, read the book by Noam Chomsky, or watch the video RequimfortheAmericandream.com.

"Today's America was shaped by the 10 Principles of Wealth & Power. One set of Rules for the Rich, and an opposite set of Rules for the Poor. That's what happens when you put Power into the hands of a narrow sector of wealth which is dedicated to increasing Power for themselves – just as you would expect."

Noam Chomsky

Women have changed a lot over the years. When I got to college as a Baby Boomer, the women wanted to get married. A joke (maybe) at the time was, "Women went to college to get a Mrs. Degree." The following Generations have been progressively less eager to marry. There has been less and less social stigma to remain Single, and all kinds of other arrangements have evolved.

Everyone I knew got married, and had good jobs with upward mobility. If not, anyone could change to a better job.

There for awhile in the 1960s, everyone thought everything was possible: war could be stopped; Civil Rights and Equal Rights were gaining momentum; there was a sense of responsibility about one another; the Black Panthers were feeding children; Tribal sovereignty was being recognized. We were moving towards the common good - it was progress in motion But then the Military Industrial Complex took over, and the Vietnam War continued until 1975. However, the music was Great.

THE NEW WAVE GENERATION
BORN 1962– 1977 AGES 58-43

It became obvious that the people 15–20 years younger than me had a different attitude, and they were a different Generation.

The Vietnam War was over by the time the oldest were 13. The World was changed by the internet, cell phones, and computers. They were the 1st to have computers as an important part of their job, or being replaced by a computer. They were a New Wave with new thinking, and they thought up new names, or new spellings of names, for their children.

The New Wave differs from the Baby Boomers in that they did not face the Draft to be sent to Vietnam; women were not so eager to marry; more women had careers of their own; there was greater access to birth control; all saw lots of divorces or got one; there was exposure of widespread abuse; explicit sex in movies or porn. They participated in the first wave of computer jobs, and the introduction of the cell phone was when they were in their 20s and 30s.

The New Wave saw a lot of change. Greater numbers needed to move out-of-state, or to travel for jobs. This trend has increased over successive generations. They were open-minded to new ways, new religious views, or no religion.

PLAID SHIRT/FREE THINKER GENERATION
BORN 1978-1993 AGES 42-27

In 2003, I had friends at work born around 1980 who I knew were against the Iraq War. They were not stupid about the war being wrong, the economy rigged, corporate government (our government) is corrupt, but they would not say or do anything. In my youth, we took to the streets to promote Civil Rights and protest the Vietnam War, but we could be drafted and sent to Vietnam to kill or be killed. Many thought the Middle East Wars were not in defense of country, but a military out of control. These younger friends were educated, but quiet about wars. In 2009, they were also quiet about the Bank Bailouts:

"The Federal Reserve provided $9.3 TRILLION DOLLARS to banks including foreign central banks with not all 'aid' disclosed."
USA Today, December 2, 2010 (underline added)

I called this age group The Ostrich Generation. We could have built a new economy for Real People with $9.3 TRILLION (revealed to be $14 TRILLION+ by today).

But in 2015 Bernie Sanders came out, and they came alive for a year. There was Occupy Wall Street, but Bernie was bigger. I finally realized my friends were quiet because they didn't feel like there was anything they could do as an individual to make a difference. Now I call them The Plaid Shirt Generation as the guys often wore Plaid Shirts. But wait, the women didn't wear Plaid Shirts so call them Free Thinkers.

The Plaid Shirt/Free Thinker Generation did not face a Draft for the Iraq War; they did not witness the Vietnam War; many have large Student Debt; the women are even less eager to marry; many women are saying they don't want to marry; more women are educated with good jobs; many women have no qualms about being a Single Mom; everyone has seen more divorces; these people focus on improving their lives as they witness economic uncertainty. They were introduced to computer Dating Sites and numerous Apps. They have used the computer and cell phone most of their lives.

The Plaid Shirt/Free Thinkers seem more Individualistic, but have great concern for the welfare of others (they buy the 2 pair of shoes so 1 pair goes to a poor person); they have concern for the welfare of the Earth; concern for pollution on their health and their children's health, and they work hard to find or keep a good job.

These people have witnessed job losses, debt loads, lowering incomes, and rising prices. I had one friend who was sent to India to train his replacement.

COURAGEOUS or MILLENNIAL GENERATION
BORN 1994-2009 AGES 26-11

These are the people born around the turn of the Century (the Millennium) in 2000. Many of these people are too young for <u>The Bullsheet,</u> but these young people are being called upon to be courageous in the face of rapid change.

They were born into a computer/smart phone savvy world. I joke, "They learned how to work the computer while in the womb. They just know which key to push."

The first I-phone was introduced in 2007. The Millennial Generation probably gets tired of being called that because it does not distinguish them except for being born near the change of the Century. Therefore, we are calling them the Courageous Generation because it is going to take Courage to reform this System (restrict lobbying, end the Revolving Door).

The economy has not improved for most. Pew Research Center reports *"52% of young adults ages 18-29 live at home in 2021."* Almost no one in America over 18 wants to live at home with their parent(s). The Courageous Generation will fight a battle against reduced purchasing power and inequality. (The battle is <u>not</u> to have "income equality", but to have way <u>less</u> "income inequality" – to pay people a <u>living</u> wage.)

The "battle for equality" is for human rights, women's rights, and to provide opportunity for Real People. There is also a battle to protect the Earth, wild animals, birds, insects, air, water, and many people who are endangered. We don't want homeless or hungry people in America. It is going to take Courage to take on the Corporate State.

The attitude of the Courageous Generation is described by 16-year-old climate activist Greta Thunberg:

"Just keep going. It may seem hopeless and impossible sometimes. It always does, so you just have to continue because if you try hard enough and long enough, you will make a difference. If enough people stand together and fight for the right thing, then anything can happen. You are never too small to make a difference."

Relationship building has taken on more meaning with the Courageous Generation. Young men ages 18-25 have been heard to say such unheard things as, "I want to have self-acceptance before I 'catch feelings'." Good for them. The young people of today want to be taken seriously.

CREATIVE GENERATION
BORN 2010-2025 AGES 10 - to being born

These are the young children of today. I heard suggestions they be called the Web or Screen Generation, but most ages could fit in that category. I don't know who is in Generation Z or what that means.

These people will need to be Creative to solve the problems we face: Never-ending Wars since 2003, Pollution, Big Banks, Tax Havens, Lobbying, Billionaires and Monopoly Power. Clean water is becoming scarce, and everyone can see the climate is changing (whether they admit it or not). WE CAN ALL DO <u>SOMETHING</u> ABOUT THESE PROBLEMS.

This challenge can't fall onto 10-year-olds, so the rest of the Generations need to rise up to help them. What kind of world are we going to leave our children and grandchildren?

Let's hope the Creative Generation does not have to turn to the rest of us and ask, "Why weren't you speaking out more and louder for Peace and to protect Nature?"

"Love is a Blessing for us humans. If we don't have love, we give up our spirit and our virtue, and then we are lost."
                                                    Philomena Franz

THE GENERATIONS BLEND INTO ONE

All the people who were alive at the turn of the Century, or are alive today, could be called Millennials. We are all part of the New Millennium.

I was cleaning out my briefcase, and found a fax (before email) dated 1999. The Dali Lama gives the instructions we need for the creative courage to make changes:

"INSTRUCTIONS FOR LIFE IN THE NEW MILLENNIUM"
1. *Take into account that great love and great achievements involve great risk.*
2. *When you lose, don't lose the lesson.*
3. *Follow the 3 R's: Respect for self, Respect for others, Responsibility for all your actions.*
4. *Remember that not getting what you want is sometimes a wonderful stroke of luck.*
5. *Learn the rules so you know how to break them properly.*
6. *Don't let a little dispute injure a great friendship.*
7. *When you realize you made a mistake, take immediate steps to correct it.*
8. *Spend some time alone every day.*
9. *Open your arms to change, but don't let go of your values.*
10. *Remember that silence sometimes is the best answer.*
11. *Live a good, honorable life. Then when you get older and think back, you will be able to enjoy it a second time.*

12. *A loving atmosphere in your home is the foundation for your life.*
13. *In disagreements with loved ones, deal only with the current situation. Don't bring up the past.*
14. *Share your knowledge. It is a way to achieve immortality.*
15. *Be gentle with the Earth.*
16. *Once a year, go someplace you have never been before.*
17. *Remember that the best relationship is one in which your love for each other exceeds your need for each other.*
18. *Judge your success by what you had to give up in order to get it.*
19. *Approach love and cooking with reckless abandon."*

"Rising Up, Standing Up, whatever the consequences, will inspire future Generations."
Elderly Seminole-Muskogee Creek Woman

WOMEN

Chapter 5

The Bullsheet doesn't know much about women, but will try to help Our Typical Guy. We do know the Women's Wave is rising.

For a comprehensive view, *The Second Sex* by Simone de Beauvoir, 1953, tells all about women. After blaming society and men for women's woes, she also acknowledges society and women cause men's woes. She concludes by the end that we all live in the Material World, and there will be problems, but Great Relationships do exist.

I heard a couple agree, "We have been together 23 years, and it seems like only yesterday."

Women realize it is a New Age. She knows the time has come for prioritizing self-care and self-love as she is not going to be able to enjoy a relationship if she feels overly burdened. Many women are going against the status quo, patriarchal society, misogyny, sexism and stereotypes.

World-wide women are demanding Dignity and Respect which translates into education, employment, equality, opportunity, consent, and they are not going to settle for less.

"We (women) get the job done – whatever it takes."
Madonna Thunder Hawk, Warrior Women, PBS

There is a movement for Gender Equality and women being recognized for the unpaid work they perform - child care, taking care of the home, etc. Women are rightfully proud of the work they do each day. Men need to respect her.

RESPECT
Women deserve Maximum Respect. In the future, women will do what they want, get the job they want, and be who they want to be. Women should make the same money as men for the same work, and women should have equal rights. A woman can be President, or anything else.

"A man does not try to find out what is inside. He does not try to scratch the surface. If he did, he might find something much more beautiful than the shape of a nose or the color of an eye."
Hedy Lamarr, Famous Actress 1940s
Co-inventor of Radio Frequency Technology

EVOLVING RELATIONSHIPS
Women and Men are still learning. Dr. John Gray in Beyond Mars and Venus **provides insights:**

"As adults we are all responsible for our own happiness, but we can certainly help each other by acting with love."

John explains that there are a lot of hormones going on in individuals and relationships. All Our Typical Guy can do is to try his best. As for actually understanding women:

A MAN WILL NEVER UNDERSTAND WOMEN ……………...REALLY

I was watching *Larry King NOW* when Larry was interviewing Stephen Hawking, the genius astrophysicist recognized as *"The Most Brilliant Mind in the Universe."*

Larry: "Six years ago you told me, "The only thing I do not fully understand is women." Do you understand them now?

Stephen: I have learned a lot about women since then. (Notice that he doesn't say he understands women — he has *'learned a lot.'*)

Stephen: Now it is my turn to ask you a personal question. You have been married 8 times to 7 different women, "Is this a triumph of over-experience?"

Larry: Yes, and it is also a triumph of hope. This last marriage has lasted 19 years."

A NEW DAY IS HERE

Women know a lot more about men than men know about women. Most men are simply trying to find a nice girlfriend, or maybe a wife. Some women would like to find her Ideal Man and are willing to marry, while some have other preferences.

In 2015, I was walking down the street in Jamaica when a friend informed me, "Men used to be in charge, but it's a Different World now. With the smart phone, women have taken over. ALL WE CAN DO IS WORK WITH THEM NOW."

Dwight's statement is an <u>important truth</u> for Our Typical Guy to remember as it describes our changing times, and a change in the nature of relationships.

I have been reflecting over the past 6 years on what he said, "With the smart phone, women have taken over. ALL WE CAN DO IS WORK WITH THEM NOW."

Dwight was speaking the truth, but it turned out to be more than the smart phone. When I first went to Jamaica in 1998, there were almost no women drivers. By 2015, around 40% of drivers were women, and if it was an expensive car, 70% had a woman driver.

So what was the extra change? In 2015, I noticed the Jamaican girls were the ones trying harder in school and going on to University. Parents have to pay for kids to go to school in Jamaica, and the classes are difficult. The girls would be studying more and getting better jobs, while too many boys didn't try in school. So it turned out to be more than the smart phone - it was also Smart Girls.

This happened earlier in the U.S. I remember when I went to law school in 1971 at Southern Methodist University, there were only 2 women in my Section of 50. When I went back to law school in 1982 at Oklahoma University, there were 20 women out of 50. The women's percentage today is probably about 50%.

INSIDE INFORMATION

A man who had older sisters or a natural ladies man would know a lot more about women than me.

We can learn from my friend J. R. who grew up with 6 older sisters. It was in the 1980s, when the family shared the home landline (no cell phones). J. R. would hear the sister's conversations, and how they would put off men. (An attractive woman will have guys calling.)
We get his Best Advice:
"There are 2 things you need to know:
1. The Good Lord gave man <u>2 eyes and 1 mouth</u>; and <u>2 ears and 1</u> <u>mouth</u>; so a man can observe and listen twice as much as he talks.
2. Women will tell you everything you want or need to know without knowing they are telling you."

After these words of wisdom, J.R. said, "I watch a woman's facial expressions. Women wear their emotions on their face. A woman's brain is wired differently than a man, and everything in their life is connected. Women attach emotion into everything. Ultimately, they outthink themselves."

J. R.'s final advice, "Focus on observing and listening to a woman is what men need to do. Men tend to talk too much."

Women often want to talk without the other person providing a solution. Talking without seeking a solution seems strange to men. Men are Problem Solvers who offer solutions, but often she just wants someone to listen. Listening in this manner is very difficult for Our Typical Guy to comprehend, so just listen and don't give advice unless asked.

THE TYPICAL WOMAN

<u>**The Bullsheet**</u> **could not possibly describe The Typical Woman, but on** Global 3000, LinkTV **they ask the question:**
"WHAT IS YOUR IDEA OF A TYPICAL WOMAN?"
Daniel (23) male : "I'd say a Typical Woman is <u>Very</u> emotional; <u>Very</u> intuitive, more so than men."
Tasmin (22) female: "They have far too many clothes in their closet. They are addicted to shopping."
Jochim (49) male: "Sensitive, led by their feelings."
Tasmin again (22): "That's right…………MOODY!!!"
Theres (26) female: "They complain about everything."…laughing
Sri (35) male: "They can cook, tidy up." (Different culture for Sri)
Anire (70) female: "A good listener………but when the man is not there, she does what she wants."……smiling
Christina (66) female: "Tough, Self-confident, Strong." thumbs up

It is unrealistic to think any person will live up to all your expectations. Maybe the seed will flower, maybe it will wilt. Life has an ebb and flow, as do relationships.

"If you can't handle me at my worst, you don't deserve me at my best."

Marilyn Monroe

Some men criticize a woman for spending money on her hair, nails, toes, accessories, and clothes. "Fixing up" seems natural and a tendency of women World-wide.

I walked to the front of a concert at St. Margaret's Bay, Jamaica and there were lots of pretty girls. I noticed every one had her hair done, nails done, nice dress, shoes, jewelry, and I knew this was World-wide. A man should appreciate the work a woman does to make herself look nice.

SEXIST

"Sexism: a way of thinking and behaving as though one sex were better than the other; especially unfair treatment of women by men, caused by such thinking."

Webster's Dictionary

The Bullsheet is not sexist and supports men and women as equals. It is ridiculous and wrong if women do not receive equal pay, equal rights, and have an equal voice.

As the burden of raising children usually falls on women, a man needs to be sure to try to do his half. (If the man actually tries to do half, he will probably be doing good to get to 40%.) Carrying half the load is to prioritize a woman and her needs. After all, if she is not there for herself, she can't be there for a man.

As a man of the 1960's, I am a Charter Member of the Women's Liberation Movement. The Bullsheet supports freedom. We have our differences in nature which makes life interesting.

I remember being with my Mom as a kid. She was red headed, fun-loving, pretty, and the boss of the family. I would hear her refer to some men as "Male Chauvinist PIGS!" (Heavy on the PIGS) I wasn't always sure what provoked her, but I learned to not be a Male Chauvinist – that's for sure!

THE MODERN WOMAN

<u>The Bullsheet</u> is for empowering women around the world as we want what is best for people. The Modern Woman feels the power to do whatever she feels she deserves. In the USA, women are not going to stand for anyone holding them back (world-wide women face greater oppression, but they try).

**WOMAN HAS FOUND THE SOURCE OF HER POWER
IT IS THE POWER OF EQUALITY**

Modern Women are more independent, and many want to stay independent.

I heard a woman say, "I don't want to marry and be dependent on any man."

This statement doesn't necessarily mean she does not want a love relationship with a man, or possible marriage someday. It means women don't want to rely on a man to bring them what they want (need) in life. They want to make sure they can fend for themselves. (However, marriage has a natural co-dependency factor. Relationships get complicated.)

We know a man feels better about himself and the world around him when he has money (*"some money in his pocket"*). The same is true for a woman.

> *"We knew that the men looked down on us, that they did not give us credit for the abilities we had, or our potential abilities, if given the experience. We knew that. But it was something that you just didn't think about. You knew what you could do."*
>
> Louise Thaden, 1930's Aviator
Fly Girls by Keith O'Brien

I heard a woman say, "Women know. They just know. Even if they didn't know, they would know. Men might not get this, but women will, because they know." (I guess this is true, but I don't know.)

THE REVERSE DOUBLE STANDARD

The Double Standard is a well known cultural misconception: the idea that men who have multiple sexual partners are seen as cool, manly or it is positive; while women who have multiple sexual partners are seen as whores, sluts or it is negative. <u>The Bullsheet</u> is letting Our Typical Guy know the Double Standard is dead. In 2021+, he could face the Reverse Double Standard.

Some women are saying, *"What's good for the goose is good for the gander."* **Men have been out doing what they do, and some women are saying they will do the same. Women are not putting up with the Double Standard, and it is a lot easier for a woman to do what she wants.**

Some men probably think the Double Standard still exists, and women do not want to known as whores or sluts (slut shaming). However, a lot of women don't care if some men think of them as whores, or anything else. She does what she wants.

The Harvey Weinstein scandal was workplace harassment, but it exposed a dumb ass man who still believed in the Double Standard and sexual harassment. Many women were rightfully pissed off, and it made all men look bad.

Actually, the Reverse Double Standard became well known in the 1950s (it has probably always existed). Kitty Wells was the first woman to top the Billboard charts with, *"It Wasn't God Who Made Honky Tonk Angels."* **The song gave notice that women waiting at home on a man was changing because too many married men were acting like they were still single.**

**IN THE REVERSE DOUBLE STANDARD
MANY WOMEN SAY "DEAL WITH IT"
BUT DOUBLE STANDARDS ARE HIDDEN AGENDAS
THEY PREVENT TRUST IN RELATIONSHIPS**

OBJECTIFICATION

Women like to be noticed, or she would not go to the trouble of doing her hair, nails, toes, eyelashes, make-up, wearing cool shoes, and pretty clothes. It is respect and appreciation to tell her she looks great, or what you like about her. It is natural that women want to feel attractive. A man will feel the uplifting effect if she is with you.

"I'm a girl and being a girl is good. I feel awesome about being a sex symbol. It's someone saying I look sexy. Why can't we be determined, athletic, strong, soft, nurturing and sexy? Why can't we be all these things? Being female and using my attributes – it works, but I never did anything I wasn't comfortable with, never."

Danica Patrick, Champion Race Car Driver, Author

Some women say they don't want to be objectified, but it depends on if the woman is interested in a man, and the circumstances (it's out if at the workplace).

"Show me a woman who does not want to feel like a sex object on occasion and I'll show you a corpse. No, we don't want to be treated like pieces of meat, but we do want to feel sought after and desired. We don't want men to become asexual wimps. We want them to feel confident in their masculinity, a very attractive trait. So men, if you want to do something for a woman's liberation, help her explore her sexuality by being tuned in to yours."

Marcy Sheiner, Sex for the Clueless

ENHANCMENT

Many women go for plastic surgery, boob jobs, botox injections, tanning, padded bras, etc so complaints of objectification are often unfounded.

"Women shouldn't point fingers at other women for whatever they are doing to enhance their body. Do whatever makes you feel good, because – trust me – if a woman isn't happy with herself, she is not going to bring nothing but pain to everybody around her."

T-Pain, Good Hair, a movie by Chris Rock

At some point a man might have to chip in, and being cool about contributing is part of building a great relationship.

However, if I hear a woman say her hobby is shopping, I run for the hills.

Some women are high maintenance, and some not. A man could soon be broke if he is not careful. However, if she is

sincere, women are usually better at managing money than men.

> *"What do I tell my daughter? The stuff on the top of your head is nowhere near as important as the stuff inside your head."*
> Chris Rock in his movie Good Hair

HER TWO BRAINS

We have established that Our Typical Guy has 2 brains, so it begs the question "DO WOMEN ALSO HAVE 2 BRAINS?" The answer is YES!

We know Nature keeps everything in balance, so women must have something comparable to trouble them. For example, men and women have genitals that are different, yet through Nature it is a perfect balance.

Man has a Big Brain in his D*** which can lead to bad decisions, and can make him predictable to a woman. Women also enjoy sex, but they do not have a brain in their P****.

The question is, WHAT DO WOMEN HAVE THAT CORRESPONDS EQUALLY AND AS POWERFULLY AS A MAN'S BIG BRAIN? We know there is something.

Our guess is...............her SHORT-TERM MOODS which can make her unpredictable - even to herself.

Rather than calling it her Big Brain, <u>The Bullsheet</u> calls it her Alternate Brain. It is not a constant impulse like with the man's Big Brain, but her Short-Term Moods can be powerful, including for sex.

SEX

There is one thing a man can't know, and I have never seen a show or read a book that answered the question:

HOW OFTEN DOES A WOMAN ACTUALLY WANT TO HAVE SEX?

One day I went to lunch with friends, a Mother age 49, and her Daughter age 30. I told them I had no way to know how often a woman would like to have sex if it was up to her. I told how if not counting her period time, a man in his 20s and 30s would probably like to have sex at least 5-6 times a week, but he is realistic enough to know that 3-4 times would be good.

So I asked, "Assuming a man does everything right, and treats her with maximum respect and courtesy, and she is under little stress: How often in a week does a woman want to have sex?"

The Mother said, "It depends on how the man treats her."

I said, "We are assuming he treats her right every day."

The Daughter answered, "I would say 5-6 times, about the same as a man."

I was struck dumbfounded. I had expected her to say 2-3 at the most, and thought her answer would be 1. All I could say was, "Equality, I should have known."

THE NEW AGE

Chapter 6

When we reflect on history, we can feel our place in time. We learn to appreciate the efforts and sacrifices of our ancestors. It's good to step back and see how things are changing, so that we can gain perspective.

"A people without knowledge of their past, origin, and culture is like a tree without roots."
Marcus Garvey

In this chapter, we look at a time period of 5125 years, and realize that 50-100 years is not very long ago. In the early 1900s, people had no cars, no phones, no radio, no TV, and few modern conveniences. It was 1925 before ½ of Americans had electricity. Mass production of cars has been for only 100 years, radio 90 years, television 70 years, cell phones 22 years, and the smart phone has existed for only 13 years. We take modern inventions for granted.

We will all see rapid change in our lifetime. My Grandparents were born in 1900. They lived from no electricity, and dating in a horse and buggy, to seeing a man land on the moon.

People have a powerful ability to adapt, even if things we think of as "normal" are not. Living in big cities or spending time on technology has many people being further removed from Nature each day. For 2021+ change is at an ever accelerating pace. This accelerated rate was proven in computers by Gordon E Moore with

"Moore's Law - we can expect the speed and capability of computers to double every 2 years."

Investopedia

My Generation, Baby Boom, grew up in the 1970s - 80s with people then age 23-43 feeling like, "Life will keep going about like it is now", but then computers emerged. Gradually, we adjusted to the changes, and now everyone knows *"change is the only constant."*

When I first started on this book, it would have been news to many that we live in a New Age. But now, it feels like everyone knows.

<u>THE BULLSHEET</u> WILL PROVE IN 3 PARTS
WHAT YOU ALREADY FEEL
WE LIVE IN A NEW AGE!!!

"On December 21, 2012, we entered the world predicted over 1300 years ago by Time's Special Witness, Pacal Vota. The 7th century Mayan prophet foretold of our accelerated technological society and the resulting damage of our collective divergence from Natural Law in exchange for materialist values."

Dr. Jose Arguelles

PART 1 – THE MAYAN LONG COUNT CALENDAR
August 13, 3013 BC to December 21, 2012

When the century changed from 1999 to 2000, we heard the scare that the World's computers would crash on the digit rollover (1999-2000). Fear and survivalist activities took place. Of course, nothing happened except "nothing happened" was

used to discredit The Mayan Long Count Calendar to say the ancient Maya predicted "The End of the World in 2000."

The ancient Maya were <u>not</u> predicting the 'End of the World' in 2000 or 2012.

"In the 1950s, Euro-American astronomers ran headlong into the stunning reality that the Ancient Maya and Native Americans were masters of a sophisticated astronomy previously unrecognized."

Mayan Prophecies and Calendar, Crystalinks

The Mayan Long Count is an ancient Mayan calendar which tracks World Ages or Creation Cycles of 5125 years. The Maya realized there were Cycles in the Cosmos.

"As avid stargazers, the ancient Maya were keen to an astrological cycle which they understood as a 26,000 year cycle compiled of five lesser cycles of 5125 years each. Each of these five cycles was considered its own 'World Age' or 'Creation Cycle'."

Mayan Prophecies and Calendar, Crystalinks

HOW DOES IT WORK?
How did the Ancient Maya determine that December 21, 2012 was the beginning of a New Age?

"Archeologists claim that the Maya began counting time as of August 31, 3113 BC. This is called the zero year and is likened to January 1, AD. All dates in the Long Count begin there, so the date of the beginning of this time cycle was written 13.0.0.0.0. That

means 13 cycles of 394 years will pass before the next cycle begins on December 21, 2012. The new cycle will begin as 1.0.0.0.0.

Another notable date is 9.9.2.4.8 or July 29, 615 AD when the great King of Palenque, Lord Pakal ascended to the throne. These dates are carved throughout Mayan territory, and the numbers can be seen by anyone."

The Maya – Riddle of the Glyphs,
National Geographic Magazine

The World did not end in 2012, but a new Creation Cycle has begun. Our lives have been transformed by computer innovation, electronic money creation, wars, extreme inequality, climate pollution, a pandemic, and the rise of new Movements.

A New Creation Cycle or World Age has relationships undergoing drastic changes with greater variations in values, sexual 'norms' and preferences. Men are discovering that women are realizing a New Reality in the New Age.

What's Our Typical Guy to do? He will need to be the Lion of the Jungle, or Jaguar of the Jungle in the Mayan World.

THE LIVING PROPHECY

"Our present great cycle from 3113 BC - 2012 AD is called the Age of the Fifth Sun in the Mayan Long Count. August 13, 3113 BC is also as precise and accurate as one can get for a beginning of our history. The first Egyptian Dynasty is dated 3100 BC; the first city, Uruk, in Mesopotamia, 3100 BC; the Hindu Kali Yuga, 3102 BC; and most interestingly, the division of time into 24 hours of 60 minutes each with 60 seconds, and the division of the circle into 360°, also around 3100 BC, in Sumaria. If the

beginning of history was so accurately placed, then must not the end of the age December 21, 2012 also be as accurate?"
Dr. Jose Arguelles, Time in the Technosphere

DECEMBER 21, 2012 WAS THE DAY WE ENTERED A NEW AGE

PART 2 – THE LAST BAKTUN
1618 AD – December 21, 2012

There are 13 *"Baktuns"* **of 394 years each that make up the 5125 years of a World Age or Creation Cycle. We reflect on the last Baktun of the Mayan Long Count.**

"Within the 5,125 year cycle lies 13 smaller cycles, known as the "13 Baktun Count." Each Baktun has its own historical epoch or Age within the Great Creation Cycle, carrying a specific destiny for the evolution of those who are incarnated.

The 13th Baktun cycle is known both as 'the triumph of materialism' and 'the transformation of matter'."
Dr. Jose Arguelles

The last Baktun (1618 – 2012) was the start of the Nation State from the Treaty of Westphalia leading on to Global Conquest in *"the triumph of materialism"*, **and Industrialization,** *"the transformation of matter."*

Global Conquest was not possible until 1618 with ocean sailing ships carrying cannons and guns:
- **Spanish and Portuguese Empires in South America**
- **British Empire around the World**
- **European Countries colonizing Africa**

- The Wars against the American Indians are told in the recommended reading Bury My Heart at Wounded Knee: An Indian History of the American West, Dee Brown
- In 1619, the 1st Africans were brought to America
- This last Baktun was a time of great expansion, but also a time of slavery, repression of women, and minorities.

"Half the story has never been told."
Saying

Globalization, Militarism, and Multi-National Corporations (wealth and power) - *"the triumph of materialism"* has left many people fighting for freedom, dignity, and a living wage. Globalization is here through the internet, privatization, big banks, supply chains, the super rich, and cheap labor while big corporations avoid helping society with off-shore accounts and shuffling accounting practices. Of course, great wealth has also been extracted and created.

With the Industrial Revolution, *"the transformation of matter",* **Mother Earth's systems are threatened by overpopulation, mining, chemicals, and pollution.** There have also been fantastic innovations to propel us into the New Age.

THE PRIOR *"HAAB"* of 52 YEARS
December 20, 1960 – December 21, 2012

As *"Avid Stargazers"*, the Maya also used many practical calendars, including a *"Haab"* for 52 year time periods. The last *"Haab"* also ended on December 21, 2012. Life in the USA was described:

"We are living in what has been called The Synthetic Age. The Age of the Atom, the Missile, the Frozen TV Dinner. It is also the Age of the Wormless Apple (pesticides) *and the Calculated Risk* (corporate profits vs. your health). *How long do pesticides persist in the environment? No one knows. We are not separate from the Natural World."*

Rachel Carson, A Silent Spring, 1962

Human arrogance and greed can outrun human wisdom. The Earth will survive, but what will human survival be like for our children/grandchildren? The Plaid Shirt/Free Thinker (they bought 2 pairs of shoes to give 1 pair to the poor)**, Courageous, and Creative Generations are our hope.**

"<u>The Maya predicted this final Baktun would be a time of great forgetting in which we drift very far from our sense of Oneness with Nature and experience a kind of collective amnesia.</u> Like a memory virus in which we begin to believe the limited reality of appearances and <u>grow dense to the Spiritual Essence which fuels this world, so humanities sense of ego and domination has grown</u>."

Dr. Jose Arguelles (underline added)

A WORLD AGE OF 5125 YEARS
ENDED ON DECEMBER 21, 2012

PART 3 - THE NEW AGE
DECEMBER 21, 2012 through TODAY+

The New Age started 8+ years ago. It is time we Wake Up to our *"Oneness with Nature."* **People should be preparing**

to rediscover their *"Spiritual Essence which fuels this world"* as we transition from one World Age to the next.

The New Age could be called the Age of Innovation and Creativity. However, we still have the Status Quo, monopoly power, militarism, and consumerism *("materialist values")* crammed down our throats from corporations, government, television, smart phones, and the internet.

The Plaid Shirt/Free Thinker and Courageous/Millennial Generations do not believe the narrative (propaganda) put out by mass media. Many in these Generations woke up and came alive for Bernie in 2012, and with the Creative Generation, they will stand up someday.

There were no homeless people in America when I was a kid. The solutions are a matter of Will Power and Creative Thinking.

"NO PROBLEM CAN BE SOLVED FROM THE SAME LEVEL OF CONSCIOUSNESS THAT CREATED IT."
Albert Einstein

The first 8 years of the New Age have been a rough start:
- **Technology Domination – Facebook, Goggle, Microsoft**
- **The Americans Surveillance State revealed by Edward Snowden (you are being spied on by your government)**
- **Terrorism increases – ISIS, many more**
- **Super hurricanes and huge storms growing stronger**
- **Epidemics - Ebola, Zika, Swine Flu, Covid-19**
- **World-Wide Migrant Crisis increasing**
- **Earthquakes around the world - 300,000 died in Haiti**
- **Pollution – CO_2 emissions rising - chemicals abound**
- **Police Brutality, Racism, Sexism exposed by videos**

- **Never-ending war in Middle East, Africa, and CIA**
- **Central Bank electronic money creation out of control**
- **Fukushima Daiichi, Japan - 3 nuclear reactors melting down now with no end in sight**
- **Earth, her people, animals, oceans, fish, plants, birds, insects, clean water and clean air are in the balance**

While we all feel the accelerating rate of change, a lot of Highlights of the first 8 years of the New Age are mostly in technology:
- **Artificial Intelligence**
- **Robotics**
- **Computer power**
- **Smart phone added features**
- **Social media**

Non-technology Highlights in the New Age could include:
- **Mindfulness**
- **Higher consciousness**
- **New ideas**
- **Movements organizing**
- **Youth in unity**

The struggle continues for a more just society with opportunity for all to display their talents. Everyone has something to contribute.

New Age Women are moving in a different way for their equal rights, and men need to move in a complementary manner.

"ONLY MAY THERE BE PEACE IN YOUR PRESENCE."
Xa Ta Zac Xa Ta Amac, Mayan

With the younger Generations, and some older people helping, a New Consciousness *("our Oneness with Nature and the Spiritual Essence")* **has arrived for the New Age. The keys to our happiness and success will be found in our patience, our actions, and our communications. We can cooperate with others.**

"I AM ANOTHER YOURSELF"

In Lak'Ech, Mayan

**NOW IS THE MOST EXCITING TIME
TO BE ALIVE
WE ARE WITNESSING
THE DAWN OF A NEW WORLD AGE**

Slow Down to live in the "now" as we are becoming more aware of our inner life.

"Self-serving egoism will be ruling and ruining the world, tricking people into forgetting their eternal natures and identifying with their most limited selves.

The second part of the prophecy is that ego (me, me, me) *must be humbled and surrender its illusory belief that it is the true center, and allow eternal wisdom to shine through. Ego grows transparent and becomes illuminated by the divine mind that was hidden underneath.*

<u>*The key to this prophecy is free will, for what we actually experience depends on our choices – whether we cling in fear to familiar illusion, or open up in love, and trust to the great mystery that seeks to transform and elevate us.*</u>*"*

John Major Jenkins, The Mystery of 2012 (underline added)

The younger Generations will *"become illuminated by the divine mind that was hidden underneath"* **to solve problems. Some Baby Boom , New Wave, and rich people or their children/grandchildren will help.**

After all, how many billion dollars does 1 person need while others go homeless and hungry in America? $1 billion is still 1000 million dollars.

We need a crackdown on off-shore bank accounts, private equity firms, tax loopholes, and monopoly power. The super rich and multi-national corporations need to pay at a tax rate that makes a significant contribution to society.

The New Age is already 8+ years old. It is sure to be the most exciting time to be alive. A. I. will prove to be powerful technology for multiple uses, rapid calculations, and spying on people. It is a new World Age, and there is a new Creation Cycle in the Cosmos. Anything is possible!
A NEW WORLD AGE BEGAN
ON DECEMBER 21, 2012

THE MAYAN PROPHESY

The Mayan Prophesy and the revealing of the New Age shows us that the time is now to make the changes within and outside ourselves to make a shift in our consciousness. We can strive to *"allow eternal wisdom to shine through"* **and** *"open up in love and trust to the great mystery that seeks to transform and elevate us."*

We need to defeat *"self-serving egoism that will be ruling and ruining the world, tricking people into forgetting their eternal natures and identifying with their most limited selves."*

In the New Age, self-doubt gives way to new realizations whereby people can change the World; people can reform the System (the way fundamental things are done); and people can treat each other with respect. But it might take some major reorganizations in the Status Quo – non-violent direct action by Climate Activists, Anti-War Activists, Anti-Surveillance, Anti-Racism, Labor Movements, Women's Rights, Protectors of Tribal Sovereignty, the Poor People's Campaign, and more in an Alliance of Movements.

"We come from the unknown. Our life is a Sunrise and a Sunset. We live in the Light. What are we going to leave our children, our descendants?
We are all part of this."
     Wayne "Vene" Chun, Breath of Life, Link TV

"Let us put our minds together and see what life we can make for our children."
     Sitting Bull, Hunkpapa Sioux, 1887

AN IDEAL PARTNER

Chapter 7

"Maybe someday I'm going to have a family and a house of my own, and I'm not going to budge from it....Am I 'IN LOVE'? 'NO', I thought I had been in love, but guess I wasn't. It just passed over. I guess I haven't met the girl yet, and I will, but I hope it won't be too long cuz I get lonesome sometimes."
Elvis Presley

Yes, you can get lonesome and it would be a Blessing to find your Ideal Partner. Our Typical Guy has asked for help to find his. He will need to date before finding her, and there must be mutual chemistry, true friendship, and great communications. It will take time, effort, and skill to find an Ideal Partner.

If you are already married, do everything to make it work. A Great Relationship can endure if you take care of yourself and help each other. Wrinkles can be covered up with a smile.

"It's a lack of faith that makes people afraid of meeting challenges. I believed in myself."
Muhammad Ali

WE ARE LEARNING AN ART
You probably won't start out dating your Ideal Partner. You are going to work your way up by learning to love, learning about women, learning about yourself, and being positive.

"The first step is to become aware that love is an art, just as living is an art. We must proceed in the same way we learn any other art, say music, carpentry, medicine, etc. I shall become a master only after a great deal of practice. There must be nothing in the world more important than the art. This is the answer!

People think that to love *is simple, but that to find the right object to love – or to be loved by – is difficult. Our fixation on the choice of 'love object' creates confusion between the initial experience of 'falling' in love, and the permanent state of being in love, or as we might better say, of 'standing' in love."*

Eric Fromm, The Art of Loving

Learning an art presents difficulties. Our Typical Guy is young and lacks experience, while an Older Man could have baggage to discard. It can be expensive to have a girlfriend and too expensive is a Warning Sign. She has to also love you, and there must be great chemistry. No wonder it looks impossible to many. Finding an Ideal Partner takes practice and patience.

Relationships do not endure when one party is more "in love" than the other. There must be mutual attraction and balance. It is important to know that you cannot buy a heartfelt loving relationship.

LOVE IS AN ART
WORTH LEARNING

CHOOSE WISELY

What is the description of an Ideal Partner? The answer is: you tell me, and tell yourself. Let your values in life guide you. What is important to you? When you are young, it can be hard to know.

The Reader realizes that no one can realistically live up to all their hopes or expectations. Ask yourself, "Do you believe it is possible to find your Ideal Partner?" Our term "Ideal" means to find someone who is as close as one feels is possible to be the best match. You could possibly find someone who is a teammate, partner, friend, and lover, but it might take awhile.

"God/The Creator shall give you the desires of your heart."

Psalm 31:4

See things for how they are, not how you would like them to be. If past behavior is a good predictor of future behavior, and <u>IT IS</u>, then you should know if to be optimistic or not. In other words, don't expect people to change. Experience will help give you that mentality.

RESPECT REALITY
DO NOT IGNORE WHAT YOU SEE AND HEAR

Equally important to finding an Ideal Partner is to <u>NOT MARRY THE WRONG PERSON!</u> It is easy to choose the Wrong Person if you <u>don't know what you value</u> (besides looks and sex). Learn to <u>not</u> ignore the Warning Signs. If the relationship has become intimate, it can be difficult to have the self-discipline required to walk away.

If you get married, the stakes are high. See what happens with a Bad Choice (Wrong Person):

"It is better to dwell in a corner of the rooftop, than with a brawling woman (or man) *in a wide house."*

Proverbs 21: 9

"It is better to dwell in the wilderness, than with a contentious and angry woman (or man)*."*

Proverbs 21: 19

THE 4 GROUPS OF PEOPLE

Building great relationships is a challenge for a lifetime. There are many different types of people in the world. It is said there are 32 different personality types and with different gender, age, race, etc it can get complicated. However, people have different attitudes about romantic relationships which <u>The Bullsheet</u> divides into 4 groups:

THE SAVERS – These are people "saving themselves" for marriage. They have faith they can find love, or that God/The Creator will lead them to their Ideal Partner. They will not be having sexual experience until their wedding. These people usually want children.

I told one of my friends who was a Saver, "I like to Test Drive the car before buying it."

Of course, that was not necessary for him. It seems from observing my friends that "the car" always works just fine.

Some people see saving themselves for religious reasons, some for other reasons, or it just happens.

THE HOPEFULS - These people want a monogamous relationship and/or marriage, but want sex in the meantime. They realize there will be non-monogamous relationships along the way. Many of these people are romantics who believe the Fairy Tale Story will come true. Maybe it will.

People who have a pattern of serial monogamy are often looking for an Ideal Partner. They know non-monogamous relationships are the majority, so they could be the only one monogamous. If Our Typical Guy finds himself in this situation, a woman might say, "Deal with it" or maybe, "I didn't want to hurt you." How each person adjusts is their problem. Our Typical Guy needs to move on if he wants to find his Ideal Woman.

If the chemistry is right, a person could find their Ideal Partner from this group.

THE PLAYERS AND GAMERS - These people want non-monogamous relationships. This is a large group today. These people do not believe it is possible to find an Ideal Partner, to have a happy marriage, to have a lasting relationship, or else that is not what they want. They probably don't want family life (even though some have children). There is no 'cheating' to them (you are supposed to know how things work).

The terms can be tricky. To have "Game" (skill) is good. When we "Step Up Our Game", we are improving our skills. But to be a "Gamer" (lying/false pretenses/hidden agenda) is <u>not good</u> (unless you don't care). Gamers are self-focused, and care only about themselves.

A question to ask yourself if you do <u>not</u> want a Player or Gamer: "What is the foundation of the relationship?" If it is only sex, you probably found a Player or Gamer. People can change, but it is far better to see change than to hope for it, or to totally rely on what someone says.

DON'T TRY - These people see the difficult side of relationships. These people might be interested, but they are not trying, so nothing will happen.

A friend at work describes himself and these people, "I don't try very hard. It seems like women are a lot of work and dating costs money. I have kind of given up."

They have given up because they believe it is impossible, or they are not willing to spend their money. Also, they lack confidence in themselves. These people don't even date. They won't be reading this book.

KEEP LOOKING

Sometimes all is not as it appears in relationships, or maybe we are not paying attention to the right things.

No one knows what will happen in relationships. My Ideal Woman turned out to be an Imagined Ideal Woman. She said, "I hate Liars and Cheaters." This sounded great as I am not a Liar or a Cheater, but she was.

It's important to stay detached in relationships, to be honest with yourself, and to <u>really</u> know each other. I followed false hope, ignored Warning Signs, and didn't listen to friends. When a person goes looking for an Ideal Partner, they are opening up to relationships. We all make mistakes, but we need to be wise.

Our Typical Guy can find his Ideal Woman, but if he is not careful, he could fall for a Manipulator along the way. I hope to prevent that from happening to you.

A relaxed approach takes the pressure off. Think long and hard about what you value because you need the greatest chance for success. Divorce is bad enough, but divorce with children is heartbreaking.

It takes positive belief and conscious effort for our desires to be fulfilled. If it seems impossible, just keep trying and believing.

"Life responds to us according to our belief about It and our use of It. If we believe and are doing everything we know to do to bring the desired good into our experience, it will manifest."
Dan Custer, The Miracle of Mind Power

AVOID MANIPULATORS

The Reader might ask, "Why would we discuss Manipulators in the chapter on an Ideal Partner?" It is because when someone is looking for an Ideal Partner they will be meeting people along the way, and some could be a Manipulator.

Avoiding manipulation is a skill to finding an Ideal Partner, and to not losing your money. You must learn to spot them and avoid emotional attachment. It sounds easy, but a man can be fooled if he meets his version of a *Femme Fatale:*

"French for an irresistibly attractive woman, especially one who leads men into different, dangerous or disastrous situations; her charms enamor her lovers. She is Attractive, Seductive, Charming, Manipulative, and Dangerous."
Dictionary.com

Anyone can be taken advantage of by a Manipulator, but how do you know? The first step is to know they exist. I was naïve to a Manipulator, so we have an Expert answer these questions:

- **What type of person is vulnerable?**

"Sensitive people seem to be the ones taken advantage of by Manipulators. We want her (him) *to be truthful, but <u>all great Manipulators are great Liars. We don't think like they do, so we need to wise up.</u>"*

- **What makes a person fall for them?**

"Manipulative people will play on your emotions, and strong emotions inhibit your ability to think clearly. Communication is a powerful weapon of a Manipulator as they can disrupt your normal thought patterns. (They make his Big Brain or her Short-Term Mood take over.)

They take their 'craft' of playing on someone else's emotions quite seriously. Persuasion is a skill you do not want used against you, especially if you are not good at resisting persuasion (temptation). <u>*They find ways to work around you, for their benefit. This includes sexual coercion.*</u>*"*

Are Manipulators fair?

"Fairness isn't an attribute they embody. They care about what they can 'get' from someone else, regardless of the magnitude of pain they inflict. Manipulators always have excuses and crafty methods."

Do you wonder whether or not they really care about you?

*"See how they make you feel - feel your gut - do you feel alone (*frustrated and confused*)?* <u>*Always trust your gut feelings*</u>*."*

- **How can you learn to avoid them?**

"<u>*Value your emotional well-being. Don't fall into their trap. Let go of harmful relationships in favor of your own well-being. You deserve someone who will nurture and balance your emotions, not someone who wants to use you*</u>*.*

<u>*Manipulators are insidious. People are just a 'means to an end', nothing more and nothing less*</u>*."*

Answers provided by Powerofpositivity.com
(underline and comments added)

The definition of *Insidious* gives us insight into their character: *"Operating in a inconspicuous and seemingly harmless way, but actually with grave effect."*
Dictionary.com

"Deceitful, or Stealthy Treacherousness, and Crafty"
Webster's Dictionary

The definition of *Crafty* tells us more:
"Clever at achieving one's aims by indirect or deceitful methods"
Oxford Dictionary

    It is clear that Manipulators will not reveal their true colors, and you might enjoy their treatment of you without realizing they have conned you. See if their actions match their words, and seek the counsel of wise friends. If friends tell you someone is "<u>not right for you</u>", they are probably right. They see things from the outside looking in. Friends guard your safety, but you will need to confide in them.

    It will probably be necessary to ask questions of your friends. My daughter recently met a friend's new boyfriend. She said the guy gave her a Bad Vibe, but she didn't know about telling her friend who thought she was 'in love.'

    Our friends care about us, but we might need to ask our friends the right questions rather than thinking they will speak up to warn us, "He's an Asshole", "She's a Bitch", "I don't feel good about him/her", "Bad Vibe." Ask your friends and family how they feel. You will need to <u>ask the right questions</u>.

A MANIPULATOR WILL NOT CHANGE
YOU CAN CONTROL YOUR ACTIONS
AVOID THEM!!!

YOUR DREAM

If you think about it too much, finding an Ideal Partner might seem too difficult to ever happen.

Yes, it takes time to find her. I was talking to a lady friend who told me her 32-year-old son ask, "Hey Mom, where can I find a woman that is smart, sweet, good-looking, fun, a good cook, keeps the house clean, and loves me?"

Mom replied, "Well, in the first place, I'm not sure if a woman like that actually exists. If she does exist, you might look at………..I don't know…………. the bookstore? But she probably doesn't want to get married."

A major problem for Our Typical Guy is his Big Brain. The Big Brain is very powerful, and IT can make it difficult to see what is true, even if he should know better.

What is Our Typical Guy going to do? He has heard the saying, *"Follow your heart"* **so the corollary must be,** *"Don't follow your Big Brain."* **Learn to use common sense and listen to your heart. Tune into your intuition. Problems arise when we do <u>not</u> follow our intuition. Our intuition is rarely wrong - <u>it knows</u>.**

"Intuition – the act or process of knowing something without actually thinking it out or studying; instant understanding."
Webster's Dictionary

LOVE IS ON THE WAY

We know there is <u>not</u> just one person in the world as our only possibility. When a relationship fails, learn the lessons, and keep trying. You can't move forward and hang on

to the past at the same time. Take risks, expect the impossible, and see your dreams come true.

It helps to be wise, trust your intuition, believe, and put out effort for your dreams to come true. It might take awhile, but remember that you don't want to marry the Wrong One!
YOU CAN FIND THE RIGHT ONE
IF YOU AVOID THE WRONG ONES

On the 75th Wedding Anniversary of Jimmy and Roselyn Carter, President Carter was asked for their secrets:

"THE SECRET IS TO PICK THE RIGHT PARTNER, AND MAKE YOUR MARRIAGE A FULL PARTNERSHIP. AND WORK OUT ANY DIFFERENCES BEFORE GOING TO SLEEP EACH NIGHT."

Don't worry - the spirit will have someone nice for you. Be patient for love.

People are finding the person of their dreams. It is important to feel you deserve someone nice. Your greatest strength is Love, but it starts within – respect yourself.

BE A COMPLETE PERSON

Chapter 8

This chapter gives practical tips for expanding your life. You can use your imagination and create a stronger version of yourself.

PART ONE: SEVEN ARROWS

Seven Arrows by Hyemeyohsts Storm invites us into the world of the American Indians:

"Sit here with me, each of you as you are in your Perceiving of yourself. Let us Teach each other in each of the Ways on this Great Medicine Wheel, our Earth."

Seven Arrows **gives us understanding through life lessons, history, storytelling, beautiful illustrations, and great photographs.** Seven Arrows **speaks to the nature of man and woman, and tells of becoming a** *"Whole Person" or "Total Being."*

o   *"Among the People, a child's first Teaching is of visiting the Four Great Powers of the Medicine Wheel:*
- *East is Illumination*
- *South is Innocence and Trust*
- *North is Wisdom*
- *West is Introspection, or the Looks-Within Place"*

o   Another teaching is to realize that each of us has a different perspective on <u>everything</u> (even a rock). Understanding that others have a different point of view shows us the need to try for dialogue and clear communications.

- **Another important lesson is** *"The Touching - No two people on the face of this earth are alike in any one thing except for their loneliness. The only way that we can overcome our loneliness is through Touching. It is only in this way that we can learn to be Total Beings."*

By reaching out to others *(the Touching)* **we can overcome loneliness. Feelings of loneliness show our need for companionship and belonging. Coronavirus has proven that people are social creatures. We all want to share love and be loved.**

I was 50 by the time I had friends tell me they were "Loners." Most of these friends had traveling jobs. Later, I guessed someone to be a Loner who was shocked but said, "Yes, I enjoy my own company."

Some people enjoy "alone time" more often. We see the difference in being alone and being lonely.

Time alone can be to relax, create, read, or reflect. By being aware that loneliness is natural, we can use our loneliness to give us energy rather than feeling anxiety, depression, or sadness.

- **We find in** Seven Arrows **that the number four is sacred, or special, among most Tribes. Four represents the Four Directions, the Four Seasons, the Four Phases of Life.**

"Any person who perceives from only one of these Four Great Directions will remain just a partial person. Even the people who have two or three of these gifts, still are not a Whole Person and must grow by seeking understanding in each of the Four Great Ways. Only in this way can we become full, capable of balance and decision in this Growing and Seeking."

WE MUST VISIT THE FOUR GREAT DIRECTIONS TO BE A *"WHOLE PERSON" OR "TOTAL BEING"*

After reading Seven Arrows, I felt a need to be a *"Whole Person" or "Total Being",* so I asked myself – "What is the meaning of Illumination, Innocence and Trust, Wisdom, and Introspection?" I realized this was going to take time, but I wanted to get started *"visiting the Four Great Powers of the Medicine Wheel."*

PART TWO: PRACTICAL ACTIVITIES

The Bullsheet introduces a Daily Practice of having **Practical Activities to assist us becoming a** *"Whole Person or Total Being by seeking understanding in each of the Four Great Ways."*

Create your own variation, but give it a try by going for a walk and take a break along the way to face each of the Four Directions while remembering the *"Power"* **or** *"Gift"* **of each direction. Start in the East with the rising Sun, and end in the West with the setting Sun.**

Next, choose some Practical Activity that will help keep you focused on what will improve your life. For examples, my current Practical Activity for each direction is listed. Change the activity to fit you, but make it a daily practice. Seven Arrows **and the definitions give added meanings.**

- *"EAST----ILLUMINATION---- WHERE WE SEE THINGS CLEARLY FAR AND WIDE."*

"Illumination: To give light to; to make clear; to explain."
Webster's Dictionary

My Practical Activity for Illumination:
FEEL THE WORLD OUTSIDE MY MIND

I don't want to live thinking all the time. With this Practical Activity, I can stop thinking for a few seconds to practice 'feeling' instead of thinking. I lose self-importance, but with a life to live.

Illumination could be bringing into the light what was in the dark. Then you could see your real situation.

Your Practical Activity for Illumination - _____

- *"SOUTH ----INNOCENCE & TRUST----- PERCEIVING CLOSELY OUR NATURE OF HEART"*

"Innocence: the ability to feel joy, passion, and desire without fear of it being wrecked; being open to the world and others without cynicism or skepticism; not intending to cause harm."

"Trust: a strong belief that some person or thing is honest or can be depended on; to have faith in; to rely or depend on; to believe."

Webster's Dictionary

My Practical Activities for Innocence and Trust:
YOGA and EXERCISE

Yoga and exercise keeps us healthy and allows us to stay calm while we work through our feelings. For innocence, I picture a smiling 2-year-old and remember that is how we are supposed to be. We can try for present moment awareness.

"If you are not living this moment, you are not really living"

Eckhart Tolle

Your Practical Activities for Innocence & Trust -_____ - _____

- *"NORTH ----WISDOM"*

"Wisdom: having a perspective that gives you good judgment coming from intuition, knowledge, common sense, and your experiences in life."

My Practical Activity for Wisdom:
MAKE GOOD DECISIONS

Wisdom includes having the strength to do what is right. Wisdom and good decisions can lead you to love.
**IT IS IN YOUR DECISIONS
THAT YOU EXECUTE YOUR POWER**

Your Practical Activity for Wisdom - _____

- *"WEST -----INTROSPECTION ----THE LOOK'S WITHIN PLACE"*

"Introspection: the process of looking into and examining one's own thoughts or feelings"

Webster's Dictionary

My Practical Activity for Introspection:
KNOW GOD LOVES ME

Knowing that God loves me gives me peace in my mind and joy in my heart. We can look within ourselves through meditation, patience, prayer, or reflection to receive guidance that is meaningful.

Why is Introspection important? *"We want to be able to distinguish between Reality and Illusion; between who we are, and who we think we are. Not having Introspection leaves us living in a trap of believing Fantasy."*

Chris Hedges

Introspection can provide insight. You might see the true nature of yourself, or your relationships. You could also see your illusions. Introspection helps you form mutually beneficial relationships, to mature, and to build the life you want.

Your Practical Activity for Introspection - _____

Additional suggestions for Practical Activities: walking more; developing patience; going to a class; reading; more time with friends or family; being in nature; deep breathing; prayer; dancing, or anything that helps you grow.

PART THREE: BE A COMPLETE PERSON

In Part Three we use our imagination to develop an analogy to a *"Whole Person"* or *"Total Being"* that we will call Be a Complete Person. We can agree that Four areas of Modern Life make us complete: OUR PHYSICAL - EMOTIONAL - SPIRITUAL & FINANCIAL LIVES.

Challenges will come and go, and deep inside you are already complete, but don't stay Too Weak – Too Long in any area, or become a Wreck!

OUR SCALE: GREAT, GOOD, FAIR, WEAK, WRECK

Of course, we want to be Great or Good in every area, but with our theory, a person could be Weak in all four areas and still be a Complete Person, <u>if they keep trying</u>.

WHEN WE STRIVE
TO STAY IN BALANCE
AND NEVER GIVE UP
OUR LIFE IMPROVES

We each have our stronger and weaker areas. For me, Financial is now my greatest problem. However, Emotional was previously my weakest, and Spiritual was my weakest before that.

SELF-ACCOUNTABILITY AND SELF-DISCIPLINE ARE REQUIRED - JUST KEEP TRYING

Self-accountability is to be honest in evaluating your actions, reactions, and current results.

Self-discipline is the ability to do what is right for you and the people you care about. Self-discipline is key to a happy/contented life built on good decisions and right effort.

SELF-DISCIPLINE IS A GOOD THING
SELF-DISCIPLINE IS HOW WE GET RESULTS

Right effort can be a foundation for inner strength. Right effort can be to imagine new possibilities for yourself, change your diet, slow down to relax, walk more, or anything that is healthy and healing for you.

Be careful to not compare yourself with others. There is always someone better looking, richer, more athletic, smarter, younger, or better at something than you are.

"Comparison is the death of joy."
                                                          Mark Twain

YOUR PHYSICAL LIFE

One day I was pumping gas and heard the people speaking to the booth in the middle. The public sounded unhappy, but the lady working in the box was so cheerful to them all. I ask her secret for having such a cheerful attitude while all the public was so grumpy.

The Cheerful Lady said, "IF I WAKE UP IN THE MORNING, AND I CAN WALK - IT'S A GOOD DAY."

START AND END EACH DAY
WITH A GRATEFUL HEART AND MIND

As you age, it would be beneficial to have short-term and long-range plans for your health and well-being. A healthy life is physical, so workout, eat right, and walk.

"You are only as young as your spine is flexible."
Richard Hittleman, Author and early TV Yoga Instructor

THE GOAL OF OUR PHYSICAL LIFE IS
TO BE HEALTHY AND FIT
TO UNITE BODY, MIND, AND SOUL

YOUR EMOTIONAL LIFE

Our Typical Guy could be unaware of his emotions. When negative emotions surface, he can be caught by surprise and overreact. <u>Overreactions can destroy your relationships</u>. Learn to take that breath of calm to react and respond in a wise manner.

Emotions are so important that we have separate chapters on Emotions, Jealousy, Anger, and Attachment. You can save yourself from a lot of bad decisions and emotional pain.

You can have great relationships with good social and emotional skills. Recognize your emotions - give them a name, process them, and understand what they represent. That allows you to control your emotions according to the situation, and you see how your emotions impact others around you.

**THE GOAL OF OUR EMOTIONAL LIFE IS
TO BE PATIENT AND CONTROL EMOTIONS
SO EMOTIONS DO NOT CONTROL US**

YOUR SPIRITUAL LIFE

When we are feeling love in our heart, appreciating life around us, or seeing/feeling God/The Creator - we are feeling the spiritual.

"In the Earth's 5 Blue Zones where people are healthy into their 100's, they have 4 things in common: 1. Good Diet 2. Physical Activity 3. Closeness of Family and or Friends 4. Spiritual Life."

Nicoya Peninsula, Costa Rica, Americas Now

The fact some people don't believe in God does not mean that God does not exist. And even if a person doesn't believe in God/The Creator/The Great Spirit, they can feel life, love, and joy in their heart.

Being spiritual and having religion are not the same. Each religion provides answers and instructions, but no religion likes another religion's answers or instructions. Everyone has a different perspective on the spiritual, but we might agree the opposite of spiritual is an egocentric (selfish) nature.

"The spiritual nature is inconceivable to us. Yet we can feel that there is something spiritual present. Even a person completely ignorant of the spiritual nature can somehow feel its presence.

We can sense the absence of spirit when a body is dead. If we witness someone dying, we can sense that something is leaving the body. Although we do not have the eyes to see it, that something is spirit."

Srila Prabhupada, The Path of Perfection

Just as our mind cannot comprehend the millions of light years to the stars, we cannot comprehend God/The Creator.

LIFE IS NOT CIRCUMSTANTIAL
LIFE IS NOT HAPPENSTANCE

"On seeking the divine within – Whether it is the godhead or not, I feel this great force, this untapped power, this dynamic something within me. This feeing defies description, and no experience with which this feeling may be compared. It is like a strong emotion mixed with faith, but a lot stronger."

Bruce Lee, Striking Thoughts

A GOAL FOR OUR SPIRITUAL LIFE IS
TO HAVE A CONNECTION
WITH GOD/THE CREATOR/THE GREAT SPIRIT

YOUR FINANCIAL LIFE

NOTE: It is difficult to address Financial Life because of disparities in income, family support, education, and life

circumstances. Of course, the more money you have, the more options become available.

You can't help someone else if you can't pay your own bills. You can't do things, buy a home, start a family, or have a girlfriend if you don't have money or income.

Not having money is stressful. Reflect on your habits and attitudes to create your budget. Look at budgeting as a way to freedom and you can find ways to avoid the Debt Trap. Once again, self-discipline is a good thing.

It's easy to borrow money, and hard to pay it back.

When you are thinking about a purchase, you can remember my Brother telling me, "All these Good Deals keep me broke."

**A GOAL FOR OUR FINANCIAL LIFE IS
TO MANAGE OUR MONEY
SO WE CAN ENJOY OUR LIFE**

**THE CHALLENGE
THE CHALLENGE IS TO KEEP IMPROVING
IN ALL FOUR AREAS EVERY DAY**

With daily effort, you will be able to keep going in our Modern World. You develop dependability that people can count on, and a mindset skill that will improve your life. Yes, you are a Complete Person already, but don't get Too Weak – Too Long in any area of your life.

"In today's rush we all think too much, seek too much, want too much, and forget about the joy of just being."

Eckhart Tolle

"THE MEDICINE WHEEL WAY"

Yes, I have been working on being a *Total Being* and Complete Person for over 30 years. Discovering the *"Power"* or *"Gift"* of each direction continues to be a reminder of how to stay balanced and improve my quality of life.

QUALITY OF LIFE
IS WHAT WE ARE WORKING ON
IT IS THE POINT OF THIS BOOK

It might take a little time for you to develop your Daily Practice with Practical Activities, but Seven Arrows **teaches us,** *"The Way of the People is learned by Seeking Understanding and then allowing it to Grow within our own Heart and Mind."*
Doubt, confusion, and fear are swept aside when you find a way to focus on what matters most. Develop your *Gifts* **to become a gift to yourself and others.**

"THIS GROWING AND SEEKING
 IS OUR LIFE'S PROGRESSION"

ARE YOU INDOCTRINATED FOR MARRIAGE?

Chapter 9

This chapter could be especially helpful for younger Readers, someone divorced, or those 27-39 who think they might be getting old. However, we should all pay attention because a lot is on the line in marriage.

In 2021, many people do not want to marry. It's not like when I was young in the 1970s, and everyone expected to get married. Everyone I knew <u>did</u> get married.

People today are asking questions about society 'norms', marriage and themselves. The definition of Indoctrination is so simple to meet that it is clear we have all been indoctrinated about marriage and much more.

"Indoctrinated: The process of teaching a person to accept a set of beliefs <u>uncritically</u>."

Oxford Dictionary (underline added)

People have been indoctrinated, programmed, and "consumerized" all their lives. We are programmed by our community and the people who raise us. Marriage has been encouraged for most of us from childhood through adulthood by our families, schools, religion, friends, television, movies, songs, and ourselves. Our feelings and beliefs could be subconscious.

Many men don't talk about marriage with their friends until they make an announcement! This is crazy. We need our friend's input all our life – this is what friends are for. He or she will have a perspective we need to consider. At times, it is helpful to hear yourself talk to see your situation.

THE MARRIAGE MINDSET

The marriage indoctrination can create the Marriage Mindset which is <u>when you feel you should, or will get married</u>. Actually, you don't know if you will ever meet someone with mutual romantic love and get married, and you sure don't want to rush into marriage. Also, if you think of actually being married to someone, you might not be so sure.

IF YOU RUSH INTO MARRIAGE
IT IS LIKE RIDING
INTO YOUR OWN AMBUSH

Seeing the Marriage Mindset indoctrination can prevent you from marrying the Wrong Person, and help you to understand the difficulty in finding the Right Person. And you have to be the Right Person for them.

Marriage could be a great thing, but it has to be a great match. Finding the Right One takes skill, luck, respect (love), and patience – a difficult combination. For a marriage to be successful, a couple will need shared interests and activities, great chemistry, and <u>both</u> will need to stay committed to building a life of friendship and love with <u>one person</u>.

Understanding the indoctrination and the Marriage Mindset is a warning to slow down, take time to get to know the other person, know yourself, and ask the right questions.

HOW CAN THE MARRIAGE MINDSET BE A TRAP?

While dating, we should go with the flow of the relationship without pressure or thinking of marriage too early. If you are just dating, but thinking of marriage, it can ruin your relationship by putting too much pressure on yourself, your date, and/or the relationship.

If in the Marriage Mindset, Our Typical Guy can goof up the relationship before giving it a real chance. For example, if he is dating an attractive woman, he might think she is so beautiful and sweet that she is the One. He might act possessive. This is crazy thinking, but some do it, and ruin what could have been a great relationship. It is easy to be jealous, but no one likes jealousy or to be pressured - it removes the fun.

If you are the one being pursued, you might be unsuspecting and pressured into marriage before thinking properly. We have all seen this happen with our friends.

A person might think they are "in love" before actually getting to know someone. You should be enjoying their company. If you give it a little time, you might find out she is pretty (or the man is handsome), but that's about it. Let the relationship evolve. There is no need to act in haste.

Yes, the attractive women seem to get 'snatched up', but it usually takes about 2 years to get to know someone. It is better to be cool about it, not indoctrinated.

The Marriage Mindset can work against Our Typical Guy even if he does not adopt it himself because women are also indoctrinated into the same Marriage Mindset. A man can be convinced to marry from his girlfriend, and some women feel the biological clock. A woman might want to marry Our Typical Guy! Watch out - they have ways of getting their way!

FREE YOUR MIND

We are not giving up on the possibility of marriage. We are simply moving thoughts of marriage from the front of our mind to the back. We are moving the idea of having a good relationship to the front. Keep it casual, and free up your mind. Maybe marriage will be good for you someday, or maybe you will never get married. Don't be concerned about marriage until you know more.

Realize the difficulty of finding the right person for a Happy Marriage. It can be fairly easy to get married, but difficult to be in a Happy Marriage. Talk about marriage with married friends, single friends, older couples, men and women, to see if they are happy. If not – WHY NOT? You will learn something.

Notice the couples you know to see if they seem happy, or if you want to be in their situation. The more you confide in friends, the more they will confide in you. The more you talk about marriage, the more you will learn. Figure out what is right for you. Know what marriage is really like - not imagination, indoctrination, or an infatuation that will wear off.

Marriage revolves around family life (usually), mutual chemistry, financial arrangements, love, and practical matters. Even if a person is married, we learned "loneliness" is something we all have in common. Look at the big picture. Learn to enjoy life while you learn what you can about yourself and relationships.

**WHEN IT COMES TO MARRIAGE
THE LITTLE BRAIN NEEDS TO TAKE CONTROL**

QUESTIONS WILL ARISE

- What are you going to do with relationships you know will not end in marriage?

Enjoy their company. You might never find a relationship that will end in marriage. However, don't fall into the Comfort Zone Trap. If the relationship is mainly about sex, calculate what it is costing in time, energy and money. Don't spend all your money chasing pleasure. It sure won't be happiness when your money is gone.

- What happens when they bring up commitment?

You can say "No" or "Yes." You do not have to be married to be in a committed relationship. If "Yes", you have agreed to focus on that relationship, but it doesn't mean it will result in marriage.

- What if you want to marry them, but they don't want to marry?

You can give it more time, enjoy the relationship as it is, or keep looking. Maybe they are against marriage, or they are not marrying <u>you</u> even if you feel they are your Ideal Partner.

- Have you overcome anger, jealousy, and other negative Emotions?

If the answer is "No" - don't get married. You can still date while you work on overcoming negative emotions. No relationship can survive abuse or disrespect. It is oppressive.

IF YOU CAN'T BE KIND
BE QUIET

- Are they your Ideal Partner?

Only you can answer this question. Are they who you would choose if you had your choice in the whole world? It can be difficult to be patient, and easy to make a bad decision. See if they are always asking for something. Do you both enjoy hanging out together for extended times? Do you participate in shared activities? Have you been on a trip together? If there are few extended times spent together, they are probably just a friend, temptation, or manipulation.

INDOCTRINATION REALIZATION

We know marriage is not for everyone. If marriage happens for you, that could be great. If marriage doesn't happen, that could also be great. How could it be great both ways? If you take your time and find the right partner, it could be great. If you take your time and still haven't found the right partner, it is great that you can keep looking for someone you love that loves you. Be content, regardless of your situation with relationships.

It could be one of the worst mistakes of your life if you marry the Wrong Person. Divorce is painful, emotional, expensive, and "everybody loses." It's going to take money to start another life. People don't get told these things in the Marriage Indoctrination. And no one should ever get married with the idea, "If it doesn't work out, I can just get a divorce."

When you contemplate your indoctrination, that fact alone will help free your mind for good decisions. You know not to pressure anyone, and not to be weak, or succumb to pressure. You are talking about the rest of your life and <u>your</u> happiness!

Freedom of mind will allow you to trust your feelings and intuition rather than trying to figure things out. You don't know what will happen. It could take a long time for a relationship to result in marriage. Free your mind, enjoy your life, and know you can share love with or without marriage.

We never know which marriages will work, but you need to feel the other is a True Friend <u>and</u> a Dream Come True for there to be the best chance of success.

BE WISE
MAKE GOOD CHOICES
YOUR HAPPINESS DEPENDS ON IT
YOU WERE INDOCTRINATED BUT NOW YOU KNOW

STARTING OUT

Chapter 10

You are starting out when you try for a new romantic relationship. A little determination and perseverance is required to get started, and to keep trying.

It can feel like a daunting task to begin looking for someone new, but the first thing to realize is that you will need to get out there and mingle. Yes, you might meet someone at work, church, the grocery store, or in everyday living, but the chances are low. Yes, you can keep your eyes open while doing regular things, but you will probably need to do more.

Make time for meeting someone new and nice by dedicating some of your time to participating in activities, going to events, or enjoying clubs to get you out. Find activities you enjoy that have a mingle factor. If you are doing things you enjoy, it should be fun. Yes, you will need to push yourself out the door on occasion, but learn to do that.

In other words, as you face apprehension and intimidation (which comes mostly from within) prepare your mind for making the effort to get out and mingle.

START FRESH
LEAVE BAGGAGE BEHIND
IMAGINE NEW POSSIBILITES FOR YOURSELF

"Nature does not hurry, yet everything is accomplished."
Lao Tzu, Ancient Chinese philosopher

We know it's going to take effort to find a nice girlfriend/boyfriend, and we can't count on someone appearing from out of the blue. Going out and being friendly is going to be up to you.

OUR TYPICAL GUY GETS STARTED

We know Our Typical Guy is relationship challenged, but he has learned to fight frustration with patience and calm to determine what he should do.

I had a Professor in law school who happened to be a friend. His Professor nickname was well deserved, 'Flunking Fred.' I should have left it at friend, but I took the most difficult class of all my schooling. I felt lucky to get a 'D.' The first day we heard, "We don't have much 'How-to' around here."

It was legal training, not practical Courthouse experience training. The Professor doesn't have time for students to ask questions. The Professor asks the questions, provides the answers, and presents the opposing and alternative views.

The Bullsheet is in the role of the Professor, and will be asking and answering the questions while presenting possible obstacles to overcome. However, it will provide some "How-to."

We discuss fundamentals so opportunity will not pass you by. There are recurring themes in The Bullsheet to help you discover your best tips. You learn to act on your intuition.

Our Typical Guy and you should know that some people are not a fit for him, and some are <u>not good</u> for him, even if he thinks they are. The important thing is to stay calm to control emotions and reactions. If one relationship fails, you will find a better relationship.

YOU HAVE TO BE STRONG
WHAT IS YOUR OTHER CHOICE?
BE WEAK AND GIVE UP?
NO!!! GET STRONGER EVERY DAY

Self-improvement makes you stronger and keeps you going. It is in everyday effort that you grow stronger or weaker - physically, emotionally, financially, and spiritually.

The ability to stay positive helps keep you on the path to happiness, contentment, and success. Being positive is simply to maintain a good attitude and to see past difficulty. It will keep you from making up excuses and procrastinating.

"You can't connect the dots looking forward; you can only connect them looking backwards. So you have to trust that the dots will somehow connect in your future. You have to trust in something - your gut, destiny, life, karma, whatever."

Steve Jobs, Inventor

GENERALIZATIONS
We can agree generalizing is impossible in the Modern World, but it is necessary to continue our story. Readers are from different backgrounds, gender, finances, age, race, and personality which add different perspectives and experiences.

I remember going on a trip to Boston after college in 1972. We went to a movie, The Last Picture Show. The theater was packed (unlike Oklahoma), and I had to sit on the front row. The irony was the movie was a relationship drama around the closing of the only movie theatre in the small Texas town of Archer City.

I lived in Wichita Falls when ages 11-15, and had been to Archer City many times to my friend's Grandparent's ranch where there were a lot of jackrabbits. We would chase jackrabbits at night in a jeep with lights. There were lots of them, and they are big with long ears and big hind legs. They can really run.

While watching the show, I got the feeling that not one of the movie goers in Boston had ever seen a jackrabbit. I looked over my shoulder and could feel from those people in Boston that they felt like they were watching a movie of life on another planet!

Where you live (big city, town, country, East Coast, West Coast, Deep South, etc) has each of us living different lives. We know there are countless variations of people, and it is impossible to generalize about relationships. We also recognize that morals have become an individual standard more than a society standard.

Women are surely impossible to speak of in general terms. When we talk about women, we are referring to a relationship with mutual attraction, respect and consent.

<u>**The Bullsheet**</u> **is NEVER saying, "All women or men are like this _____". We could say,**

WOMEN WANT FREEDOM
FREEDOM TO HAVE CHOICES
FREEDOM TO BE AN INDIVIDUAL

VITALITY

The world of relationships is undergoing drastic change as men and women are adjusting to the New Age and Modern Women. However, the fundamentals stay the same as basic desires and needs don't change. Most people have a longing for love and the *"Gift of Companionship."*

We need respect and wisdom to bring love into our lives and to sustain our relationships. We will be tested by our

desires, emotions, other people, making a living, and what happens in life. We need to maintain vitality to persevere.

"Vitality: gives us energy, vigor, strength of mind and body. Vitality is the power to keep on living, and to be full of life and energy."
Webster's Dictionary

With vitality, you stay determined, passionate, and reinvigorated about your vision. If something or some relationship doesn't work - a new vision is coming. Each relationship you engage can change your perspective. Vitality is the power to feel the life force within you. Vitality is part of your VIBE.

IT'S ALL ABOUT THE VIBE
LIFE IS ABOUT BEING AWARE
AND MAKING GOOD CHOICES

SEX

All types of relationship arrangements are possible in the Modern World. However, <u>The Bullsheet</u> is focusing on a man/woman relationship – that's complicated enough!

While in Colombia, I mentioned lesbians.

A lady said, "What's wrong with that? It's normal."

I didn't say anything. Actually, I understand lesbians as I like women myself.

Sex is a personal matter, and can be a wonderful experience. God is Good, Life is the Greatest, Great Relationships and Great Sex are part of Nature and part of what most want.

"Go the way your blood beats. All True Love is Holy"
James Baldwin

True Love can be difficult to find. There has to be mutual attraction and a strong bond for a relationship to succeed. Therefore, we will be vulnerable, but fearless, as we walk into the fire of relationships – a person could get Burned or ignite a Big Fire.

BEAUTY

Beauty is illusive. (Even the most beautiful woman knows she will not always be young and beautiful, and she is more conscious of this than any man.) When <u>The Bullsheet</u> mentions "beautiful", we define it as "attractive to a man to where he is interested in being intimate with her"; "beauty fitting the concept, there is someone for everyone"; "beauty is only skin deep"; "beauty is in the eye of the beholder"; and

"Beauty: That quality in a woman that makes her pleasant to look at, listen to, or think about."
Webster's Dictionary

Our Typical Guy should quickly learn that there is a lot more to a woman than her looks, and that being a *"Shallow Hal"* can lead to trouble. My Mom would say,
"PRETTY IS
AS PRETTY DOES."

PROCRASTINATION

Starting Out is always the hardest part of any project. Procrastination is a formidable enemy that blocks success. The

word "procrastination" comes from 2 Latin words "go forward – tomorrow." We are starting <u>today</u> – not tomorrow.

We are agreeing to leave baggage, jealousy, fear, anxiety, and judgments at the door. We are ridding ourselves of poisonous self-doubt, impatience, and negative self-image.

I tell myself, "I look kind of like Brad Pitt" and just go on with it. I try to stay away from mirrors.

Just get out there, be friendly, and enjoy yourself. Good things will happen. It might take a little time and practice, but good things will happen.

"PROCRASTINATION IS THE THIEF OF TIME."
                                                        Brother Martin Luther King Jr.

DISTRACTION

Distraction is something I would not have considered a problem, but I recently encountered an Easily Distracted Person. Also, our own distractions can turn into excuses that keep us from going out to socialize and mingle.

The Modern World has increasingly greater distractions from computers, social media, cell phones, etc. Easily Distracted People are not lazy or afraid of failure like someone who procrastinates. They simply get too many activities going on.

If you discover yourself trying to be in a relationship with an Easily Distracted Person, it can be frustrating. These people have good intentions, but they lose focus easily. However, they might not realize they are living that way so, "Why do some people live an Easily Distracted lifestyle?"

They might be a "people pleaser" (not good at telling people "No.") They are usually behind on their efforts, so they have a lot to do. Because they are active, they keep getting more and more activities. And they don't realize they are losing focus because of how they don't prioritize. They can always justify their over-activity, and fit the saying. *"They can't see the forest for the trees."*

There is good news: distractions can be easily eliminated. A person can learn to say "No", or "I would love to but_____", or simply not respond to requests.

However, it is difficult to be in a relationship with an Easily Distracted Person because they are busy all the time. They might not change, but you can express how you feel. You might want to move on. Yes, distraction can ruin a relationship.

IF SOMEONE IS OVERDOING
THEY PROBABLY WON'T HAVE TIME FOR YOU
IT COULD BE TIME TO FIND SOMEONE NEW

Take authority over your life. Understanding people and avoiding distractions will give you added freedom. Focus on the people and activities that matter the most to you, not someone who doesn't make time for you.

INSECURITIES

Don't feel alone as we all have insecurities. They come from anxiety or doubt, and a lack of trust or confidence. Insecurities are a form of low self-esteem or negative self-image which manifests as feeling like, "not being good enough" or "I have made too many mistakes." We all make mistakes.

Insecurities can be greater when Our Typical Guy is starting out because he is lacking emotional intimacy and relationship stability. But these things will be coming as he grows.

Sometimes we "beat ourselves up" when what we tell ourselves is emotional poison: "I'm too old", "It won't happen for me", "I'm ugly", "I can't get well", "I'm too shy", or whatever that is negative. Don't believe it and don't do it. When you identify your feelings, you can confront personal issues.

Be yourself - there is no need to prove anything to anyone. If you do not currently have a romantic relationship, you can keep trying. A good disposition and pleasant personality will make up for a lot of looks. Be friendly.

BE AROUND PEOPLE YOU LOVE
DO THINGS YOU ENJOY

WHAT TO DO

Our Typical Guy will need to Step Up His Game to make his relationships better. What is Game?

"Game: It is confidently using your attributes and overall personality to win the affection of a woman (or man) *you want. A measure of smoothness with the opposite sex. You can't have 'Game' if you doubt yourself."*

Urbandictionary.com

When you are friendly and feel joy in your heart, you will be able to meet someone nice. You could meet them anywhere or anytime. There is the saying, *"Love is where you find it."* Wisdom and guidance comes from many sources, but it is up to you to apply common sense. <u>The Bullsheet</u> is offering tips. These tips are like love - they are where you find them.

THINK
<u>THE BULLSHEET</u> IS NOT TELLING YOU "WHAT" TO THINK BUT TELLING YOU "TO THINK"

I found many helpful self-improvement books, but only a few on relationships were helpful. However, I did read a book by a woman author who agreed that a woman should <u>not settle</u> for someone less than her Dream Man (Ideal Man). She agreed that if we know what to look for, we can find the Right Person. However, we are just looking for someone to go on a date when we are starting out.

It would be a Blessing to most of us to have great relationship(s) so that we are not always on our own. It will probably take years to find an Ideal Partner, so most people will live non-monogamous or going without for some time. In the meantime, be working on personal growth, developing relationship skills, and keeping your eyes open. We are starting out with the short-term goal to meet someone attractive and go on dates.

Starting out is to live in the moment and to do what you can to be happy. If you are motivated by the prospect of romance, you will not be scared or frustrated. Going out to mingle is like going to work-out in that your mind will come up with excuses for why not to go. Yes, some outings will be better than others, but you can't meet anyone by sitting at home.

Most people would enjoy some romance and companionship in their life, but they need to meet someone. Yes, it feels difficult when starting out, but you can find the

courage and confidence for good things to happen. Of course, online dating might be how you meet in 2021+. Remember that it could be worth the effort when she/he comes over.

It might take a few months, but know that good things will happen if you do things you enjoy. Have a friend go with you sometimes. You should have a good time, regardless of who you see.

THE BEST THINGS IN LIFE

On a trip to Jamaica in 2000, there were a lot more Rasta restaurants than in 2015. They are not fancy, but serve healthy Jamaican vegetarian food. After eating Rasta for a week, my son and I changed our diets to mostly vegetarian for the rest of our lives. You get to a point to where you don't even want the food that is not good for you. In one of these Rasta restaurants, I took a photo of a wall painting *"Haile Selassie Says"*, and framed it for my bookcase at home.

REMEMBER THESE THINGS
TO START OUT – START OVER – OR TO KEEP GOING:

HAILE SELASSIE SAYS

"THE GREATEST SIN....FEAR
THE BEST DAY....TODAY
THE BEST TOWN....WHERE YOU SUCCEED
THE BEST WORK....WHAT YOU LIKE
THE BEST PLAY....WORK
THE SECRET OF PRODUCTION....SAVING
THE CHEAPEST THING....FINDING FAULT
THE MOST DANGROUS PERSON....LIAR
THE GREATEST MISTAKE....GIVING UP
THE BEST THING IN THE WORLD....LOVE"

A GOOD ATTITUDE

Chapter 11

Being comfortable with yourself is elementary to enjoying life and being able to participate in a great relationship. Preparation and a positive attitude will be a key to our success. However, there will be disappointments.

"Disappointments are inevitable, Misery is Optional."
Saying

With a Good Attitude we are looking at the dating process and relationships as a challenge that is fun. We are transforming ourselves to be mentally and emotionally strong. It's like doing homework.

IMPORTANT MINDSETS

RESPECT

The most important attitude is Respect. There is no love without respect. One way we respect ourselves is in having boundary lines. If Our Typical Guy doesn't know where his line exists, he cannot enforce it. Boundaries – What's that?

Yes, most need to determine and enforce their boundary lines. The importance of boundary lines is to learn about yourself, to keep from being a Fool, and to be able to observe other's intentions. Boundaries are about who you will let into your life (remember Manipulators).

Questions will arise: What will you tolerate? How will you adjust? Do you still want to see them? (You could be with a Manipulator.) Your kindness can be taken as weakness. Do they show real interest in your life and spend time with you? What kind of relationship do you want?

**MUTUAL RESPECT IS THE
BASIS OF A GREAT RELATIONSHIP**

PATIENCE
In retrospect, I have not been very good at being patient. I have been good at waiting, but that is not the same.

"Patience: 1. Able to put up with pain, trouble, delay, boredom, etc. without complaining, 2. Working steadily without giving up."
Webster's Dictionary

"Wait: 1. To stay in a place or do nothing while expecting a certain thing to happen. 2, To keep expecting, or look forward to."
Webster's Dictionary

One quickly sees that with waiting, not much will happen in life, and with patience, everything is possible - even finding love.

At times we are required to wait as a part of patience, so patience can be waiting without anxiety, worrying, or apprehension.

Discover and adopt the power and peace that comes to you with having Enduring Patience.

"HE WHO IS NOT COURAGEOUS ENOUGH TO TAKE RISKS WILL ACCOMPLISH NOTHING IN LIFE."
Muhammad Ali

It takes confidence to accomplish anything. Our Typical Guy will need confidence to approach a woman he finds attractive.

A Lady in Jamaica told me,

"YOU HAVE TO STEP UP TO THE ONE YOU LIKE AND BE ABLE TO TAKE YOUR REJECTION."

I didn't like hearing this observation of me, but it's the truth. For many Americans, rejection is like a boxer getting his head knocked back from a strong jab. When an American gets rejection, he often stops trying.

I commented to Jamaican friends, "Rejection doesn't bother you guys at all."

They smiled and said, "Not at all." One guy told me he uses rejection to give him more inspiration. Another guy said, "I find one I like better."

I realize that asking you to step up to a woman you think you would like to go out with is not easy, and it can be intimidating. Whether it be at a club, church, grocery store, or wherever, having courage and self-confidence is often necessary if you are to go out with someone new.

When you are able to strike up a conversation with someone you would like to go out with, it would be so simple to get excited and blurt out, "Let's go out to lunch or dinner sometime." Say something! And don't forget to Smile! When she is gone, the feeling of her "getting away" without your saying anything is worse than what the rejection would have been. We all get rejection. No one likes rejection. We have to be strong in this world. Otherwise, we keep getting the same results.

A man is required to "step up" and say something to the woman. None of us like rejection, but <u>to step up and say</u>

something to the woman you like is a must. If you are not willing to do this, you might as well forget it.

I read the travel guide for Colombia saying that South American countries have a "macho environment." It explained, "This means the man is usually required to make the first move with a woman."

We know it doesn't always happen like this in the Modern World, but it's still the way it usually works.
A MAN HAS TO SHOW HER
SHE IS THE ONE HE LIKES

For various reasons, you could be rejected. It doesn't mean she doesn't like you. She might have a boyfriend, maybe she just ended a relationship, or there could be no reason. Fear of rejection can stop a man in his tracks, but as long as you are polite, it is part of the dating process.

"Thinking will not overcome fear, but action will."

W. Clement Stone

A Jamaican friend trying to help me, "If you walk up to 20 women, one of them has to say 'Yes'."

That approach sounded brutal. I wasn't going to walk up and talk to 20 women to get 19 rejections, but a lot can be 'lost in translation.'

He was actually saying, "If you keep trying, you will find one you like that will respond favorably." With 20 women, he was only saying to keep trying (although it would be nice to get lucky in the early going).

Rejection is part of the process. Have courage and confidence (even if faking it) to talk to a woman you find attractive. But you still have to SAY SOMETHING!

What are you going to say? In a way, it doesn't matter because you only want to see if she responds favorably. If nothing else, you can be polite, "You look nice" or say something about her outfit, hair, eyes, etc. Just be ready and be yourself. However, the better your conversation, the better your chances.

DON'T SHY AWAY FROM HER
SAY SOMETHING ABOUT SOMETHING!

It would be good form to carry the conversation long enough to get her phone number. If you don't get her number, you probably won't ever see her again. There may be exceptions if she works at a certain place, or if you have a connection through a friend, etc. It could be said,
" RULES #1 - #10 are GET HER NUMBER!!!"

You can also give them your number, or try to get contact information to follow up – at least Ask! Remind yourself, the time is "now." Otherwise, you will never see them again.

"Self-confidence is critical to happiness and success. When we lack it, we dwell on our flaws. We fail to embrace new challenges and learn new skills. We hesitate to take even a small risk that can lead to a big opportunity. We decide not to apply for a new job or we don't muster the courage to ask for a first date, and the future love of our life becomes the one who got away."
Sheryl Sandberg and Adam Grant, Option B

BE SWEET

Being sweet means having the nature of a sweet heart or sweet disposition: affectionate, helpful, kind, and pleasant. We can learn to be sweet by not being selfish.

In Jamaica, friends helped me calculate that a man needs SWEET AGGRESSIVE DETERMINATION to engage in conversation with a woman. I told the CD Mixer Man that I had this attitude down.

He added, "AND SMILE."

If Our Typical Guy goes around with SWEET AGGRESSIVE DETERMINATION and DOESN'T SMILE, he is going to come across as some kind of Creep.

"Aggressive" is used in The Bullsheet to mean being courageous enough to walk up to the woman you like to say something, to propose a fun activity, or suggest a date.

Being sweet is being friendly and caring about others.

HAVE A GOOD PLAN

A good plan could be to work on yourself, and see who you meet in the process. She might appear when you least expect it. A relaxed approach works in your favor.

"I believe in everything we do to trust the process. The process is important and sometimes things may not come together now, but later on it will. No two people are alike. I am always Positive and work hard and rely on experience."

Shelly-Ann Fraser-Pryce, Jamaican sprinter,
Olympic Champion, 2019 World Champion

Your plan could be to find events or activities you enjoy, and get a friend to go with you. Our Typical Guy needs good ideas, and the ability to make them come to life.

The world is connected in ways we can't see, so the magic works when you are in the right place at the right time. Dating is to have fun and share life. Figure out how to flirt, and be playful.

WHAT NOT TO DO!
DON'T TRY TO BE COOL
Learn to relax like a cat. Watch how cats completely relax, yet remain alert. You might have to pretend "to have it all going on." But don't put unnecessary pressure on yourself or a woman - just have a good time.

Talking to women is kind of like sales, you have to act successful even if you haven't ever sold one thing. If you are relaxed, she can relax.

"Humility connects and Arrogance separates"

Paula Burks

DON'T HAVE A VIBE OF DESPERATION
Women pick up on desperation as a big turn off. A woman will never know how much a man's Big Brain can trouble him, but the process of being with a woman takes finesse. When you are not desperate she wonders about you, and your confidence can be impressive.

"Your own style is the best style."

Bruce Lee, Striking Thoughts

DON'T HAVE A NEGATIVE MINDSET

We all make mistakes, get negative results, or get hurt. To let go, learn, and move on, we should examine our thoughts.

Shortly after my divorce, my secretary at my law office told me about a book that discussed *"Victim Mentality."* It sounded awful, so I asked, "What's that?"

She explained, "It is when a person feels that things are happening to them, or not happening for them because they are victims of circumstances, situations, other people, their shortcomings, or society."

I told her, "That sounds terrible. I think I could have it! What does a person do to not have Victim Mentality?"

She said, "You have to be *"Proactive."* That means to determine what you want to achieve, and then go about working on it each day until it becomes a reality. It helps to keep lists to feel see you are making progress."

You can accomplish things one step at a time. Be *Proactive* to work for the changes you want in life. You might find your own mind can be your enemy if you have *Victim Mentality*.

AVOID BAD CHOICES

Part of a Good Plan could be to make good decisions and good choices. Jesse James had it together with his marriage to actress Sandra Bullock, but he "blew it" through infidelity. He was asked, *"What did you learn?"*

"To change and be a better person I had to be accountable for all I did wrong and take it. I learned to stay away from negative influences. I was drinking a lot with the wrong crowd and

banged a stripper. That was stupid and wrong. I had a lot of resentment.

I thought there must have been a flaw in my personality to make me think it was OK, so I went to re-hab where I learned that you can't pull a weed out unless you go in there and get the root. You got to figure out what the problem is and what you need to do to rectify it. Then, (throwing a weed over his shoulder) *leave it all there."*

THINGS TO KNOW
BE CONSCIOUS OF YOUR VIBE

What would be a good Vibe? It is the Positive Vibration you give the world from your inner being. You have to be authentic and believe in yourself. If you don't believe in yourself, no one else will believe in you.

CHANGE PLANS WHEN NEED BE

If the Little Brain is in charge of your Plan, it will lead to progress. Be flexible to go with the flow. If one plan doesn't work, develop another. Keep working on today, but pointed towards tomorrow. Don't let the Big Brain lead you to the wrong places or the wrong people.

GREAT EFFORT IS REQUIRED

Yes, you will need to put more effort into Relationship Building than what you originally thought, but that is true for everything in life. In your failures, you learn to do things better. You can surrender to freedom when you detach from people or things that hold you back. You leave behind what didn't work, and open your mind to find what will work.

It is unlikely someone will just appear, so get out there and mingle. You will meet someone you like that likes you. If you are married, trust in your marriage and put your effort into it.

YOUR LOOK

A part of having a good attitude is in being confident about your look. Your look includes your car, clothes, grooming, etc. Actually, your look is more about your attitude and your Vibe. If you and your car are clean, that's good enough. Have good posture, be friendly, and Smile.

LEARN TO LEAVE

Our Typical Guy needs to be able to feel when he should leave places and people that don't feel right. Knowing this could save your life!

The test is to be able to feel the vibe of places and other people. Stay away from drama, negativity, and needy people. Be honest with yourself. Some people you are attracted to are a Wrong Choice. Find someone good for you, or keep looking. We need to trust our intuition everywhere we go and in every circumstance.

MENTAL HEALTH

NOTE: In 2021+, many people have Mental Health concerns that could be helped by Mental Health Professionals who are trained to help through counseling, medication, diet, exercise, etc. To "go it alone" is a bad idea when there is a problem. There is a lot to learn about mental health.

We know that our mind is linked with our Physical, Emotional, Spiritual, and ultimately, Financial lives. In our

fast-paced world, the importance of Mental Health has come to the forefront.

I was watching a TV show about young people in America who told about their mental health problems. It was disturbing to me to see that so many of America's youth are struggling to adjust. There were good jobs and families were not under so much stress while I was growing up. There was not so much divorce, pills, abuse, and trauma. We are all struggling, but many people struggle on their own until they get help.

We remember from Seven Arrows, *"the Touching – No two people on the face of this Earth are alike in any one thing except for their loneliness. The only way we can overcome our loneliness is through Touching. It is only in this way that we can learn to be Total Beings."* If something is discouraging in your life, don't dwell on it, but find someone to talk to or to hang out with.

When young people speak of Mental Health, we know it is difficult to grow up, and many are not able to get outdoors in nature enough, to play with others enough, to have safe places to play, good food, and friends. Coronavirus has proven we are social creatures.

Most of the people in the TV show looked perfectly "normal" so things can be Hidden In Plain Sight (the name of the show). The young people improved by connecting with others, having access to mental health professionals, being in nature, <u>and</u> often a dog or cat or a horse. Mental Health can be a struggle. A message for healing: *"there will always be someone to help you."*

If adversity strikes - reflect on your inner self, but reach out to friends, counselors, or nature. Have courage and build bonds by connecting with others – in-person is better than

online. It feels good to share your feelings when there is mutual respect and dialogue (openness). You can make new friends and strengthen current friendships.

Our mind is very important – it is our connection to the world, to ourselves, and to the spiritual. <u>The Bullsheet</u> offers these observations about mental health;
- **Don't let frustration (resentment) build**
- **Overcome everyday troubles – we all have troubles and anxieties**
- **If discouraged, don't dwell on it – find something to do, someone to talk to, or go for a walk**
- **Make time for meaningful connections**
- **Free up your mind**

> *"None but ourselves can free our mind."*
> Bob Marley and the Wailers

- **Share your feelings – don't keep things inside**
- **No one feels outgoing every day**
- **Ask for what you need**
- **Most things in life are not "quick and easy" - adopting patience is a key to mental health**
- **Examine your reactions – find what is helping you**
- **You can upgrade your mind (brain)**
- **Self-discipline is the way to accomplish things, build good habits, and establish your boundaries. Set aside time each day.**
- **It's a process – our body and mind can heal**
- **Listen to your voice of self-care – respect yourself**

"You have to be your own best friend Instead of your own worst enemy."

Amy Winehouse, British singer

NEVER GIVE UP

Building great relationships will improve your mental health. Some great sex could give you a good attitude adjustment. You can also enjoy life on your own as you go for a walk and feel a connection with Nature.

People need intimate relationships - lovers, friends, family. When you have a Good Attitude, things will fall into place.

"My secret is: 'Don't Worry', let things go and laugh a lot."

Stella at 95. PBS

MEETING SOMEONE YOU LIKE THAT LIKES YOU

Chapter 12

Before Our Typical Guy meets a possible Ideal Woman, he will be dating and making new friends. To do these things, he will need to meet someone he likes that likes him.

We know it is natural to have competition for an attractive woman who has personality and confidence. She is fun, and men want to go out with her, but you are better off not paying attention to the competition. See if she is friendly and not wearing a wedding ring.

There will be rare (magical) times that she "pops up" when you least expect it. Be aware of this phenomenon so you will be sure to say something. Remember to be friendly for her to be friendly. You will miss opportunities, but you have learned there will be new opportunities. Dating is for fun, so there is never pressure on her or yourself.

WAYS OF MEETING

DANCING might be the way to meet her. Dancing is fun. Dancing can be connecting on an emotional and physical level. Ask her to dance.

I noticed from watching dancing that the women are loose and move with the music. Usually, more women are dancing. Most men appear to be more inhibited, tight, and sway to the music while dancing is going on.

Feel the music, feel the beat, don't think, dance with someone.

IF YOU DON'T ASK HER TO DANCE IT'S ON YOU

Being playful and confident is something women like. If she is having fun, she won't care about your looks, your current circumstances, or how good of a dancer you are.

"If you can dance, you have a chance."

Country and Western saying

FLIRTING can be a way of meeting someone. <u>The Bullsheet</u> defines Flirting: joking with a woman, asking her enticing questions, teasing, or complimenting her to see if there is a positive response. Webster's Dictionary is more precise:

"Flirting: 1. To act amorously without serious intention. 2. To trifle, or toy with an idea (or a woman/man).*"*

Be playful and be yourself. Say something to compliment her. Compliments are to recognize a woman's strengths and to show your appreciation.

I saw in Jamaica that compliments can work even if what you say is "corny" or "gushy."

Michael demonstrated: "You make my Heart warm like the Sun when in the presence of your Beauty that lights up the World", then he would emotionally and dramatically clasp his heart as if he was about to faint.

She might laugh out loud (I did), but she admires his effort. Try your version. Great flirting and compliments might intrigue her. Notice her mannerisms, her looks, or what she is wearing. Put her at ease, and see if you get a response. Let her know you are interested and try to get her number.

Flirting is a skill to develop. Wynton Marsalis commented on Duke Ellington and his flirting ability:

"You're not going to get to know him (Duke) *too well because he has a certain space he has reserved for himself.*
And he has a great understanding.

He's a great listener.
He's always listening.
As a great observer, a woman might not know it, but he is observing everything. The way she walks, says things, what she has on, little mannerisms, things you wouldn't know.
He was a great flirter; Always flirting,
And the ladies loved him because he is such a great flirter.
But it's not just that he flirts, but that his flirtations are accurate. And the best flirt is always accurate. He's almost always accurate because he is always observing. So he could look at a woman and tell she was a singer, or what kind of job she has. So his flirt was going to coax.
She asked, 'How did you know that Duke?'
Duke would just look at her.
She would say, 'Oh.'
It was an uncanny understanding."

This level of uncanny understanding can be achieved by slowing down, being polite, and being a great listener. You learn how to flirt so she will talk, and you can make friends. Like dancing, it is fun to flirt. Practice flirting to show her a good time.

GOOD CONVERSATION is definitely a way of meeting, but you will be on your own, just like with dancing and flirting. Our Typical Guy needs to have a balance between being interesting and building a friendship i.e. light-hearted conversation. You should understand the other person's point of view and their perspective.

The man is projecting his image. You will surely meet some nice women if you are persistent, cheerful, and positive. Some will go on dates – if you ask!

ONLINE DATING is a common way couples meet today. I do not participate in online dating, so you already know more. All I know about it is: In 2009 <u>EVERYTHING</u> WENT ONLINE

A person can probably find every type of woman/man through the internet. A lot of people don't go to clubs and bars, and it appears easy to meet people through the internet or smart phone.

Meeting someone online might not be too difficult, but you still need mutual attraction and enjoyable conversation when you meet in person.

WARNINGS!!! There are hazards in Online Dating: the possibility of fake photos, getting robbed by the boyfriend or girlfriend, someone looking for money, and/or liars with a hidden agenda. Always arrange the 1st meeting in a public place, and make it short (a drink not dinner) in case there is little chemistry.

Some older men have technology problems, but it is easy to get help. However, it can be difficult to tell who, or what, is honest reality online. These new terms reveal possible problems:

"Catfishing: Deceptive activity to lure someone into a relationship or a meeting by means of a fictional online persona. These are romance scams on dating websites."

"Sadfishing: Someone making exaggerated claims about their emotional problems to generate sympathy."

Internet definitions

There is a lot of *sadfishing* in the world today, on and offline. These claims for sympathy include emotional pleas for money and/or "crocodile tears." Be careful out there. Don't get caught up in a Fairy Tale Fantasy.

THE WORKPLACE - <u>The Bullsheet</u> recommends <u>not</u> dating people from your job as this can backfire in numerous ways. It could make the fun you had cost a lot at the end. It is different if you feel they are your Ideal Partner, but there are so many people in the world that we should be able to meet someone outside our job.

How can the workplace romance backfire? While dating, people naturally reveal a lot about themselves. The more you feel like they could be an Ideal Partner, you might tell them anything while assuming they won't repeat it at work. They probably won't, unless they get hurt or angry. At that point, the workplace romance could backfire into your needing a new workplace.

Be careful about who you trust and how loyal they will be. However, about 20% of married people met their spouse at work.

THE CLUB/ BAR OR AN EVENT - Shortly before Coronavirus hit, it appeared that Clubs and Bars were losing purpose as the internet and smart phones seemed to be taking over social activity. However, by 2021+ it appears that Clubs and Bars have a permanent place as a way for people to meet and socialize. After our experience with social-isolationism, it is good to go out.

Clubs and bars are the same for discussion, but Clubs include a dance floor. The secret to having fun at the Club is to not have high expectations. Good music, attractive women, and a chance to use your tips should meet your highest level of expectation for having a good time that night. If you get a name and contact information, that would be a bonus.

You will need friendly energy to meet someone. If you are planning to go to the Club, but don't feel like being friendly, it is better to wait until another night. The Club will be open next week, or the next, when you are more cheerful.

If there is good music and some attractive women, you should not be disappointed at the Club. Maybe you can dance with one. Be a friendly person, move to the music, and be alert to talk to her. It can feel daunting, but magic can happen. Watch out or she could leave before you know it!

SOMETIMES YOU MUST ACT QUICKLY OR OPPORTUNITY WILL PASS YOU BY

A NIGHT AT THE CLUB, OR AT AN EVENT

I am low-tech, old-fashioned, and old-school, so the Club is where I go to meet women when nothing is going on in my romantic life. There are 4 factors for a Club to be fun:

1. Good Music
2. Attractive Women
3. Mingling
4. Good Ratio

When you have the 4 factors, you should succeed in meeting someone.

A Good Ratio would be 60% men and 40% women. If the ratio is 50-50, a man needs serious analysis if he does not make a contact. At 50%, women have a natural competitive nature among themselves.

Clubs or Events get people out of their house to socialize. By an Event, it could be arts and craft shows, music, sports, amusement parks, or any event. Dancing or a Concert/Event without assigned seating helps with the Mingle Factor.

There are people who talk down about women who go to clubs. But if you meet someone with mutual attraction, who cares? My perspective on the women in the Club is they are at least trying to have fun. They like to dance, and dancing is fun. There are some women that are out with friends for birthdays or special occasions that are not 'regulars.' Regulars should probably be approached with caution.

It was a lot a easier to meet a woman at a Club a few years ago than it is today. A man would be competing only among the other guys in the Club. Now, the women can spend their time looking at texts or other things on their phone. That leaves the man competing with the men in the Club <u>and</u> the men she already knows that are sending her texts, etc. Don't be discouraged, and remember to keep expectations (frustrations) low. Remember that you only need one.

I learned a woman can look a whole lot different the next morning than they did that night in the Club. I don't go home with any woman from a Club. She can look a lot different in the light. A few times the woman looked so different that I couldn't recognize her!

When an woman takes you out of your comfort zone, know you need to step up to her and take your best shot. Don't be shy! Ask her to dance, and try to talk to her. I remember younger guys encouraging me, "Go out there and pick you one out." I wish it was that easy.

ACTIVITIES are the best way to meet someone. This includes business socials, sports, grocery store, health club, private parties, church, yoga class, or anything you like to do. You could possibly join a co-ed sports team. If you meet them doing something you like, you have something you both enjoy. People need to work-out to stay in shape, so get in yoga class if nothing else.

MUTUAL FRIENDS is the way a lot of people meet. A good recommendation could help you avoid a lot of trouble. The friend feels there might be chemistry, so it is worth a try. With mutual friends, there is a sense of built-in trust.

IT TAKES TIME to move from looking for potential relationships - to meeting someone good for you - to a great relationship, so take it easy. **Don't rush into anything.**

Remember to not go on looks alone (this is a common mistake). I remember one time I picked the prettiest one (it's not a Beauty Contest). Her boyfriend's name turned out to be Hulk and for good reason. That was the end. I should have talked more with the group of friends to try to find one with mutual interest, and tried to go out with her. Once you pick (approach one in a group), it is difficult (impossible) to keep picking from among their friends.

Watch mannerisms for awhile to see who looks like fun (pleasant to be around); a genuine person (not a Gamer), and possibly interested in you.

If you really like someone, relax, and have a good time. When you are relaxed, they can relax. If you feel like you have missed the boat – be patient and you will find someone nice to date.

"'BUT STILL DO IT'
THE MOTTO GIVES YOU THE WILL AND BRAVERY
TO 'STEP UP' EVEN IF YOU DO NOT KNOW
IF YOU WILL BE SUCCESSFUL."
Takashi Nemoto, Japanese musician

Just be yourself. Do things you enjoy to meet people you enjoy, but try new things for new experiences (or a different crowd). Imagination and desire are natural and good for keeping you going.

Have enthusiasm for life in your voice and it will only be a matter of time until you will meet someone you like that likes you.

MAKE YOURSELF MORE INTERESTING

Chapter 13

We describe a Supplemental Invention: the automobile was a Primary Invention before windshield wipers were a necessary Supplemental Invention. <u>The Bullsheet</u> is ranking Mankind's Greatest Supplemental Inventions:
#1 Caller ID
#2 Remote Control
#3 DVR
#4 Mute

Caller ID is the winner for obvious reasons. The others are important so we are not forced to watch or listen to the zillion commercials that interrupt and annoy. A lifetime of advertising has more effect than we realize. What is the problem with advertising?

"What advertising tries to do is convince us that above average products can compensate for below average traits. A belief comes from advertising is that if you are not funny, not verbally creative or artistic (none of the romantic skills) then you can compensate. Don't worry - you can earn a respectable living, buy a bunch of stuff, a new car, house, clothes, and still be viable and attractive on the dating market. So consumers do not develop crucial romantically attractive traits. Many men will buy things they think makes them 'cool.' However, only saying "I have a Mercedes" is superficial and does not make you interesting as a person. The problem is you may attract a spouse or girlfriend for a while, but they will get bored, and leave you or divorce you for someone more interesting."

Consumed, LinkTV

Advertising tries to makes you feel inadequate so you will buy the product. Don't feel inadequate, or that finding someone nice won't happen for you.

Being interesting will improve all your relationships: business, family, friends, romantic, and even with yourself. You don't need to be the most successful. You are trying for the quality of doing your best - that makes you interesting. The task is perseverance in pursuing your genuine interests.

Confidence and patience are the keys. You can work on your weaknesses, improve your strengths, and have fun doing it. Even the effort will make you more interesting. You are especially interesting when you are grateful for life and have a Cheerful Attitude. Then you are creating Allure.

She might think, "He looks happy. What's up with him?"

DO SOMETHING TO BE INTERESTING

We all have gifts, talents, and interests. Many of the things we take for granted could be regarded as Gifts or Special Powers. No one is totally handsome, has lots of money, a big Thing, funny, etc. We can be interested <u>in</u> something, and there are many talents we can develop:

Music	Athletic	Coach	Travel	Singing
Hobbies	Camping	Dancing	Volunteer	Cooking
Gardening	Activist	Language	Biking	Artistic

...and there are many more

In America we ask: "Who is the best or the greatest?"
PARTICIPATING IS ENOUGH
IMPROVING IS ENOUGH
ENJOYING IS ENOUGH

Do more with friends and build a strong support group. If you open up and talk to your friends about your personal situations and relationships, you will make better decisions and better friends. Sometimes we need new friends.

Take a break from sedentary habits to go for a walk, ride a bike, get a dog, take a class, join a team, be open to the New Age.

DEVELOP YOUR GIFTS

"You are special because you are different from any other person in the world. You have special gifts, unique capabilities. You are able to express Life in a special way, able to do something in a special way that no one else in the world can do.

Dan Custer, The Miracle of Mind Power

- **YOUR EYES – Most people take their health for granted. It is a miracle how the mind and body work to perfection – all the tiny parts and connections. We can see from the way our body works that it is God in Action. Our eyes, brain, and all our body are the perfect gift.**

- **BE YOURSELF - Don't be the guy who tries too hard to be cool. Some guys try to cater to a woman's whims, but she knows that will wear off, and the man will spend more money than necessary.**

    I knew a guy who was handsome and had a good job, but he tried so hard it was ridiculous. He had a 240Z which was cool enough, but he spent a ton of money to have the doors so they would open up towards the sky. They were so heavy that his dates couldn't open the door. I am sure she wondered when she couldn't get out of the car, "What kind of creep is he?"

We need to relax, and know we have Special Gifts to develop that make us attractive.

- **GOOD POSTURE – It might not sound like good posture makes a difference, but it does, both physically and subconsciously. When you stand and sit up straight, you give off confidence as well as protecting your back and neck.**

    I heard a little short woman say, "Pretend you have a string pulling you up through the top of your head." She was so short, she had to stand up straight, and so do we. Good posture is part of a Good Vibe.

- **TRAVEL – Travel broadens your horizons. It is healthy and educational to travel as your finances and opportunity permits (don't take a trip on a credit card). Overseas travel is especially beneficial. You can experience different cultures, perspectives, and gain greater appreciation for your home. Travel will surely make you more interesting.**

    "Travel is fatal to prejudice, bigotry, and narrow-mindedness."

    Mark Twain

- **EDUCATION - Knowledge can make you more interesting. Almost everyone enjoys hearing interesting stories from books, or from what you have learned. Education doesn't always include school.**

    My Grandfather told me, "Son, you can't learn it all from a book." I learned the difference between book smart, street smart, and common sense.

**THE MORE YOU READ AND LEARN
THE MORE YOU CARE ABOUT OTHERS
THE MORE INTERESTING YOU WILL BECOME
AND THE BETTER YOUR SOCIAL LIFE WILL BE**

Your brain needs new challenges to thrive. Learning something new creates physical changes in the brain's wiring as you acquire new skills and gain the ability for continued improvement and growth.

I could have stayed longer in Colombia and have had more fun if I could have spoken Spanish. Speaking Spanish would have made my travel more interesting, allowed for possible relationships, and created new pathways in my brain.

I heard that the younger a person is the easier it is to learn a new language. It would be good to start on learning your new language today. If you have children – learn together for more fun.

- **ACTIVITIES – Our Typical Guy needs to get out there and do something. He can do things he enjoys, try new activities, or get in a new class. It would be nice to meet someone who enjoys the same activity.**

**DO WHAT YOU LIKE
SO YOU WILL KEEP GOING
WHAT DO YOU LIKE TO DO?**

- **GOOD MANNERS - Always be polite with good manners. You can make your life a lot easier by being polite rather than rude or selfish. Good manners show respect.**

I know manners matter because my daughter told me, "Good manners are important to a woman."

- **CONFIDENCE – If we lack confidence, we will probably not be interesting.**

- **BE CREATIVE – there is music, art, sports, writing, being fun, being funny, etc. Invite her to join in your creative activity to see if there is mutual chemistry.**

- **ALLURE – Allure is abstract, similar to our Vibe. We are definitely interesting if we can create** *"Allure: to entice by charm or attraction"*

Webster's Dictionary

A woman creates Allure with her looks, mannerisms, mystery, clothes, being friendly, charming, confident, sexy, and we want to get to know her.

A man creates Allure by being confident, well-groomed, friendly, interesting, and the right balance of respect, persistence, and fun. Let her know you are interested. Flirting creates Allure (at least it should).

- **MAKE MONEY - Having money or a good job makes you more interesting. Money gives a person more freedom, options, and possibilities. You need money for dating, looking for your Ideal Partner, or having a family. You need money to take care of yourself.**

A friend told me, "George, the World looks a lot better out there when you have some money in your pocket." It's stressful to be broke.

Ambition and drive makes you more interesting. However, allow life to unfold rather than trying to force things. Doors will open.

Don't give up if you currently don't have money. Women are more patient and forgiving than men. She will see potential if you put out effort with hope, patience, and participation. Good things will happen.

- **BE THANKFUL** - Of course, the Special Gifts of real handsome and lots of money open doors. However, we can be thankful for what we have. We are more interesting when we are Thankful.

- **STAY IN SHAPE** – Work-out and walk every day.

- **LET GO OF MENTAL BAGGAGE** – Free your mind.

- **EMPATHY** – Why is empathy a Special Gift? The reason is because no one wants to be with someone who cares only about themselves.

<u>The Bullsheet</u> defines Empathy: 1. the ability to feel or understand another person's feelings or thoughts and realizing their feelings are important to them; 2. trying to understand other people through listening and observing to see what they value."

When you have empathy, you become attuned to a heartfelt connection by showing them you care about their feelings and well-being. Understand that their family might rank higher than you, depending on the situation, and pets can be family too.

It is important to have empathy when she is upset, even if you don't understand "Why?" However, don't believe all you see and hear. Some people's crying can be crocodile tears. They might not really be upset, but trying to get their way, or to make you feel sorry for them so that you will do something (usually involving money). You might have met a Manipulator. But relationships can be tricky. Often crying is not crocodile tears, so be careful if compassion is needed. You will need to be aware and trust your intuition.

- A GOOD SENSE OF HUMOR - Everyone loves to be around someone with a good sense of humor. Being funny is attractive. Even if you are not very funny, a pleasant disposition is attractive. Some humor is not funny. We all know people who make sarcastic or cynical comments. Every now and then these comments can be funny but usually not. Sarcasm and cynicism often reflect a bitter person who is disrespectful and demeaning of others. However, it could possibly be funny, so maybe let them know ahead if it is sarcasm or cynicism.
BE FUN
TO HAVE FUN

- BE NICE – Being nice shows Respect. Know what NOT to say. Mean, demeaning, or blaming comments can do untold damage to relationships.

- EACH PERSON HAS THEIR OWN GIFTS – Respect yourself, respect God, respect others.

WHAT'S THE POINT?

When we develop patience, being sweet, and good conversation, we can enjoy their company. We will notice when someone has these traits, and when they don't. When we are interested in life and interested in being in great relationships, we are interesting.

"In nature, it is the blending of sunshine and rain that gives rise to a beautiful rainbow. In a similar way, we, too, can gradually develop and express all of the different talents and gifts that remain dormant within us."
John Gray, Beyond Mars and Venus

FEEL THE VIBE

When you feel someone doesn't care about you, it is time to head for the door! The same is true for negative people. Negative people are toxic to our happiness and self-esteem. Life is too short to let people waste our time. You might as well know <u>now</u> if people are true friends or not. There are times that changing you social circle can be a good idea.

We can Step Up Our Game by becoming an Observer. My daughter is an Observer. When she was a little girl 10-13, she would go with me to the ranches on sales calls for the horse insurance. After we were back in the car, she would tell me all kinds of things about the other person. She would figure them out by watching their mannerisms, their eyes, little things they would say, and their tone of voice. She would tell me some people didn't like me, but I didn't know.

Men, especially salesmen (or when we think she is attractive) feel a need to impress, but you are stepping up your game when you become an Observer.

THESE THINGS WILL <u>NOT</u> MAKE YOU INTERESTING!

- **DON'T STARE** –A man needs to approach a woman before she will find out he is interesting and fun. It is always better to walk up and try to talk to her than to get caught staring at her from a distance. It sounds ridiculous, but Our Typical Guy has been known to stare.

- **DON'T GET DRUNK** - Don't get drunk, unless maybe at the House Party and she is drinking with you (and no one is driving). If at the Bar or Club, drinking can be good for letting inhibitions down, but it is a huge turn if a person is drunk.

    I remember going to the Club and drinking two Crown and Coke to get my inhibitions down. One night, I told a woman at the bar that the drinks got me into Club Mode.

    She said, "You shouldn't need two Crown and Coke to get into Club Mode."

    When I went for walks for the next 3 months, I couldn't get what she said out of my mind. It finally sank in. Now, I can go out and be in Club Mode without alcohol. I get a beer to join the party, move with the music, let inhibitions go, and Club Mode is easy.

    Drinking with a woman can be fun. Find out her preference and have it at your place in case the liquor stores are closed. There could be a surprise House Party!

- **DON'T WORRY** - The Great Spirit will make a way if you are trying and both are interested. You don't have to make a lot of money, but something. Don't dwell on the past, feel lonely, be judgmental, be angry, have fear, or let emotions and thinking rule (ruin) your life.

IMPROVE ON YOUR OWN

Create a better present and future for yourself. When you are interesting, you will have fun and your confidence goes up. There will be ups and downs, but never lose confidence. Confidence gives you the strength and courage to be friendly.

See if she is enjoying the conversation. If the woman is not interested in your conversation, change the conversation or you will soon be changing women. Be enthusiastic and make sure she is engaged.

We know self-improvement will lead to good things happening. We are not getting anywhere by blaming someone or something for our situation.

We have all been told negative things. For example, my Dad would tell me I was ugly. I didn't necessarily believe I was ugly, but it didn't do much for my confidence. I sure didn't consider myself handsome.

One time a woman said to me, "Hey, Sexy Man", and that planted a seed. I didn't consider myself to be a Sexy Man, but ever since that night I adopted the attitude "I am a Sexy Man." Smile, be friendly, have good posture, and you can be a Sexy Man.

What's strange is telling yourself you are a Sexy Man actually works as long as you believe it. For example, I had not been out to the Club in a long time, and forgot the part about being a Sexy Man. I was getting no response or interest from any women. I even had one say, "You look sooooooo old, what are you doing out here?" This was discouraging and made me think I was losing my touch even though I did ask her about her cute friend. She stumbled off shaking her head, and I went home.

I went out again a few weeks later, but remembered that I am a Sexy Man. The difference was like night and day. The women were friendly and a few came over to talk, and I was able to dance. Give it a try.

It actually works because it adds to your confidence. Self-projection is key. Most women don't care so much about your looks, so don't worry about it. What we say, our Vibe, feeling good about yourself, being interesting, being fun, and showing interest in her might get you where you think you want to go.

<u>The trick is in the doing</u>. You can get more interesting every day. All you need is to have activities, be a Sexy Man/Woman, try to control your thoughts and emotions, and you will meet someone nice that fits you. You can do it, and your life will be more interesting.

"When we live from the Mind
We think all the time and the mind can be out of control.
When we learn to live by feeling from the Heart
We calm down, make good decisions, and become more interesting."

Vedic teachings

DIFFERENT CREATIONS

Chapter 14

That men and women are Different Creations has been known since the dawn of time. Emotional differences are described in the book and phrase, *Men are from Mars, Women are from Venus* by John Gray. We realize that people and relationships are far more complex than the sex involved.

The terms feminine and masculine often portray stereotypes rather than real life today. We are all a mixture of feminine and masculine traits as stereotypes are becoming a thing of the past. However, there are differences in the brain's wiring and body chemistry between men and women which result in different ways of thinking, reacting, and feeling. And men do have their troublesome Big Brain.

It's a changing world with changing roles and changing hormones which can make it very difficult for Our Typical Guy to understand and relate to a woman. Just listening has proven to be difficult, but he can learn how to say things and when to keep quiet. A relationship that maintains passion and love is a real challenge, but it would be a wonderful thing.

SOME DIFFERENCES IN MEN AND WOMEN
#1 MISUNDERSTANDINGS
Our Typical Guy doesn't want to hold misconceptions or keep repeating mistakes. Alison Armstrong answers the question, *"WHICH CORE DIFFERENCES BETWEEN MEN AND WOMEN CAUSE EVERYDAY MISUNDERSTANDINGS?"*

"<u>The biggest mischief is denying that differences exist. Both assume that each is a version of the other, which creates misunderstandings</u>.
- *We interact with our Partners by doing or saying what works for us.*
- *When that doesn't get the response we are expecting, we usually draw incorrect conclusions and act in counterproductive ways.*
- *Men and women relate to feelings differently. Women often make important life decisions based on their feelings about something or someone. Men tend to rely on facts.*
- *To some men, the women's approach (basing decisions on feelings) can seem rational. Relating to women as rational has predictably bad outcomes.*

The most powerful thing men and women can do is to address misunderstandings with openness and curiosity rather than assuming we know why our partner did or said something."

(emphasis added)

One misconception Our Typical Guy might have is if he thinks his Lady Friend will be like his Guy Friend, but with sex. This is not reality.

It feels like the key to avoid misunderstandings is for the man and woman to reach an understanding. If there is disagreement, each could peacefully present their perspective and the other listen. Then they could see: "What is the problem?"

There might not be a problem, but only a misunderstanding. If there is a problem, it can be fixed through an agreement or compromise. The ability to compromise is an important part of great relationships.

However, it is important that neither party feels resentment as a result of the compromise.

No matter the result of the conversation, she will appreciate your effort to understand her feelings.

#2 DIFFERENCES IN NEEDS

The best and easiest way for someone to understand the differences in 'needs' is to read and understand the book *His Needs, Her Needs* by William F. Harley, Jr.

I remembered reading the book as life changing, so I went to find a copy at the bookstore. I told the Clerk that it is a great book. He said, "I don't have a girlfriend, so I don't need to read it." I told him, "If you read the book, you might get a girlfriend."

The Author includes lists of His and Her Top 5 Needs that must be met to have a Great Relationship:

"His #1 Sexual Fulfillment	*Her #1 Affection*
His #2 Recreational Companionship	*Her #2 Intimate Conversation*
His #3 Physically Attractive	*Her #3 Honesty & Openness*
His #4 Domestic Support	*Her #4 Financial Support*
His #5 Admiration	*Her #5 Family Commitment"*

It is very important to understand Affection - Her #1. Affection could be a lot of little things one does like calling her to show you care, a nice card, cleaning house, massage, candles, cooking, flowers, favors, hugs and kisses. Affection is genuine caring, and not just to get something.

"Affection: fond or tender feeling; warm liking; loving."
Webster's Dictionary

I heard a woman say, "Affection is for a man to do everything he can to help her feel, 'I AM IMPORTANT' – 'I AM GOOD ENOUGH'." Show her she is important to you and good enough to you - just like she is.

**IF HER NEEDS ARE NOT MET
THE MAN'S NEEDS ARE NOT GOING TO BE MET**

#3 MEN ARE EXPERIENCERS

Men are Experiencers in that they often do what they want without thinking of the long-term consequences. He might do whatever it is: change jobs, vacation, move residences, buy something, go somewhere, chase women, drink - then enjoy and/or suffer the consequences.

I have done this too often in my life. I went to great effort and expense to coach football, to own horses, to go on trips, and other unwise decisions. I didn't think things all the way through, but wanted the experience. We will get experience living this way, but it might not be a good experience in the end.

Men often do what they want without thinking of how stupid it might be (emotion-based bad decisions), or who it might hurt - which usually includes himself. Even in children, we see it is the boys that are more likely to do wild impulsive things.

Maybe what a man does is fun or a healthy experience. We do have a life to live. But if it's a bad decision, then pain is on the way. An Experiencer with a Right Now trait can leave himself with short-term experiences and bad results.

My daughter called one day after Sociology class at the university, and said they learned about the frontal lobe in humans.

She reported, "The frontal lobe is the part of the brain that controls our ability to reason and to see the consequences of our actions. The frontal lobe in a female is fully developed by age 18, and in a male it is fully developed at age 32."

I told her I did not believe those statistics. I believed that the frontal lobe in a female is fully developed by age 18, and in a male it is fully developed at age 60.

She said, "I'm afraid you are right!"

I was 65 at the time, and my cousin said, "Knowing you, it must be 67 for men."

Make that 73 now, and it's feeling like it is finally almost fully developed. I tell my daughter, "It is rough out here in the world with one of these smaller frontal lobes."

#4 WOMEN ARE PLANNERS

Women think and plan ahead to be able to see the consequences of their actions. Before they act, they think, "If I do this - this will happen - then this will happen - then this will happen, and that is a result I do not want." She will then <u>not do the first act</u> that ultimately brings a result she does not want. Women think through to the consequences before acting and plan accordingly.

**IT IS NOT WISE TO BE AN EXPERIENCER
BEFORE BECOMING A PLANNER**

#5 MEN AND WOMEN SPEAK DIFFERENT LANGUAGES

The greatest cause of breakdowns in any relationship (romantic, friend, relative, business, etc) is a Breakdown in Communications or Poor Communications.

A man or woman might face a challenge in developing communication skills. Accepting the differences in men and women can require humility, but great communications leads to great relationships.

"There is a reason that getting your message heard and understood by your Partner is tricky business, especially when the purpose of what we are saying is to get some form of action or response out of the other. Men and women speak different languages. The following observations illustrate differences in the way we communicate:

- *Men use talk to gain status and attention - women use conversation to connect and maintain relationships.*
- *It is common for men to tell jokes or stories, which serves as a fun way to get attention. The purpose of conversation for women is to build intimacy and connection.*
- *Men and women talk about problems differently. Men share frustrations and problems with other men, but they will bond over minimizing* (sports, music, etc) *because men look at problems as things to be solved.* <u>*Women use problems to build closeness.*</u>

It is important to remember it is not about right or wrong, good or bad, it is simply about being different. Wise men and women will learn to understand the language of their Partner."

Charlotte Lankard, licensed therapist (emphasis added)

A breakdown in communications can also be characterized by my old habit of keeping things inside (we are not communicating if we don't say anything).

#6 MEN AND WOMEN ARE ON DIFFERENT TEAMS
WOMEN ARE PLAYING ON THE WINNING TEAM
MEN ARE PLAYING ON THE LOSING TEAM

My observation of the Single World is that women come out of relationships far better than men. Women seem to not be getting hurt as bad (maybe women are better at letting go and moving on). I started seeing women as <u>playing together</u> on The Winning Team and men are <u>playing separately</u> on The Losing Team.

I observed the tendencies that create this situation, and decided to adopt the strategies of The Winning Team. I got tired of losing. What are some of the characteristics of these two teams?

WINNING TEAM #1 – WOMEN HAVE SUPPORT GROUPS
Women build their support groups for their entire life. They get together and talk things over. They tell each other about relationships, and talk about their problems before making decisions. They usually have men friends they can talk to for a different perspective. Women discuss and adjust.

A woman is able to accurately evaluate a relationship because a man is often predictable. But regardless of how certain she is about someone, she will still confide in her support group.

LOSING TEAM #1– MANY MEN THINK THEY DO NOT NEED A SUPPORT GROUP, AND THEY DO NOT HAVE A SCOUT
Our Typical Guy operates on his own - he doesn't confide in others about his relationships. A man might tell a friend of his success, but he won't discuss the overall relationship or any problems. This is Losing Team mentality.

<u>The Bullsheet</u> **calls a woman that will help a man with women, his communications, and his perspective - his Scout.**

A man needs a Scout, or he might not get close to a woman he wants to approach.

A MAN NEEDS A WOMAN FRIEND
TO TELL HIM THE WAYS OF WOMEN

She helps a man with meeting women, his dating, and the details of the relationship. When you get a Scout, your chances go up. Your Scout is like your Coach or Advisor. She can tell you what you are doing right or wrong. She knows what women are thinking, can tell if a woman is being honest, and knows what your next move should be.

You are looking for a woman you can confide in that will tell you how women feel. She is your friend, knows your current situation, and she sees the dynamics of relationships in their entirety. This process will create a fun friendship bond with your Scout. It is good to talk to someone about your progress. She can see things you can't. She can lead you to the right woman, and equally important, lead you away from the wrong women.

Our Typical Guy often needs help. He should realize that to ask for help is a strength, not a weakness. If you look, there will always be someone to help.

"A PROBLEM SHARED
IS A PROBLEM SOLVED"

Saying

Your Scout does not have to be a woman. Some men have Game, and they can help you just as well. He might be a Player. They could probably write a better book, but they don't see the problems – it's easy for them.

WINNING TEAM #2 – WOMEN ARE ACCEPTING OF SITUATIONS (REALITY) AND DEAL ACCORDINGLY

If the relationship does not have enough mutual chemistry or if he has "deal breaker" traits - she accepts the fact, and lets him go. She lets herself move on.

Women are not so focused on looks as a man, and usually not as anxious for sex. These traits free her mind to notice all the other parts of a relationship to see if it might work.

LOSING TEAM #2 – MEN ARE OFTEN IN DENIAL OF SITUATIONS

Men often deny or ignore problems, while women discuss them. Denial is a bad habit that will lead to she's gone and Our Typical Guy left with hurt feelings.

Many men can be blinded by a woman's looks, or what he wants to be true about a relationship. It is Wishful Thinking or Willful Blindness when a man denies things happening within his relationship. For example, he might be crazy over her while she does not show nearly as much interest in him. A man might imagine things he wants to happen that are far removed from reality. He might be blind to things she does that should be obvious (he does not want to see).

"Denial Psychology: the reduction of anxiety by the unconscious exclusion from the mind of intolerable thoughts, feelings, or facts."
Webster's Dictionary

The denial could be when he should know there is not mutual attraction, or when she has others. When pleasure is involved, Our Typical Guy is good at denial, but denial is not good for him.

Some men don't want to open up, or they feel in charge by keeping their feelings inside. Maybe he has hope for the relationship (or her) to change (this probably won't happen). By not seeing and discussing problems, a man might feel like the Ruler or the King in his life. But there can be problems from not opening up with friends, and for not having a Scout.

"THE DANGER OF BEING AN ABSOLUTE RULER IS THAT NO ONE DARES TELL YOU THAT WHAT YOU HAVE JUST DECREED IS NOT A GOOD IDEA."
Amama Project, Akhenaten, National Geographic

WINNING TEAM #3 – WOMEN ARE MORE AWARE OF FEELINGS - HER OWN <u>AND</u> HIS

Women look into the potential of the overall relationship and how it makes her feel.

LOSING TEAM #3 – MEN ARE NOT SO AWARE OF FEELINGS - HIS OWN <u>OR</u> HERS

Men are more Problem Solvers than being in touch with feelings or emotions. Many men are heavily influenced by what their Big Brain promotes. It is good to tune into your feelings – they could be telling you something.

I heard that a man should listen to her without trying to solve her problem. If we listen, we learn the importance of <u>her</u> feelings. Be a Great Listener to become aware of her feelings. Get her to talk to tune into her feelings.

"I never learned anything while I was talking,"
Larry King, legendary talk show host

DEALING WITH THE DIFFERENCES

Relationships are fragile, so handle them with care. Listen carefully to what your dates and friends have to say. If something is bothering you - get it out. When the love could be only one-way, don't let hopes or expectations cloud your view. Go with the flow, and do the best you can.

"What gets you in trouble is not what you don't know – it's what you know for sure, but it ain't so."

Mark Twain

THE ART OF DATING

Chapter 15

The Art of Dating is the relationship you create with your dates as Co-Creators. Hopefully, some dates will lead to romance.

"ROMANCE: IS A WONDERFUL, EXTRAORDINARY EVENT OF LOVE, ADVENTURE AND EXCITEMENT. ROMANCE IS COURTSHIP, TRYING TO GET THE LOVE OF THE ONE WE FIND SUITED FOR LOVE."
Webster's Dictionary

People should relax and enjoy dating while trying to create friendship, fun conversation, excitement, and possibly romance. It can happen, but finding one to date might take awhile.

"HE WHO WANTS A ROSE MUST RESPECT THE THORN."
Persian Proverb

The Reader is reminded there is no strategy or plan to <u>The Bullsheet</u>. It is a book of tips, reminders, discussions, definitions, quotes, speculation, and stories.

We can't accurately predict or control what will happen in our relationships, but self-discipline and patience will help make dating enjoyable. Self-discipline means controlling emotions and not to spend money that will put you in a bind. It is natural that you will need to fight frustrations or foolish behavior.

Our Typical Guy is trying to build relationships on a foundation of respect, love, and connection. He knows to open

the doors of communication to understand her the best he can. Dating and building great relationships is not going to be all fun, but it could be special beyond belief!!!

MODERN DATING

Modern Dating is fluid. It is a New Age and a fast-paced world. A person might find a lifelong partner, but many people consider 1 or 2 years to be a good relationship, and 5 or 6 years could be considered long-term. Some people are serial monogamous and date one person until they figure out the other is not their Ideal Partner, or they are the only one being monogamous.

Notice to see if the same things happen to you over and over again. If it does, it is you, and not the people you date. You might need more lively conversation, or new places to go and new people to see.

In dating, a person can get caught up in desire, hopes, expectations, and lose our sense of being kind above all.

"Plant kindness and gather love."

Proverb

It helps to have money, but no one wants someone who 'loves' (needs) them for their money (that won't work). You can do better. You will need to be strong-minded to not feel obligated to other's requests. However, sometimes you help by giving. It can be tricky, so you learn as you go. It is better to say "No" than to oblige with reluctance (that causes resentment). Keep a positive attitude to prepare your emotions for the ups and downs of dating.

Dating sites make it look easy to arrange a hook-up. (The term "hook-up" could include a wide range of activities from meeting to kissing+.) However, even after you arrange to meet, there is still the one-on-one relationship, and a lot of women are not going to be on dating apps.

Dating can be expensive, but you do not need to spend a lot of money. Of course, the man is usually expected to pay, and she wants to "do something", but you can work together to find activities that are inexpensive.

Be relaxed and open-minded. Get to know her. See if she laughs at your jokes, there is respect, and you enjoy each other. You don't want to miss opportunities if there are small things to overlook (both are going to be overlooking quirks and shortcomings).

DATING CAN BE SIMPLE
YOU NEED MUTUAL ATTRACTION
TO GET INTO ACTION

FUNDAMENTALS

People have to be what they want to be - not what someone else wants them to be. We all want something, but no one wants someone else to dictate what is best for them.

A man needs to listen to a woman. Work with her to create an environment for each to open up and relax.

Our Typical Guy needs to learn how to discover <u>her</u> concerns in life. The Big Brain is concerned with sex, so the Little Brain is often not so concerned about her goals or problems. However, her problems could be real problems to discuss, or to understand her, or to appreciate her more.

It is going to take time to get to know each other. Know that people will probably not change, so it would be better to change dating partners than to think someone is going to change. Of course, you can change, but that takes your own dedicated effort.

In the Single World, everyone is free to date who they want, unless they have agreed to commitment. And we learn there will not be a relationship for long if jealousy is involved.

The times and the dating scene are changing rapidly, but Our Typical Guy is trying to go on dates, build great relationships, and try to find his Ideal Woman.

**DATING IS FOR FUN
AND GETTING TO KNOW SOMEONE**

WATCH OUT WHAT YOU WISH FOR
When a person is dating, they will encounter people from all 4 Groups of People, including Players and Gamers. A challenge in dating is to choose the right people to date and to not spend a lot of time and money on people you should know are Players or Gamers (Manipulators).

"Player or Gamer: can be a Male or Female. They are usually slick, dress nicely and Very Charming. They prey on people socially usually looking for sex or money. They have a way of befriending people and making them feel important (or loved), *before they use them to their own ends. They have no loyalty to anyone but themselves."*

Ian De La Rosa, internet definition

A Player or Gamer makes their date think they care about them while they are only out for what they can get. They are smooth talkers (*"Very Charming"*) **who often lie.**

I had a woman friend tell me, "Some of these women have too much Game for you." I thought she meant that I wasn't game enough to do a good job.

That is not what she meant. She was saying, "Some women are playing too many Games for you." She was right.

I was looking for someone serious or honest+ , but it seems like I have learned all these things the hard way.

Players and Gamers are out there. They are playing too many games for Our Typical Guy.

AVOID THE PITFALLS

Our Typical Guy wants his dates to have a good time, and to see if she is _____ (Ideal Woman, or whatever your stage). "Looking for Love" might sound corny, but that is what Our Typical Guy is trying for with dating.

Good relationships are the key to just about everything in life (family, friends, business, romance). We don't want to be a hermit. However, we don't want to fall into any of the pits that can open up to consume someone. Many of the PITFALLS are our own doing.

PITFALL #1 - NEGATIVE THINKING causes us to lose patience and perseverance. For example, a woman might think that all men cheat and lie, or just want sex. A man might think that all women lie, or are just out for money.

What is the point? We can't develop intimacy when we hold onto wrong thinking or past hurt. If a prior relationship failed - accept what happened, your part in things, forgive yourself, forgive the other party, learn your lessons, change your behavior, and keep moving on.

Making assumptions leads to negative thinking. A person might make good assumptions – seeing your dates through rose-colored glasses (wishful thinking), or bad assumptions of imaginary misconduct (tripping). The assumption could turn into a whole story in a person's mind, and little or none of it is true! Know it is not wise to make assumptions.

NO NEGATIVE SELF TALK
NO SELF-PITY
PATIENCE ALLOWS YOU TO BE POSITIVE

PITFALL #2 - A COMFORT ZONE can keep you from meeting someone that is better for you. You will spend time and money in the Comfort Zone rather than dating or finding activities to meet someone new. In this way, you miss your opportunities. Our Typical Guy can find his Ideal Woman if he doesn't get stuck in a Comfort Zone.

PITFALL #3 - NOT HAVING BOUNDARIES will set you up to be used. Try to find someone honest (everyone lies some), but when you know they are not honest about important matters - move on. Don't let sex and/or fear of loss paralyze you.

TAKE YOUR TIME
DRAW YOUR LINE
AND KEEP LOOKING

PITFALL #4 – LIARS are out there. As the saying goes, "Actions speak louder than words." **The person you are dating might have an agenda besides an interest in you. Therefore, your Bull Shit Detector needs to be ON, and don't believe everything you hear. You need your mind (Little Brain) in the game to see if they are playing games with you.**

We hope people are honest, but be realistic to see if they exclude you from a big part of their life; makes lots of excuses (battery down, lost phone, sleeping, forgot, etc); or if one of you seems a lot more interested than the other. You don't want to be 'crazy' about someone while they are not serious (don't care) about you, or they are with someone else.

"The person who is infatuated is always the last to know."
Saying

PITFALL #5 – THE BIG BRAIN leads the chase, but it should not be in charge of his thinking. Yes, Our Typical Guy wants sex. The Big Brain can help him step up to get the ball rolling, but a man needs his Little Brain, intuition, and friends to help him see the real situation.

PITFALL #6 – MANIPULATORS - Try to avoid dating these people - even if they look good.

MASTER THE DATING PROCESS

FRIENDSHIP is the first thing we are trying to accomplish with dating. We are dating to also have a good time and see what the relationship becomes.

"Friendship is a sheltering tree."
Samuel Taylor Coleridge

However, relationships can be tricky. If they feel like "just a friend" (The Friend Zone), or "she feels like a sister" - this is still a great relationship, but it will not work romantically. There has to be that special chemistry for romance.

Anyone can go on a date, talk, go to a movie, go out to eat, and more talking, talking. Our Typical Guy needs skills to get more action than talking. However, more action in a relationship could start out with something different than sex. See if you enjoy activities together. Find activities that have more action than talking like riding bikes, hiking, dancing, traveling, kayaking (not a canoe) etc.

My daughter heard from a Doctor friend, "Canoes lead to divorce – kayaking is each has fun."

With interaction, you both have fun, or know you are not right for each other.

"There ain't no surer way to figure out whether we like people or hate them, than to travel with them,"
Mark Twain

ENGAGING CONVERSATION is a key to compatibility. Make sure they stay engaged by keeping the conversation two-way. Of course, the conversation does not involve talking all the time.
BODY LANGUAGE & TONE OF VOICE
ARE IMPORTANT PARTS OF CONVERSATION
PAY ATTENTION
TO SEE AND HEAR

Have enthusiasm for life in your voice. You can listen for the expression in their voice to understand the emotion behind their words. Listening will help to show you a path forward, or a need to change direction.

PATIENCE will help you enjoy life and be happy/content. If patient, you immediately relax and proceed steadily without giving up.

Patience will allow your relationship to unfold, but there is a time Our Typical Guy will need to make a move. He learns to be calm, and wait until the time is right. It's no wonder that a woman would be attracted to a man that is patient.

BEING SWEET is having joy in your heart and being open to others. Don't let it be said you have an attitude, and don't date people with an attitude.

"Attitude: A Slang definition of attitude is a way of acting that suggests a person is angry, hard to get along with, conceited, haughty, etc."

Webster's Dictionary

A person with an attitude will often make hateful, sarcastic, or petty comments. There is no room for meanness in relationships.

Down in Ardmore they say, "Don't shit in your own nest."

Most people hate to be criticized. "Don't criticize a woman" should go without saying. By thinking about it, we can say what we want to say in a way that is not critical.

We know it is bad manners and rude to interrupt. To listen and care will make you sweet. Being sweet is kindness, affection, and respect towards others.

"It does not cost a penny; to speak loveful, true, sweet words."
Brahma Kumari, Thought for Today

We develop honest sweetness by emptying ourselves of negativity, anger, jealousy, and controlling behavior. If you are patient and sweet, they will be a friend, and maybe more.

CONFIDENCE is needed for everything we do, especially dating. Confidence is looking forward to the future as you live in the present. Confidence is feeling good about life, yourself, and your gifts.
BE THANKFUL

"CONSENT : ENTHUSIASTIC – ONGOING – INFORMED– VOLUNTARY – COHERENT"
This definition from a woman's t-shirt about sums up an understanding of Consent. You might find a better definition, or need to talk it over with someone, but Respect and Consent are <u>always</u> at the forefront of intimacy.

HOW YOU SAY IT

There are many ways to say the same thing, but it is often "How you say it" that makes the difference.

I learned during my 18 years in the horse insurance business that <u>the way we ask for something can make the difference</u>. I feel from my time as an insurance salesman, lawyer, football coach, school teacher, husband, and Dad that we are all involved in Sales in almost everything we do. A person has to say things properly in different situations to have a successful outcome. Dating is no exception.

I remember the day I knew I would succeed in the horse insurance business. There was an important 2-day horse sale resulting from a divorce that was held in 2 giant air-conditioned tents with free food in true Texas Style. There were expensive mares-in-foal, colts, fillies, and yearlings sired by World Champion Quarter Horse – Dash For Cash.

As the sale progressed, I was having little luck (skill) in selling any insurance. I would step up and ask buyers, "Would you like to have insurance on that horse?" I was getting nowhere, and thought I needed to change my approach. I had been asking for a sale by asking "Yes" or "No" questions. It was too easy for them to say "No", so I changed to something that did not have a "Yes" or "No" answer. My new idea was to say, "I have great rates on horse insurance." This change resulted in my insuring 11 out of 14 yearlings, and the 2 most expensive horses in the sale. I was in the race horse insurance business to stay!

After that big horse sale, I learned to not phrase important matters in ways that have a "Yes" or "No" answer. You might have to think awhile, but you can come up with something.

The experience gave me a flashback to a date back in college. I was on a date with a woman I thought was really cute. We went 'parking' in the car, and I wanted some action. I asked her, "Would you like to get in the back seat?"

She said, "No, I think I will stay up here in the front seat with you."

THE FIRST DATE

Our Typical Guy is a Hopeful, and there will be the first date. Some books tell women to not be sexual on the first date, but <u>The Bullsheet</u> knows it can be the best time for both (unless you are a Saver).

The man's role is to be sweet, patient, and interesting. She wouldn't be with you if she wasn't interested. Early in the relationship, she might be more likely to overlook the things you do that annoy her. (You can work on those after you figure out what they are.)

Let her unwind and relax. Concentrate on her to make her comfortable. She already knows what you have in mind, but there is always more to discover when she comes over.

I saw an eye-catching ad in the local paper from a bakery. It was the same day that I had a first date. The ad ran only one time as it showed a woman lying back in sexy panties wearing net hose and said,

"Le sort d'un ménage depend de la premiere nuit."

Balzac

"A COUPLES'S DESTINY DEPENDS ON THEIR FIRST NIGHT"

The first date can turn into a magical opportunity. Magic might not happen on the first date, but if she is willing, you should know it can be more difficult to be intimate the longer things drag out.

It can be great if the first date is a House Party (or Car Party). If the date is not a House Party (movie, eating out, activity), then try to have as much fun as possible through flirting. That takes the pressure (anxiety) away. Depending on the woman and other factors, Our Typical Guy will probably need more than one date. If you are having fun dates and enjoying her company, that is all that matters.

All women are different, and most need more time than the first date, but it doesn't hurt to try so long as both are having a good time and the chemistry is there. Be calm and cool because the Big Brain wants to rush it!

DON'T REJECT WHAT IS COMING TO YOU

When I first re-entered the Single World at 50, I was not having any luck with women, including with one I was attracted to. A friend told me to not continue suggesting an activity, or asking her out. He said to wait and have her suggest something. This advice sounded like nothing would happen, but I was wrong.

Sometimes Our Typical Guy spends time and energy pursuing a woman, but the relationship is not going the way he would like. He might think it has ended. He was attracted to her, and he tried, but finally gave up. Then one day she calls and says she is coming over, or invites him over to her place. Surprisingly, many men might tell her "No."

Our mind can play tricks on us. Why do men say "No"? Maybe his ego thinks he did not plan it, maybe he is too surprised, maybe he is stupid or naïve, maybe scared of intimacy, and he rejects seeing her.

If you feel attraction, go with the flow, and say "YES" when she says she wants to do something. Don't shy away from it. You know the time is right when she calls. Women can be unpredictable (Short-Term Moods), so men can be caught by surprise. However, you will not be surprised if you make her feel that she can give you a call to have a good time.
DON'T REJECT WHAT IS COMING TO YOU!

Get your place ready as fast as you can, and enjoy it as it is. It is about when she is in the mood, not when you are in the mood.

MY GREATEST TIP

I do not know which will be your Greatest Tip, but my Greatest Tip worked like magic for me. It does not work every time, but there have been many times nothing would have happened had I not used my Greatest Tip. I did not originate the tip as it came from Cousin Al.

As a story within a story, we remember from Cousin Al that *"Every Day is a Blessing."* Al ended this life at age 45 on a traveling job when he pulled into his space at a motel, and had a massive heart attack. But Cousin Al was a Ladies Man and that is also how he is remembered.

It had been 2 years after my divorce, and I had not had any luck with the ladies. I was at a friend's house, and his Cousin Al was visiting. I had heard from my friend that Cousin Al was quite the Ladies Man and sex was no problem for him. He had the traveling job, girlfriends in different areas, and he had no problem in dating quality women. He knew how to work internet dating when it first came out. I was also told he had a big Thing. Maybe that had something to do with it, but I don't know about that. I just knew Cousin Al was getting a lot, and I wasn't getting any. I told him my situation, and ask him to give me a tip. I told him <u>I wanted a tip that really worked</u>. Cousin Al examined me, and finally said, "YOU HAVE TO PLACE THE ORDER TO GET THE BURGER."

I thought, "That doesn't sound like much of a tip."
I asked Cousin Al, "Do you have anything else?"
Cousin Al stared at me and said, "NO."

After that tip, there were a lot of dates that were starting to move to the end and I would think, "Have I placed the order?" The answer was "NO." ('Place the order' simply means to 'make a request', or to 'present a good idea.')

It is amazing, but there were numerous times I would proceed to place the order and get the burger!

SEX

Chapter 16

"Dear God: Please let me survive this skydiving. I still have to lose my virginity, and I don't know what I'm missing yet, but I've heard it's really good. Amen"
Colton, The Bachelor, ABC

He heard right. Sex can be wonderful beyond description. A healthy sexual relationship can decrease stress and increase well-being. With great sex, time seems to disappear.

"When you are happy sexually,
It kind of balances the rest of the stuff out."
Candace Cameron Bure

Men and women often live in different worlds.

I told a woman, "It can be a project for a man to have sex. He has to meet the woman, make arrangements, and go to extra efforts. For a pretty woman, it's easy. Men are always trying to talk to her. If she wants, she can call a guy and he will be over at her house."

She smiled, "Yes, we can call Mr. Fix-it."

Sex is natural so it can be great, and sometimes perfect. Sex can be spiritual as well as physical. <u>The Bullsheet</u> gives the highest rating Heavenly Sex. Great sex can go beyond words as your efforts can be rewarded in spectacular fashion.

However, sex is not always a good experience, so choose wisely. Sex is special, so be careful. You need to be smart about it.

There are kinds of sex we are <u>not including</u>: gay, bisexual, swingers, lesbian, and more too numerous to name. Prostitution and extramarital would fit the definition of sex, but it is not our goal.

If married, make your sex life better. The grass is not always greener on the other side of the fence. The grass might look greener, but there are hidden weeds. Looks can fool!

RELATIONSHIPS TAKE TIME

Many people are chasing something without realizing that a happy life can be found in the joy of everyday moments. To be at peace would ease your mind and give your relationships a better chance.

In Beyond Mars and Venus, John Gray **informs us that relationships have changed over the past 25 years as people face greater stress resulting in many fluctuating hormones. He tells 'How-to' create a** *"Complaint –Free Relationship."* **However, it is questionable if such a relationship is actually possible, but this much is true:**

"If men and women are to be happy together, they must clearly take responsibility to first be happy on their own."
John Gray

GREAT SEX IS HEALTHY FOR YOU

Sex provides health benefits, and puts a smile on your face (for about a week). We must Step Up Our Game for great relationships and great sex.

Medical studies show that great sex is proven to:

1. **Improve your quality of life** (the world looks a lot brighter)

2. **Helps you focus on your job** (you are not frustrated)
3. **Has mood lifting effects** (puts a smile on your face)
4. **Improves heart rate and blood pressure**
5. **Good for your skin**
6. **Sex reduces anxiety** (an Attitude Adjustment)
7. **Sex helps get more blood to both brains** (but medical studies do not recognize the Big Brain's intelligence)
8. **Sex helps you sleep** (like a baby when 'rolling eyes syndrome' kicks in)
9. **It helps with your weight as you burn calories** (*"sexexercising"*)
10. **It decreases your risk for disease** (sex has proven benefits for stress-related problems - like going crazy!)
11. **Sex eases tension and encourages peace over discord**
12. **Sex lets you have bedroom fun as you experience life's greatest pleasure**

SEX CAN BE GIVING AND RECEIVING LOVE
SEX WITH LOVE IS HER SPECIAL GIFT

Great sex includes the right time, right place, and <u>right partner</u> for what is natural. When sex is exciting, healthy, and loving - it would be a Blessing. It is natural for people to want to enjoy themselves, and to be with someone nice.

I remember hearing about sex on a high school summer job in Ardmore, Oklahoma working for the natural gas company. There were older countrymen buddies on the Gas Crew. My favorite was Boolie Brown.

Boolie and the co-workers would go coon hunting on Friday nights with dogs and donkeys. When they got to a fence, they would throw a blanket on the fence for the donkey to jump over, and then they would get on the donkey to ride through the woods after the dogs to tree raccoons (it was only for sport – you don't eat raccoons).

But back to Boolie Brown and the fact that he had 4 kids. The Gas Company Crew was on a break, and I was young. As a practical thinker, I thought, "How can a guy on his salary afford 4 kids?" I asked him why he had so many kids.

Boolie explained, "George, when you're up on top of her and it's about to go off - you feel like you can hold the Whole World on your shoulders!!!"

Everyone laughed, and we knew it was a wonderful feeling!!!

WOMEN READERS: IT'S YOUR PARTY

"When we allow our Partners to fulfill our needs, it can help us unlock our own greatness, as well as theirs..... By asking for what we need, women create opportunities for partnership, satisfaction and fulfillment for both Partners. When we allow the man in our life to contribute to us and learn to receive graciously, we discover that it doesn't diminish our power."

Alison Armstrong, Author

*"DESIRE IS THE FIRE THAT BURNS WITHIN
IT'S OUR NEED THAT HAS TO BE MET"*
Karen Blessen, Keys to the Kingdom of Good Fortune

"Women should take control of their own satisfaction. Some resist that idea because society tells us that the right partner will know what to do, or that love always leads to great sex. But those ideas discount the power of a woman's sexuality because they put pleasure in someone else's hands. Be selfish! Prioritize your own erotic needs."

Madeleine Castellanos, MD, Wanting To Want

MORALS

Sex involves morals. Morals change with the times, and each individual has their own morals. Morals seem to be subjective in the Modern World.

"Morals: 1. Having to do with right and wrong in conduct (cheating is a moral issue.) 2. Good or right according to ideas of being decent and respectable."

Webster's Dictionary

Our Typical Guy is asking about sex, so <u>The Bullsheet</u> is trying to help him, not judge his morals. It is up to each person to have the quality of relationship and sex that is within their skill and moral bounds.

Why are morals important? When we feel that both are honest, we can care. We can move into the future relaxed. If you want a long-term relationship, you should discuss morals. What kind of relationship do you have? What is right and wrong conduct in your relationship?

Some people will lie about their morals. A lot of people are said to have "loose morals." Some will say cheating is wrong, and do it anyway. Lying can be a real problem. The world is not composed of all fair, ethical and honest people so Our Typical Guy doesn't want to set himself up for heartache.

How religion affects your morals (perspective on sex) is your business, but sexual energy is part of our life-force.

"When you experience pleasure, God comes through and you become aware of your divine nature. You'll find that joy comes in the ways that are unique to you. Connection with the natural world is an essential element of agelessness. Agelessness is all about vitality."

Dr. Christinae Northrop, Health expert

GREAT SEX

Our Typical Guy needs to realize that within a long-term relationship or marriage, the sex varies. A man does **not** have to be with a new woman to have better sex. It can get better and better with the one you love. It is a matter of enjoying each other and working together.

Variety does not mean to find a variety of women. You can have variety with the same woman as long as both are creative and play along. You need a **willing partner**.

THE STRENGTH OF THE RELATIONSHIP EQUALS THE INTENSITY OF THE INTIMACY

Great sex would include the ability to abandon yourself to love, desire, and pleasure; or you could feel the mood as respectful, amorous, and sensitive. Whatever works for both of you is how it works.

ENERGIZE THE RELATIONSHIP
FEEL GOOD ABOUT YOURSELF
BE HAPPY TO BE ALIVE
USE YOUR IMAGINATION FOR ROMANCE

"There are two ways to reach me; by way of kisses or by way of the imagination. But there is a hierarchy; the kisses alone don't work."

Anais Nin, Author

Intimacy is a part of Great Sex. Intimacy is closeness, private, personal, and associated with a good friend and the

senses. Take your time, and tell her the things you love about her. Put her at ease, and appreciate her gifts.

Great sex can change a person's attitude. It can make us see the World in a different light. One day, my boss came in the office, and the ladies guessed he had "got some" the night before.

He said cheerfully, "It's amazing how that stuff works!!!" Everyone smiled!!!!

SEXLESS

Our Typical Guy should know that some women <u>don't care for sex very much</u>. It would be great if he figured this out before he gets in too deep i.e. marriage.

My friend Fred was enjoying the Single World, and was a genuine Lady's Man. He was previously married, but divorced. Then he met a pretty girl and got married. He liked to fish, and we would talk.

Fred would complain of not near enough sex (we know most men want more than they get). But Fred was super frustrated. She would tell him "later" or "maybe tomorrow", but "later" rarely arrived, and tomorrow never got here. He was staying married because of the kids. Of course, Fred was trying and doing what's necessary. After all, he had been a Natural Ladies Man in the Single World (there were stories of him with 2 women at once).

After several frustrating years, Fred went on a family vacation with his wife's family. There was an evening around the table with the wife, her sister, her Mother, and Fred. The subject of sex came up and her Mother stated out loud, "I don't care for sex and neither do either of my daughters." The three women proceeded to laugh in Fred's face! Laughing like, "<u>You are not getting much of any, and you are never going to get much of any</u>!"

The Bullsheet is making you aware this situation could happen to you if you are not observant. What can you do to prevent this frustration? You can watch to see if she is aggressive or freaky for sex. Feel to see if she really enjoys it, and if she is adventuresome. Trust your intuition, and you could find out if she really enjoys sex. Take the time to get to know your prospective partner if you are contemplating marriage.

Great advice comes from my favorite movie *Little Big Man*. The Chief asked his adopted White son, *"Does she show enthusiasm when you mount her?"*

"Enthusiasm: showing great interest or strong liking for something along with an eagerness to seek or follow it. As passion, it is strong love between a man and a woman."
Webster's Dictionary

Feel if she is enthusiastic to have sex with you (if she is not at the start, she sure won't be later on). Ask your girlfriend about her sisters and notice her Mother. She might not know about her relatives, but we don't want to end up like Fred. Our Typical Guy needs to try to figure out what his woman friend is really like before he gets married, gets frustrated, goes broke, and/or doesn't see his kids.

SEX AND LOVE

As a Single Man, Our Typical Guy needs to know that he may be the only one serious, even if sex is involved. Many men struggle with attachment and jealousy when she has Great Stuff. After great sex, Our Typical Guy can start to have emotional feelings, but some people are better at not getting so emotionally involved.

BE CAREFUL WITH YOUR HEART

When we discuss sex, we are back to a problem with generalizing. There are all kinds of people (different ages, gender, race, beliefs), and everyone has a different perspective on sex and love. Also, we could agree on a definition for "sex", but everyone has a different concept of "love."

Religious upbringings (or none) can influence the way people view sex and love. There are also many people who have had unpleasant experiences or a childhood upbringing that gives them problems. And some people have sexual hang-ups. We know it takes time to get over bad experiences, and some need professional help or spiritual healing. Psychological healing is not presented in <u>The Bullsheet</u>, but therapy has helped a lot of people.

We should be able to see by now that the Players and Gamers are surely excellent at separating sex and love. (If you do not understand this, re-read about Manipulators).

Remember to not compare yourself to others. People can put pressure on themselves to perform well, but confidence is a key.

In 2000, when I joined the Single World, I would hear songs about doing it "all night long." I learned that "all night long" means, "until the woman climaxes."

But by 2015 in Jamaica, men were still talking about doing it "all night long", and said the women would go along. I still don't believe that story.

They would ask me, "Can you *do it* all night long?" I said, "No." "What about ½ a night?" I said, "No." "What about 2 hours?" I said, "No." "What about 1 hour?" I said, "Maybe, if she told me ahead, and she wanted me to." (One hour was an exaggeration, but I had to claim something.)

As for all night long, if your woman climaxes, you did a good job. She will let you know if she is in the mood for more.

There are times that sex and love are not separated, and join together for a sacred act. It feels like Divine Intervention when each is right for the other, and they join together through sex and love. This type of exciting climax would get the highest rating - Heavenly Sex.

SATISFACTION

Of course, a man wants to satisfy the woman he loves. However, there are many little things to satisfy her not included in the physical act. The different kinds of love a woman needs include all the little things a man can do to show respect, love, affection, and to support her. Relationships can get complicated, but if a man can remember to do the following things, it should be a Great Relationship:

"THE DIFFERENT KINDS OF LOVE A WOMAN NEEDS"
- *"He provides reassurance*
- *Gives romantic attention*
- *Shows interest in her feelings and experiences*
- *Provides affection and hugs*
- *Anticipates her needs and offers to help*
- *Listens more and does not interrupt with solutions*
- *Shows empathy*
- *Apologizes*
- *He acknowledges how much she gives*

- *Compliments her beauty and attractiveness*
- *Considers her needs equal to his own*
- *Validates her feelings and contributes*
- *Provides foreplay and plans dates*
- *Gives her the space to be and express her authentic self*
- *He compromises"*

                    John Gray, *Beyond Mars and Venus* (bullets added)

Good Luck!!! If a man does all this, there is not much more he needs to know or do for a woman. Of course, John has a corresponding list for a Man's Needs, but they all connect to his Big Brain.

LIVE AND LEARN

Women are a mystery, so besides direct experience or a girlfriend providing personal lessons, what would be a way for a man to improve sexually? Our Typical Guy could study anatomy books, or do his own research.

I have seen only one anatomy book that showed a woman's clitoris being more than a tiny bump full of sensitive nerves, or something difficult to find. One book showed the clitoris can be stimulated to be an inside-out length of 3 to 5 inches. It can also swell up to 3 times larger with proper arousal. Medical research has shown that her clitoris has twice the nerve endings as is in a man's penis. No wonder we read about the man not knowing of its importance in her sexual satisfaction. It would be nice if she would help, but maybe she doesn't know.

A Scout told me, "I never met a man who didn't like to have his D*** sucked." This tells you there might be something you could do for her. There is a lot to learn - men need to be cliterate.

Anatomy books will show how a man ejaculates, but I have yet to see the same for a woman. However, we know she does.

My Grandfather told me, "You can't learn everything in a book." He wasn't talking about sex, and like with dancing, flirting, and conversation - you are on your own.

However, the internet says there are glands on the inside of a woman that ejaculate a fluid chemically similar to a man's ejaculation. Believe it or not, many Scientists state, "It is uncertain or doubtful if a woman can ejaculate at climax." I suggest those Scientists get up there and try it for themselves. If they do a good job, they will no longer be uncertain or doubtful.

ATTACHMENT

Chapter 17

ATTACHMENT COULD BE YOUR BEST TIP ESPECIALLY IF YOU ARE UNAWARE OF THIS SUBTLE TRAP

The trap is in how attachment can be a good thing or a bad thing. A person needs to know the difference before it is too late. The tricky part is a degree of attachment is natural. When we are attracted to someone, we can develop feelings of affection and loyalty. If the resulting attachment is based on Mutual Love and Respect, it is a good thing, and attachment would be a natural part of a Great Love Relationship. However, you can trick yourself if you are attached, and they are not.

If you were highly attracted to them, and they told you everything you wanted to hear, you might want the relationship to be serious. But the feelings could be unfounded attachment (wishful thinking). Maybe what you were told is leading you on, or you are rushing the matter.

In the Single World, attachment can be a big mistake. I thought it was natural to find a woman I loved, and it would evolve into a lasting relationship. Well it might, but I was the only one serious. Attachment limited my thinking, and I didn't meet anyone new.

I did not see my feelings as attachment. I thought it was love. It is easy to have attachment if she is beautiful, you have been intimate, she says she loves you, and she has great stuff. We hope for the best in relationships, but many people do not want a serious relationship. You might be the only one attached.

Although wanting love to last and attachment can be a natural reaction, I can testify that attachment can lead to disappointment and pain if you take a relationship too serious. They can let you stay in your world of One-Way Attachment as long as they are getting what they want.

We could be doing what we think is right – but it's wrong for us. It is good to stay open-minded and to be lighthearted.

The Reader's views on attachment will differ based on whether you are looking for a monogamous relationship or not. If you don't care about a monogamous romantic relationship, attachment should not be a problem. However, if you are dating someone and feel you are "in love", Attachment vs. Detachment can be a challenge as you open up and become vulnerable.

I was talking to a friend about my last relationship. He told me I made the mistake of becoming Too Attached to the woman. Michael is 35, and a natural ladies man. He told me attachment was a bad thing because one will take advantage of the other. He said about attachment, "She has you where she wants you." That was a shock!

I didn't realize attachment was my problem, but I could feel what he was saying fit my situation. I told Michael he was right, but I didn't understand attachment.

Michael gave a definition, "Attachment is being concerned with the ultimate outcome of the relationship."

I told him I wanted to talk more about Attachment. His only reply was to text a photo for which I later found the source:

THE LAW OF DETACHMENT
"In Detachment lies the wisdom of uncertainty. In the wisdom of uncertainty lies freedom from our past, from the known,

which is the prison of past conditioning. And in our willingness to step into the unknown, the field of all possibilities, we surrender ourselves to the creative mind that orchestrates the dance of the universe."

Deepak Chopra, The Seven Spiritual Laws of Success

This was my final lesson from Michael. I am to learn to live by the *Law of Detachment*. I tried to find out more, but that was it.

I finally realized that what I thought was Love was really Attachment. We have all seen relationships where one party has far more feelings of love for the other than what is given in return. <u>These type relationships never work. Even if they do result in marriage, there will be a Divorce</u> (married the Wrong Person).

Many people would like to find that special someone – someone to live with and enjoy life together. (Our Typical Guy is looking for his Ideal Woman.) Maybe this longing is part of human nature, but it might be unrealistic imagination or wishful thinking.

NON-ATTACHMENT

The following wisdom allows us to see the need to learn to live Detached (Non-Attachment) to enjoy life:

"*Sutra 1.12 introduces two essential elements of yogic philosophy: <u>'Persistent Effort'</u> and <u>'Non-attachment to the result'</u>. When practiced together, they serve as a spiritual and practical roadmap for navigating almost every aspect of life with greater equanimity. The basic gist: If you can be resolute in your efforts and, in equal measure, <u>not be fixated on the outcome of those efforts, your consciousness will become less hectic, and your mental modifications or habitual thought patterns will still or settle.</u>"*

Natasha Rizopoulos, Sutra 1.12, Patanjali (underline added)

LET PEOPLE COME AND GO AS THEY PLEASE
THAT IS WHAT THEY ARE GOING TO DO ANYWAY
YOU MIGHT NEED TO KEEP LOOKING

HOW IS ATTACHMET A BAD THING?

It stuck in my mind what Michael said of attachment, "She has you where she wants you." It is nice to have a girlfriend, but we don't want to be "played", be a fool, or ignore the reality of our situations. When you are the only one attached, you can have anxious feelings of being disconnected, but helpless.

Let life unfold, and people will reveal themselves. If you are not attached, you will figure out their intentions (if a manipulator, or if you are truly good for each other).

Attachment can be a feeling like, "If I don't have _____ (name) I won't be whole" or "I want her, and she is the One for me." And if you act jealous or possessive, that would be a sense of ownership you don't have a right to, especially if you are just dating.

> *"ATTACHMENT IS A FORM OF DEPENDENCY*
> *BASED ON EGO,*
> *LOVE IS NON-ATTACHMENT BASED ON SPIRIT."*
> Deepok Chopra, The Path of Love

BEING DETACHED

<u>**The Bullsheet**</u> **defines "Detached (Non-Attachment): Having to do with things as they actually exist outside of what is in your mind and thoughts;** *"to not be fixated on the outcome of your efforts."* Sutra 1.12

We need to face Reality. Ask yourself, "Are you on the same team?" OR "Are you 2 teams that get together to play?" There is no reason to be attached if you are on 2 separate teams. Either enjoy their company, or move on. There will always be competition for an attractive woman.
"HOW MANY ROADS MUST A MAN TRAVEL DOWN BEFORE HE ADMITS HE IS LOST!"
Barn Burner Inc.

If you have "the talk" and agree it is a monogamous relationship, it is natural to be attached. It is a good thing to find a good Partner. However, in today's Single World, a lot of people will say they are being monogamous when they are not.

Attachment can be confusing when you are not being told the truth. If you are attached to that person, you are placing your energy and love into that relationship. Many men and women have spent emotions and what money they had to end up feeling heartbroken, stupid, and betrayed.

If the relationship turns out to not be monogamous, you will receive some Warning Signs. But in the end, it is better to be aware of the dynamics of the Single World, and to trust your intuition than to believe everything you hear. Great relationships and love are about a lot more than sex.

ATTACHMENT CAN BE TRICKY

"Attachment: a strong liking or love, friendship, affection, to bring together by feelings of love or affection"
Webster's Dictionary

So what is wrong with Attachment? Isn't this what we are looking for in our relationships? YES, if it is <u>mutual</u>. We

could say the problem is: TOO ATTACHED --- TOO SOON. Relationship building takes time.

If you are <u>not</u> Too Attached - Too Soon, you gain greater independence of mind and can follow *"The Law of Detachment."* A non-monogamous relationship, or going without, might be all there is for now.

Set boundaries to avoid attachment. Without boundaries, you can be taken advantage of. Be bold enough to face reality. You need inner strength to not be Too Attached-Too Soon.

If you enjoy each other's company and want to hang out together, a serious relationship could possibly evolve. Otherwise, surrender to freedom for yourself and others. Live by *"The Law of Detachment."*

A HIDDEN AGENDA

People need to be aware that some romantic partners might have a Hidden Agenda. A Hidden Agenda can be hard to detect. Sometimes all is not as it appears, but how do you know?

"LISTEN WITH YOUR EYES, MIND AND HEART NOT JUST WITH YOUR EARS!"

Unknown

Even if a person wants to marry, or have a monogamous relationship, it will take time for a relationship to evolve into love and commitment. And many people have chosen a non-monogamous lifestyle. It is common sense to know not to expect people to honestly tell you if they are having sex with others.

Get to know them over time to keep from making mistakes. People reveal their true nature if you are honest with yourself so as to recognize it. When you have strong feelings for someone, you need to surrender your understanding to the higher powers of intuition and common sense. And talk to your friends.

I can testify that a woman (or man) can look a man straight in the eye and say it is monogamous when it is not. We feel she is beautiful, fun, and we love her (or think we do - it could be "need" or "want"). This "love" makes us vulnerable.

Attachment can leave a person with feelings of being exploited and used. Hopefully, Our Typical Guy learns before getting this ending.

Be aware that relationships create Natural Attachment (that's why it hurts when you break up, even when you know a break-up is needed). Attachment that is Misplaced Loyalty or a Fantasy Bond that is fueled by the other person's Hidden Agenda will leave you feeling disappointed. Rather than wanting a specific outcome, you should want what is best for you, your finances, your life, and that will give you the best chance for a great relationship.

Master *"The Law of Detachment"* **to be happy/content in the Dating World. With Detachment, you will enjoy your relationships and your mind will be less hectic. You can let relationships evolve while you work to be a Complete Person.**

**THE IDEA IS TO NOT TRY TO CREATE
A SERIOUS RELATIONSHIP
WHERE THERE IS NONE**

CO-DEPENDENCY

Attachment is closely related to co-dependency. Attachment and co-dependency are normal/natural in a Great Relationship where teamwork and love are required.

However, co-dependency also has a dark side. If you have fallen into a Comfort Zone, found a Manipulator, or are in an unbalanced relationship, you will need to examine your areas and levels of co-dependency. Often people don't get out when they should. Here is the problem and a solution:

"The definition of 'co-dependency' is when you make the relationship more important than you make yourself. When you are trying to please others, you are not an authentic version of yourself, so what you attract into your life doesn't really fit you.

Start with loving the person you are right now. The more you are true to yourself, the better boundaries you have. You might piss off the people used to you doing things for them, they might start to leave, and you might feel lonely and afraid. But nature abhors a vacuum, so what will come into that space is people who empower and cherish you."

Renee Linnell, The Burn Zone

THE STRUGGLE

NOTE: IF THE READER IS MARRIED, THE FOLLOWING DOES NOT NECESSARILY APPLY TO YOU AS MARRIAGE IS A RELATIONSHIP WITH EXISTING TRUST.

Powerful feelings can arise when you are with someone you think you love. By staying detached, you can avoid bringing jealousy, anger, or resentment into your life. There is great wisdom in the following lesson if you can find the strength to follow his advice.

"You know that you cannot make the assumption that others are going to be what you want them to be....With awareness and practice, you are going to take all the action necessary to enjoy your life, and detach from whatever is gone.

For example: I may love a woman very deeply, but as soon as I want to own her, I am attached, and I don't want to let her go. No matter what I do, she is free, and every time she walks away from me, if I am attached, it's going to hurt. If I am detached, I respect her freedom. She can do whatever she wants to do, and it doesn't hurt me at all.

By being detached, I respect my freedom as well. When you are around me, I enjoy your beauty and your presence, and I attach to you. But when I walk out the door and do not see you, then I detach because if I don't detach, it's going to hurt. The key is to find an equilibrium between attachment and detachment.

Attachment helps you live your life intensely in the present moment. With attachment you can increase your desire to accomplish whatever you want to accomplish, and with detachment you don't have to suffer what you didn't accomplish. You simply let go."

Don Miguel Ruiz, The Four Agreements Companion Book

To master this attitude would help a lot, but it can be a lot easier said than done. Having powerful feelings for someone can be natural, but we need to be mindful to not be Too Attached – Too Soon.

"THE STORY OF LIFE IS QUICKER
THAN THE WINK OF AN EYE
THE STORY OF LOVE IS HELLO & GOODBYE
UNTIL WE MEET AGAIN"

Jimi Hendrix

WARNING SIGNS

Chapter 18

While you are driving down the Road of Life, you will approach intersections. You know when the light turns yellow, it is a warning to not run a red light. It is better to stop than to crash or pay that big ticket.

In relationships, the lights could be telling you to slow down your pursuit, or to stop, or go in a different direction. Driving and dating can result in expensive wrecks – financially, emotionally, and even physically.

DON'T SPEED THROUGH LIFE
DRIVE AND DATE WITH CAUTION

When someone wants to be closer to a love interest, they reveal hopes and wishes. It is only natural. Most people (usually men) love to talk about themselves, especially when life is going good. Your love interest might be interested, but do they really care about you? If you are getting serious, you should pay attention to the Warning Signs.

WHERE IS THE RELATIONSHIP?

Do you want a serious relationship? Do you really love them? Do they really love you? Many people do not consider the difference between need, like, and love.

"A person who marries for money, because of loneliness, or to get away - is in 'need.'

A person who marries for excitement, objectification, or sex – 'likes' the other person."

Roy Masters, How Your Mind Can Keep You Well

The Warning Signs help us to not get serious about a relationship that we should know is <u>not</u> going any further than it has been. We might have been going too fast, daydreaming (wishful thinking), or we could be making wrong assumptions.

People overlook Warning Signs because they know that no one is perfect, there will be compromise in relationships, and you won't know a lot of things about them until you have dated awhile. However, small moments can be revealing.

SLOW DOWN

If you are trying for a long-term romantic relationship, you should know when you see these Warnings Signs that it could be time to STOP! It could be time to look for someone new.

- ❖ **One of you <u>likes</u> (or loves) the other a lot more than is reciprocal.**

  These relationships don't work because there is a need for near equally balanced attraction and dedication. Consider how long you have been dating, and see how much affection each shows the other. <u>Observe your relationship</u> to see if there is equal interest and enthusiasm. Who is putting out effort to initiate activities?

- ❖ **If they come to you in a desperate situation time after time.**

  They are too dependent (needy), especially if it is about money.

- ❖ **If you don't like their friends.**

  Sayings are for good reason, *"Birds of a feather flock together."*

- **If either of you is overly jealous, or has an anger problem, it will be a difficult (impossible) relationship.**
  Don't ignore anger or jealousy.

- **If you have been dating and they don't invite you to their house for dinner, or introduce you to family and friends - even if you are older.**
  They are ashamed of you or the relationship. They probably have a Hidden Agenda.

- **It is a problem if you don't enjoy the same food. Sharing good food with a Pleasant Vibe is a great connector.**
  If a man doesn't like to cook, he can learn to help with the cooking and cleaning. In the Modern Age of sometimes role reversal, the man often does the cooking if the woman works a job. Also, it can be romantic when a man cooks for a woman. Cooking is a great skill to develop!

- **If watching TV, movies, eating out, and sex is all that happens in the relationship.**
  These activities alone are not enough to show a relationship is serious.

- **They like music you can't stand, or vice versa.**
  Music likes might sound trivial, and it's possible music interests will change over time, but relationships are about enjoying things together. Music is an important part of relationships, and it can lead to dancing and romance.

❖ **You want to change something about them that gets on your nerves, or they have a habit (smoking, drinking, pills, etc) you want to stop.**

People are not going to change <u>unless they are in the process</u>. Don't ignore these traits or habits as they will be amplified over time.

❖ **If you don't like their kids, or they do not like you.**

This is a Big Warning Sign (unless the kids are grown, but it still could be a Big Warning Sign).

PROBABLY <u>NOT</u> A MONOGAMOUS RELATIONSHIP

If you want a monogamous relationship, you are forced to trust your intuition, observations, friends, and your Partner (until you <u>know</u> otherwise). However, unless you are a Saver dating a Saver, you are forewarned that Modern Relationships are often non-monogamous. Don't assume anything (good or bad), and be careful to not get serious with the Wrong One.

❖ **Watch out if they flatter you only to ask for something (manipulation).**

If you want to help - OK, but learn to graciously say "No" or "I would love to but _____."

❖ **You find yourself writing a letter, email, or text that you feel your heart was broken.**

That relationship has probably suffered irreparable damage and/or they are probably having sex with someone else. They don't really care about your broken heart. Find someone good for you.

❖ **They come over to visit, and possibly include sex, but they do not hang out (spend time) with you.**

If sex is involved, a lot of men will be paying (helping out with something), but overlook her not spending time with him. However, if you do <u>not</u> want a monogamous relationship, hanging out should not matter.

❖ **You don't have a date for your Birthday, their Birthday, or Valentine's Day.**

❖ **You tell them something like, "I couldn't help but fall in love with you", or "I really care about you", and they don't respond, change the subject, or walk away.**

They are probably reminding you to not be so serious. The message could be that the relationship is not reciprocal in terms of wanting to be in a relationship.

❖ **The worst happens in secrecy and silence.**

It is rude if someone while dating you is frequently texting others. *"Phubbing"* is a new word combining phone and snub. They are snubbing you in favor of their mobile phone and others. If not their kids or something important, texting during a date is rude and creates suspicion among romantic partners.

A similar silence is when they rarely call to talk, but only to arrange a visit. This is a shallow relationship even if it is fun when they come over.

❖ **They "stand you up" for a date with a weak or no excuse (especially if at the last minute).**

In relationships, you often don't know if something is true or not. <u>Therefore, notice if it is at the last minute and how</u>

frequently they have excuses that stand you up. If frequent, they found someone else to go out with, or they are not truly interested in you. Trust your intuition and common sense.

- ❖ **They are frequently 'missing in action' when you call or text.**

It is a Warning Sign if they frequently do not answer your calls or texts. If they say they fell asleep from 6 - 10 pm, this is possible a few times, but if it is frequent, you know they are lying or lazy. People can have a lot of excuses.

Of course, no one is available to talk on the phone at any time, so be careful about overreacting. You should be able to feel if "missing in action" becomes a frequent pattern. But be careful you don't ruin the relationship because of your assumptions or suspicions.

In other words, you could risk a huge disappointment (ruin your relationship) by saying something (an accusation) based on a wrong assumption, or by being overly attached. The Warning Sign is to notice if they seem too unavailable, but then don't make it into too big of a deal because of your risk of being too needy or Too-Attached Too-Soon.

Be patient, but pay attention so you are not caught by surprise. You could invest (emotionally or financially) too hastily in a relationship before really knowing someone.

STAY ON THE RIGHT ROAD

Romantic relationships can be tricky because it depends on circumstances and the people involved. When you call or text and there is no answer, you might see yellow lights flashing and feel a Warning Sign that makes you feel the need to see

what is true. However, the problem with no answer is that it doesn't tell you anything.

On one hand, people can always make up excuses, while on the other hand, they could simply be visiting friends, family, or be away from their phone. After all, women and men need time alone, or to do what they enjoy doing without being disturbed by a phone. We forget the smart phone has been around for only 14 years.

I heard a guy ask, "Do you control your phone, or does your phone control you?" At first, I thought it was a stupid question, but I couldn't get it out of mind. After a few months of observing my phone as a frequent pest, I paid more attention. I heard scholars tell the "tricks" that Goggle and advertisers use to keep people engaged with the phone.

It sounds crazy to discuss my phone controlling me. No wonder anyone would want time away from their phone.

However, the phone has almost turned into a body part. I call mine "my left leg." When I go off and leave it, I will say, "I left my left leg behind", and often go get it. Who is in control?

It's difficult to know what someone else is doing, so don't make accusations just because someone wants time to themselves. Assumptions or accusations can be a relationship killer.

As for excuses, you cannot pin someone down if they are lying, so don't even try. It is better to give the relationship time to evolve. However, love of self is not tolerating lies, disrespect, or suffering in silence. It's OK if someone doesn't really love you. You can keep looking.

**BE PATIENT
FOR THE TRUTH TO COME OUT**

KEEP DRIVING

Do your best, and notice the Warning Signs. It is going to be difficult to find an Ideal Partner, and it seems to be getting more difficult every day.

Know that you cannot change anyone except yourself, so don't let people take advantage of you. See if both are working towards building Trust, Love, and Friendship. You have to be honest with yourself.

It's possible the Warning Signs are only telling you to control your speed so you can discuss a potential problem, or date longer before getting serious.

If they are the Right One, maybe everything will happen naturally – that would be Love.

"MAYBE I'M LUCKY TO BE GOING SO SLOWLY BECAUSE I MAY BE GOING IN THE WRONG DIRECTION"
                                    Ashleigh Brilliant

DON'T LOSE YOUR MONEY

Chapter 19

"Beware of little expenses. A small leak will sink a great ship."

Benjamin Franklin

A person can spend what money they had on someone that did not truly care about them. They think there is mutual love, but finally realize it was only their perspective. It would be good to avoid miscalculations.

IT WORKS BOTH WAYS

Until 2020, I thought men were about 80%+ more likely than women to lose their money in relationships. Then I saw an episode of Showtime's *"Love Fraud."* It showed that a lot of women get caught up in internet scams by manipulative men (this guy used different names and married several). These women would lose a <u>lot</u> of money ($50,000.+ was common).

Our conversation is often with Our Typical Guy, but we know that everything about relationships can apply both ways. Women Readers can simply switch the gender to fit.

People can also lose their money in a relationship where both put out honest effort, but it just didn't work out. We can learn to have the relationship, but to not spend too much.

There are lots of ways to lose your money, and chasing pleasure is included, as is trying to rid ourselves of loneliness.

"No two people on the face of this earth are alike in any one thing except for their loneliness."

Seven Arrows

SPENDING

Some people do not place a high priority on their own security because they do not consider its importance.

"Security: 1 the condition of being safe or sure; freedom from danger, fear, doubt, etc. 2 something that protects"
Webster's Dictionary

Security can add to your confidence. Before spending too much money on dating, be comfortable in being able to pay your bills and saving some money. You don't want to *"sink a great ship"* (lose your car, the place you live, or have the electricity cut off). You want to enjoy life, but life will be more difficult if you are broke.

As for chasing pleasure, it sounds simple to not spend too much, but the pleasure can be so great that money can feel like "only paper", or people can rationalize or justify their behavior. Our Typical Guy can find it hard to resist someone attractive who makes it fun. The process is described:

When the heat of passion is over and she is gone, and "it's the 'morning after the night before" or a week later, Our Typical Guy wakes up to realize the excitement has subsided and his money is gone. It is then that he might wonder if it was all a good idea. A Comfort Zone can be hard to resist.

It takes patience and self-discipline to make good decisions. It is especially difficult for a man if the Big Brain is making the decisions. It takes strength to resist temptation even if you know they are not good for you.

"A FOOL AND HIS MONEY ARE SOON PARTED"
Proverbs 21:20

If a man thinks he is "in love", he might lose his mind (the Big Brain takes over). Be honest with yourself to check out the real situation.

YOU CAN KEEP LOOKING
FOR THE RIGHT ONE
IF YOU DON'T GET SIDE-TRACKED
BY THE WRONG ONES

LOOK OUT!!!

Dating happens on many different levels, and some of the people Our Typical Guy dates might have no real interest in him, but they might tell him what he wants to hear. They are gone when he is out of money.

Therefore, Our Typical Guy needs to not be "addickted" to sex. Addickted is a new word which applies to men only:

Addickted 1. when sex has the man's D***, or Big Brain, in such a condition that he cannot stay away from a woman, or say "No Thanks"; 2. when the man is highly attracted, attached, or "in love", but it is not mutual; 3. addickted happens when a man is only pleasure driven.

One problem with being addickted is when he thinks it isn't costing much, and he is having fun, but then "the bite" comes for a car, a loan, help with bills, or co-sign a note. (Of course, he could also get the bite without getting sex).

It's OK to be generous if you have money, but it's also OK to say "No", or "I would love to but _____."

When you can't keep up financially, you might feel like a victim of circumstances. However, if it is not a relationship of teamwork and mutual attraction, the day will surely come when you can't keep up with the requests.

All of this can be tricky when a man has feelings of love, but a man should keep his Little Brain in control or he could soon be broke. People (men and women) 40, 50, 60+ are also vulnerable, and it hurts a lot more when their money is gone.

PAY CLOSE ATTENTION

A person can spend a lot of money if they think someone is an Ideal Partner. Be a Great Listener and Observer. Keep your money for future security in case the relationship turns out to not be as honest as you thought.

DON'T IGNORE THE WARNING SIGNS
TRUST YOUR INTUITION
LISTEN TO FRIENDS

There will be clues if they are acting, or if you are deluding yourself. Some examples:

1. If you should confront them that the relationship is not serious and say, "I will never be more than a _____ (friend/sugar daddy/ fuck buddy) to you." They respond, "Baby, please don't feel that way" or "I wish you didn't feel that way." Notice that they didn't say your statement wasn't true - they said they didn't want you to feel that way.

2. A person can delude themselves (willfully ignorant) by wanting someone for more than a girlfriend/boyfriend, but the feelings are not mutual. You can notice how much genuine affection they show for you.

3. You can fuel your own delusion: They tell you what you want to hear, and you assume (want) the relationship to be for real. A man might be mesmerized by her beauty, what she tells him, and/or the wonderful night together. The relationship evolves into sex, and he gets addickted. She says, "I love you." She might love him to some degree, but love has different depths and meanings. It could be love and lust, but mainly lust. It is easy to fall into the trap because it is a trap he set for himself.

4. Pay attention for Bitches and Assholes, and either sex can be one or both. <u>The Bullsheet</u> provides definitions:

Bitch: 1. someone with frequent daily complaining; 2. a Bitch is demanding, very bossy; 3. Bitches talk bad about others.

Asshole: 1. someone who cares only about themselves; 2. Assholes insist on having their way; 3. Assholes are inconsiderate of others, even their partner; 4. Assholes want their way every time on important matters; 5. Assholes often have a Hidden Agenda; 6. selfish people.

Bitches and Assholes are self-centered, secretly plotting, and both think the world revolves around them.

HAVE YOUR BITCH AND ASSHOLE DETECTOR "ON"
IF YOU LISTEN & OBSERVE
YOU CAN FIGURE THEM OUT

You have to trust your intuition in the Dating World. The gold that glitters might be Fool's Gold (Golddiggers or Manipulators). It's time to notice relationships that are one-sided or lack equality. If someone is interested, they will find time for you (more than a fleeting moment or a quick fling, but at times that could be what people want).
LOOKS AREN'T EVERYTHING
COURAGE AND PATIENCE ARE NEEDED
THERE CAN COME A TIME
TO KEEP LOOKING

FACTORS TO CONSIDER

- Are you a 'Sugar Daddy'? Regardless of if a man is the same age or a lot older, if the relationship is about paying for sex, he is a Sugar Daddy. She has others, and he becomes vulnerable to manipulation. A woman would be a Sugar Momma.
- Do you think a young woman or man (20-30s) is going to be in a long-term romantic relationship with a man or woman in their 50s+? Maybe, if the older person is rich. Otherwise, true love and friendship is possible, but rare.
- Delusion can come from either direction:
    1. **They lie to you.** (Women and men probably lie about the same.)
    2. **You lie to yourself, and they let you believe it.**

For example, Our Typical Guy can be infatuated and the Big Brain takes over. They encourage or allow him to believe his delusion or his illusions of a serious relationship. In the end, when his money is gone, he won't be able to blame anyone but himself. He should only spend what is comfortable with his budget.

- What if she gets pregnant and you are not married? This mistake could cost for 18 years. Child support for 18 years would be a least $100,000+ with additional payments. When a relationship with children falls apart, how are you going to have money for another girlfriend, or extra time/money to spend on the child?

PEOPLE SHOULD...THINK!
SO THEY WILL HAVE MONEY
WHEN THEY MEET THEIR IDEAL PARTNER

SOLUTIONS
SOLUTION #1. THE LITTLE BRAIN BEING IN CONTROL
This is Our Typical Guy's Best Solution. Most men don't (won't) admit to their friends the amount of money they spend on their girlfriend. (If you can't, then that's probably a Warning Sign.) Every man has to spend some money, but it is a matter of how much.

SOLUTION #2. HAVE LIMITS AND BOUNDARIES
Many people do not understand the importance of setting boundaries, or even consider boundaries. Boundaries in relationships are what you should do for others, or what you tolerate in their behavior. When you cross that line or give in by saying "Yes", you could feel taken advantage of which creates resentment.

Without boundaries a person can be "played." Understand the process. Do you pour creative energy and money into someone else's life plan and neglect your own? Rather than giving in - think of saying "No" as a way of staying strong with healthy boundaries.

"Setting limits allows us to be more, not less compassionate. Limits bring better health, emotional balance, creative fulfillment, and creates stronger relationships."
                                    Brene Brown, PhD, Social Scientist

YOU NEED TO PREPARE YOUR BOUNDARIES <u>NOW</u> HAVE THEM IN MIND....
<u>BEFORE</u> A RELATIONSHIP BEGINS
OR YOU WILL NOT BE ABLE TO ENFORCE THEM!

Boundaries help sort out the truth in your relationships. If someone shows up only when they need help - set a boundary. It might be time to Move On.

Remember that boundaries are a safe place from which you can remain stable. Boundaries are <u>not restrictive</u>, but to guide you to a safe place with the choices you make.

SOLUTION #3 PROTECT YOUR HEART AND ASSETS

You might have the urge to relieve their suffering or give in to requests without thinking of the emotional or financial cost to yourself. (You will feel it later.)

If someone is frequently "in a jam", the key is to feel compassion without taking on their suffering. If you are Too Attached – Too Soon, think you are in love, or afraid of losing them if you say "No", you will be the one suffering because of not having boundaries. <u>You can be empathetic without being used.</u>

THINK ABOUT WHAT IS BEST FOR YOU
DON'T FOLD UNDER PRESSURE

BE STRONG TO FACE REALITY

You have worked hard for your money, or even if your money was inherited - don't blow it. Be strong to get out of sacrificial insincere relationships. Watch out for yourself.

From the movie Body Heat, **there are lessons to be learned:**

A friend says, *"Stay away from her."*

He replies, *"Sorry guys, I can't do that. Did you see how good she looked?"*

Friend, *"You think you are having fun. Some men like you mess up again and again as it is your nature. Most of our mess ups are small, but she could be big time trouble. Watch yourself."*

Of course, he doesn't quit seeing her. She tells him things I have heard, *"I would never do anything to hurt you"* and *"No matter what you think, I love you."* Not to be a spoiler, but he ends up in prison.

Listen with more than your ears (and eyes) because no matter what anyone says, some people don't listen. There is the saying,

"Love is blind" (and hard of hearing)

Some people are stubborn or wishful thinkers. If you haven't learned to listen to friends, there are moments your body might tell you something is wrong:

- **You suddenly pause or freeze in a moment of realization.**
- **You <u>feel</u> something is wrong in the relationship - remember boundaries and your intuition.**

- You reflect on your relationship, and know they are not your Ideal Partner (A True Friend/Lover).
- They are "missing in action" (don't answer calls, texts, show up) far more than someone who truly cares.

IT'S TIME FOR GOOD DECISIONS
YOU ARE NOT GOING TO CHANGE ANYONE
EXCEPT MAYBE YOURSELF

INTO THE FUTURE

In a rapidly evolving world, many people are losing their jobs, money, connections, and relationships. Try to keep all four together. Your dreams can come true, but it will probably take longer and be in a different way than you expect (imagine).

Some people (especially men) never grow up, and few can afford the price. Be willing to walk away from demanding people and one-way relationships. You will find someone nice.

IF SOMEONE IS CONTROLLING YOU
IT'S YOUR FAULT – NOT THEIRS
TRY FOR SOMEONE HONEST

We all make mistakes, but we can take heart in the following story:

" I started to get over the shame from telling my story when I realized we all have incredible stories. We think something shouldn't have happened to us, or we are embarrassed it happened to us. Or we are ashamed we made a bad decision.

I realized it's time for us to be proud of our stories, and the stuff that happened to us is actually part of our destiny. I call them 'Divine Wounds', and everything that happened 'to' us actually happened 'for' us. My story is to help us heal and Move On."
Renee Linnell, The Burn Zone

"KEEP IT REAL"
IS OUR MOTTO

EVERYONE'S EMOTIONAL

Chapter 20

Single Life has not been as easy as I thought, especially since I started out an emotional wreck. I was like, "Emotions – What's that?"

"Emotion: 1. Strong feeling 2. Any particular feeling, such as love, hate, joy, or fear 3. Emotion is any of the ways in which one reacts to something without careful thinking."
Webster's Dictionary

This definition is a start, but too basic for the complexity of emotions. Emotions are like feelings, but people can justify or rationalize feeling a certain way, or any way. For example, a person can feel jealous, or even "in love", based on a wrong assumption or incorrect rationalization.

Whether emotions and feelings are the same or not, our emotions and brain are connected, and we want them working for us. The Latin root for emotion means "to move", so there is "motion" in emotions. Emotions can move our thinking, or move us to take action.

If we develop understanding, we can calm down to observe ourselves and to control our emotions.

WHAT ARE EMOTIONS?

"Emotions are brain generated physical and mental states that both motivate people to take action and energize their behavior. Emotions may or may not be conscious. People can come under the sway of their emotions without realizing they have been impacted. Each emotion can evoke an automatic reaction.

For example, when anger is the issue, they say we have a short fuse or a quick trigger."
Ronald Potter-Efron, Healing the Angry Brain

The Bullsheet is not an expert as Dr. Potter-Efron who goes on to discuss *"Primary and Social Emotions."* **Emotions make individuals and relationships complicated. For now, our discussion will simplify the matter to Negative and Positive Emotions.**

HAVE THE COURAGE
TO CONFRONT YOUR EMOTIONS

NEGATIVE EMOTIONS
Negative Emotions are disturbances to our happiness. A person can waste a lot of energy and life-force on hard feelings, anxiety, and/or self-judgment. However, we can overcome negative emotions by becoming aware of them and our contributions to sustain them. We can open our mind to move to the positive side of life.

*"THE MIND IS LIKE A PARCHUTE
IT ONLY WORKS WHEN IT IS OPEN"*
Unknown

There will be situations, circumstances, or things people say or do that are going to upset you. It can be tricky. For example, anger has its place, and a person can be justified in speaking up about being angry. But it is important to stay calm, so you say or do what is needed without an angry reaction. You can be assertive without being aggressive.

NAME THE EMOTION TO FIND THE PROBLEM

Regardless of whether self-inflicted, tragedy, or "just life", we all experience Negative Emotions. However, we often bring Negative Emotions on ourselves with wrong thinking and wrong reactions.

Now we call out Negative Emotions as Enemies for our awareness to recognize. Each one is negativity to rid from your life. If you feel any of these, understand the emotion and let that go.

NEGATIVE EMOTIONS

Scared	Hate	Dread	Fear
Overwhelmed	Accusing	Greedy	Desperate
Guilt	Despair	Envy	Shame
Blaming	Grudges	Critical	Suffering
Arrogant	Bitter	Pessimistic	Depressed
Ashamed	Annoyed	Worried	Insulting
Harsh	Hurtful	Revenge	Belligerent

Each of these emotions has its own energy. It would be good practice to write out the definition of each to see the meaning so you are able to recognize when you have that emotional feeling.

The definition gives insight, and puts you in touch with your feelings. When you indentify your emotions, you might uncover that they have been with you for a long time, or were unconscious.

Negative Emotions can turn into habits - like worrying. Instead of worry, we can learn to accept a situation and then do something to improve it or improve ourselves. For example, we know worry won't help anything, so we can learn good habits instead.

"The root of our negative thinking lies in the emotions. Nobody but you can overcome your problems. You have one because you allow people to trigger you emotionally, thereby giving their words and actions the power to direct you. You must learn to lead your own emotions."

Roy Masters

POSITIVE EMOTIONS

When you learn Patience, you learn to be positive. Being positive will help you live happier and longer. We call out Positive Emotions as Friends, or emotions we try to build on to keep our life improving.

POSITIVE EMOTIONS

Kind	Enthusiastic	Calm	Inspired
Relaxed	Accepting	Brave	Compassionate
Content	Cheerful	Hopeful	Faith
Friendly	Playful	Romantic	Sweet
Vibrant	Confident	Optimistic	Strong
Humble	Courageous	Forgiveness	Thankful
Grateful	Happy	Passionate	Energetic

It would also be good practice to write out the definition of these words so you know the feeling and mindset you are trying for.

How do we fall from Positive to Negative Emotions? We forget to be thankful, we let in resentment, or we forget to feel love, gratitude, and joy in our heart.

"The emotions that drain you are the emotions that come from fear; the emotions that give you more energy are those that come from love."

Don Miguel Ruiz, The Four Agreements Companion Book

Don Miguel's book explains how we are the Judge of ourselves, have a Victim inside, and how we can rise above being a Victim through boundaries based on love and respect. Don't disrespect yourself, or let others disrespect you.

With Positive Emotions you have a Good Vibe, and never underestimate the importance of having a Good Vibe. Good fortune will be heading your way if you persevere and maintain a positive attitude.

I must tell you it usually takes time for things to change. It feels like our lives move in 2-year increments, and over that time, we have some changes. So "patience" does not mean "for just a little while." It will probably take some time, but positive emotions will bring positive change. But regardless of how long it takes, you can count on patience and being positive to help you enjoy life.

Through self-reflection, you will be able to accurately evaluate emotions and your relationships. If you enjoy their company, get to know them before becoming emotionally involved, and know it can take longer than you think to get to know someone (some people don't know themselves).

Emotions cause us liberation or bondage - choose liberation. Life will support you when you learn to let go of negativity. However, it is going to take conscious effort.

CHOOSE POSITIVITY
CEASE TO REACT AS BEFORE
PATIENCE IS THE KEY

NOT SO SIMPLE
This chapter was to end here with emotions arranged into Negative and Positive. We were to recognize our Negative Emotions and with the strength gained there, we would deal

with future Negative Emotions. On the other hand, we would try to be positive.

It was neatly arranged for us to sail on the Sea of Life, but it turned out to be only a start. Emotions are not so simple because there are so many; they are so different; they are tied to our brain and heart; they can be created from circumstances; they can be created by other people; they can depend on how we respond; they can be unconscious (emotions are in our convictions); they are not totally under our control, and they are not understood. We are each a complicated mix of emotions.

THE SEA OF LIFE

We want the Sea of Life to be smooth sailing with calm waters and beautiful destinations. We would even enjoy a few waves at times to make life exciting, and some great sex would be nice. But powerful storms can blow in to rock our boat (world). The Sea of Life can rise up with great winds and waves capable of sinking weak boats (people). And regardless of how choppy or smooth it is on the Sea of Life, we know we must keep sailing.

As Captain of our ship, we realize:
Uncertainty is the only certainty in life - be prepared for storms
We can't control everything & control is an illusion - the Sea is vast
We sail into uncharted waters - go with the flow
Big waves are natural - some stress is good for us to elevate our skill
Never panic - increase awareness to survive
Run a tight ship - control emotions
If you have a Co-Captain - work together
Enjoy your voyage!!!

MAJOR PROBLEMS

Emotions, feelings, talking, and thinking make up a big part of who we are and how we live. We need increased effort to enjoy life and enjoy ourselves as we face problems on the Sea of Life.

PROBLEM #1 – Negative Emotions Can Be Natural

Negative emotions are <u>natural</u> at times. It would ridiculous to think a person could live positive all the time as that would be <u>unnatural</u>. Loss or tragic things will happen.

We accept we cannot be 100% Positive all the time, but it sounds like a worthy goal at 90%. A goal of 90% would make us aware to fight off negativity. If we focus on positive things, those are the things we are most likely to remember.

PROBLEM #2 – "Be Strong"

To try "be strong" to get through every situation would be <u>impossible</u>. We know it would be rude and not very understanding to tell someone suffering, "Be strong." That would not be comforting, and will not work even if you try it on yourself. People have emotions, and people have a heart. Our hearts will be tested more that "be strong" can bear.

The Buddha taught us that suffering is part of life in this world. We all need to learn how to work our way through suffering and negative emotions without it being long-term. We can learn to process our problems (emotions). Professional help is available if needed.

OUR TRANSFORMATION IS IN HOW WE RELATE TO PEOPLE, CIRCUMSTANCES, AND OURSELVES

PROBLEM #3 – Negative Thinking

Another disconnect that makes emotions not so simple is when we involve THINKING. We cannot keep from thinking, and some of it will be negative.

Thinking mixes up our conversation. Instead of just Negative and Positive Emotions, we must consider Negative Thinking and Positive Thinking. Emotions are often related to our thinking, but they are not the same. We can just think up stuff, make wrong assumptions, or tell ourselves stories that are not true.

PROBLEM #4 – Fear, Worry, Anxiety

A lot of fears are said to be based on fear of being alone or insecurities. Don't be afraid and don't worry. Anxiety and worry can destroy your peace and your relationships.

Reactions are often an emotional response, and we can make emotional responses that are not in our best interest. Think of the consequences before overreacting.

Emotion-based bad decisions are often based on frustration, pride, or ambition. Emotions can be difficult to control, so back away before you end up saying or doing something you will regret.

"One who controls occurring anger as one would control a chariot gone off the track, that one I call a charioteer - other people just hold the reins."

The Buddha

**YOU CONTOL YOUR EMOTIONS
OR THEY CONTROL YOU**

GAIN CONTROL

For better or worse, our brain is constantly reprogramming, and it is proven that we can *"control the brain's reprogramming process."* **Dr. David Hanscom tells us how:**

*"It's **not** helpful to cope with repetitive negative thoughts by suffering, suppressing them, or masking them with obsessive behavior. <u>To really break the cycle, you have to reprogram your thoughts.</u> In my experience with thousands of patients, it's the only method that works.*

*<u>In dealing with the root problem, you cannot control your mind **with** your mind very long. In other words, you can't "out-think" your own thoughts.</u> If you are upset, you are upset. More importantly, see how much mental energy you can waste on just one situation.*

*<u>It's critical to understand that **you can control** the brain's reprogramming process. To overcome negative thinking, there are three phases to forming alternative neurological pathways:</u>*

1. ***An awareness of the thoughts that incites your pain, <u>and</u>***
2. ***Detaching from the thoughts, <u>and</u>***
3. ***Burning a pathway of new and different thoughts."***

David Hanscom MD, Back In Control (emphasis added)

Create your reality as a participant (not a victim). You create a world you like, or live in a world with troublesome thoughts. The emotions must be dealt with. It's like doing homework with determination.

When you realize your thoughts can make you suffer, you will leave behind old ways of thinking. It's easy to play the blame game, but if something is going to change, you have to

be the one who changes. Rethinking painful memories only brings things back. That pain is already part of you, so you don't need to think about it. For peace of mind, have positive thinking.

**CONNECT THOUGHTS THAT ARE POSITIVE
TO YOUR EMOTIONS
DISCONNECT FROM THOUGHTS THAT ARE NEGATIVE
DISCONNECT FROM DISCONTENT**

YOU ARE NOT YOUR THOUGHTS
We hear this and we know this, but it can be difficult to internalize. Most of us go around thinking too much, and think it is natural. But you can change your focus or stop thinking about something at any time. Also, recognize that your thinking could be sending you false messages.

*"If you experience anxiety-producing thoughts, they become stronger over time. If you suppress them they become much worse. The **only** effective way to deal with these thoughts is to detach from them.*
<u>Detachment, or meditation, involves watching thoughts come in and out of your mind, and learning not to respond to them. You observe the thoughts as a separate entity without reacting.</u>"
David Hanscom MD, Back In Control (emphasis added)

**DON'T LET NEGATIVE THINKING
CAUSE YOU TO HAVE NEGATIVE EMOTIONS**

RESENTMENT & HOSTILITY

We recognize Negative Emotions are natural in some cases. For example, if our beloved dog or family member dies, or if some unfortunate event, it is natural to have negative emotions. But in daily life events, negative thinking leads to negative emotions which create resentment. It is resentment that we need to end.

"Resentment: A feeling of hurt and anger at being wronged, insulted, slighted, snubbed, neglected, mistreated, etc."
Webster's Dictionary

In other words, we don't just "get angry." We resent something about a situation or person (slighted, mistreated, jealous etc), and that "made us angry." **But if we can identify what we resent, and let that go, we can end most of the Negative Emotions we create.**

NEGATIVE THINKING LEADS TO RESENTMENT
RESENTMENT LEADS TO HOSTILITY

"Hostility: A feeling of dislike or hate; unfriendly; the bitter feeling."
Webster's Dictionary

HOSTILITY BYPASSES REASON
CAUSING PEOPLE TO ACT OUT

Not letting resentment into your life will end hostility before it arrives. Remember that you can also resent little things that happen throughout your day including your job, co-workers, traffic, etc. You might need to make some changes.

For example, if you didn't think of _____ (something that's bothering you), you would not have an emotion or feeling about it. If you suffer negative emotions: Search inside to discover things you resent and let resentments go.

"Resentment and rage (hostility) *are like swallowing poison pills and hoping the other person dies."*

Saying

RESENTMENT & HOSTILITY
CAUSE US NEGATIVE EMOTIONS

If you need to deal with something, then do it with calmness. Some things you will need to overlook, or forgive, and move on.

If you can develop patience, you will have more positive emotions. It might take time to develop patience, but the result will be positive. It's a constant battle: do not let Resentment into your life while developing more and more Patience.

HOLDING ON TO GRUDGES
IS A WASTE OF YOUR LIFE-FORCE

Use your thinking to help yourself. If a relationship is not working, do something or talk to someone – friends, family, a counselor, or your romantic interest.

NEGATIVE PEOPLE

All of us encounter Negative People, but it will be good when their part of our story is over. These people contribute to our negative emotions. They plant poison seeds, and listening to them puts doubt and negative thinking into our mind. Know

that you cannot change them, or their assessments and judgments. They will need to change on their own.

We all know Negative People, and some are a "Malcontent: 1. a dissatisfied person with unreasonable complaining and faultfinding 2. Chronically discontented; bears a grudge from a sense of grievance or thwarted ambition 3. Bitter and complaining from self-pity; feels disadvantaged 4. Unhappy, blaming, constantly displeased with the world 5. A person who is difficult to deal with, and they show little empathy or sympathy for others."

Even after hearing the correct diagnosis, we might keep reaching out to them for years. It's more difficult to avoid them when they are family or friends.

In reading the definition, you might think it describes a poor or disadvantaged person, but some are blessed with wealth and health. They are not focused on their blessings, but on their perceptions of the world.

A Malcontent can be friendly, or even charming at first, but conversations will change to something negative about someone or a group they despise (immigrants, politics, etc). They act like the conversation is open for discussion, and it might be, but only for as long as you agree, or do not dispute what they say. They are a conditional friend.

Although they talk of change for others, they will probably not change themselves. In their mind, they are always correct. To be their friend, it is their way or the highway – take the highway.

Yes, take the highway. If the Malcontent is a family member, you can be manipulated by a sense of affection, or a

duty to family. There is no such duty to listen to negativity from anyone. We do not want to reinforce negativity by continuing to engage with a Malcontent.

It is not healthy to hear their negative opinions. You will be thankful when you no longer have a Malcontent's negative thinking influencing you (it can be subconscious). Some relationships get to be too much trouble, especially if we are empowering a Malcontent or a Manipulator.

However, because of family or friends, there are times you must be with a Malcontent. You can't pretend they are not happening, so what do you say? You could say, "That's not helpful to me" (your boundary) or "I'm feeling overwhelmed by what you are saying" or simply, "I don't want to talk about it," or "you already told me that" instead of letting them go on and on. It's OK, and even natural, when some people don't like you, especially if they are a Negative Person.

Of course, there could be many other ways of dealing with Negative People. I have one friend who is 38, but he still has an overbearing Malcontent Mother and a Dad who meekly stays quiet. My friend's Mother is one of those types that no matter what you do - they don't like it and they are unhappy about it.

My friend told me his coping technique: "I pretend like they are dead. Then I am always surprised when they call. I can enjoy visiting with them."

Whatever works for you would be a good idea. It is difficult to deal with Negative People and Malcontents, so professional help could help those who can afford it. It could be the best money some people ever spend if they gain peace of mind.

When you identify Negative People, remember to not be resentful towards them so you can save your strength to deal with life's other pressures. It is your task to be discerning in

determining if you should avoid them. In other words, it is not your place to judge them, but to identify them and stay away, or whatever your technique. You simply do not want their emotional poison. Realize that Negative people are Stressors to you. Forgiveness (accepting other's shortcomings) will be necessary. However, you can be patient to hope that something happens in their life or yours to make them see a need to change.

PATIENCE CAN PAY OFF

Time has passed since I wrote the above, and I have new hope that a Malcontent or Negative Person can change to where you can at least have a pleasant relationship with them. But don't press your luck. It's tricky because being nice to them by itself doesn't work because they can take advantage of the friendliness you have to offer.

A Malcontent might not ever be content/happy, but they might see their negative behavior is chasing off others. They can learn to not be so opinionated (they remember the conversations that went bad). At some point, a person realizes their individual opinion matters little, and there are many things beyond their control (other people, government, almost everything). With time, people can learn to not be antagonistic.

Patience and time are your best hope with a Malcontent. There are many paths to peace.

**OF COURSE YOU SHOULD BE KIND
TO MALCONTENTS AND MANIPULATORS
BUT DON'T EXPECT OR THINK
THEY WILL CHANGE**

THE LAST LINE

In August of 2000, I was sent to Atlanta for training in my telecommunications site-acquisition job. I had heard Atlanta was fun, so on my last night I wanted to go out to a club.

It was about 10:00 o'clock on that last night when I rode the trolley to Buckhead District and got off at a nice hotel. I went in and came out as if I was staying there, and got a ride on their Hospitality Van. The Driver was a Black Man who asked where I wanted to go. I ask him which club he would go to. He said "Club Plush" so I asked him to take me there.

At 12 o'clock the night was still young, and I had become familiar with Club Plush. I figured out that Plush was mostly (95%) a Black Club. It was about that same time I heard from the crowd "buzz" that the Up In Smoke Concert was to be in Atlanta the next night. The Club was already a lot of fun with the people and the music, but at 12:30 the vibe picked way up when Dr Dre, Snoop Dog, and their Entourage actually arrived inside Plush. They walked right by where I was standing, and I shook hands with Snoop Dog.

Word must have gotten out across Atlanta because the place started to fill up with pretty women, and it was packed. The music played all Dr Dre, Snoop Dog, and Warren G as he was there too. Smoke was in the air. It was so much fun. I was having a fantastic time!

The stars and their entourage left by 2:30, so I drifted to another room to sit down a minute. It was there that a Black Man befriended me. I think he saw how much I enjoyed everything. Have you ever met someone where you know that you will see them for only a short time and never see them again, yet you meet a Friend you will never forget? That is how this man was to me - maybe he was a Spiritual Friend. Anyway, we were visiting and he told me, "Black People will let you party with them" and the reasons why.

The clubs in Atlanta stay open until 4, and I got to dance with a beautiful woman that was 28 for an unforgettable dance. She invited me to her upcoming Birthday Party. When she asked me if I lived in Atlanta, I nearly cried when I had to say "No."

It was the most fun I ever had in a club.

After returning from Atlanta, I started going out to the Black Clubs (95% of the people were Black, but they were inviting and called it a "mixed crowd"). Gradually, I made friends over the following years.

In January 2003, I saw my friend Andy in the club, and we were visiting about the possibility of the U.S. invading Iraq. We agreed it was inevitable, and that nothing could (would) stop it from happening. The rest is history. I was already 56 so I stayed at my job, but Andy went to Active Duty in the Army as a Drill Sergeant for the Infantry at Ft. Sill.

Over the years, I learned that Black People will let you party with them, and that Black People make Great Friends.

By 2013, Andy was back in Oklahoma City where he started a boxing gym. I had been in boxing class for 4 years, so I went to his gym for a work-out. Andy had a drill that was new to me where I was to flip a giant truck tire over and over the length of a 50+ yard driveway and back. There were spacer lines in the concrete about 8 yards apart. On my turn, I got busy flipping the tire, but it was really heavy. When I got to the next-to-last line, I saw if I went to the last line that I would have to flip it back to exactly the line I was on. I was relying on my age, being a friend, and being a guest to ask, "Can I stop here and not go to the last line?"

Andy said, "George, I would like to let you do that, but I just can't. You have to go to the last line." I went on to the last line, and all the way back to the start.

What is the point of this story for Our Typical Guy, or you?

As with the lines in the concrete, we often think we are at the end of a relationship, but there is more to do. We might still need to "flip our tire" to the last line.

IT WOULD BE NICE
IF SIMPLY AVOIDING NEGATIVE PEOPLE
WAS GOOD ENOUGH
BUT IT'S NOT

To get to the last line, you need to do more to free yourself from Negative People, and that would be to <u>not think about them</u>.

When we think about the Negative Person, we have negative thoughts which evoke negative emotions. Thinking about them makes you resent something about them, or your involvement in the relationship. You could feel used or stupid for your participation in having had anything to do with them. You might resent your own actions and contributions (guilt, blame, etc).

<u>The Negative Person is no longer around so there is no point in thinking about them</u>. Thinking of Negative People only creates resentment and hostility in the Thinker.

Are you finished when you get to the 'last line' by avoiding and not thinking of Negative People?

NO, because you still have to flip your tire back to the start. In other words, you need to minimize seeing and thinking about Negative People for <u>the rest of your life</u>.

Even when you do get back to the start, it turns out that it was a good work-out, but you need to come back to class (life) every day until your reprogrammed mind has conquered negative people, negative thinking, and negativity within. We are flipping our way to the Positive Side of Life.

YOU NEED TO BE CAREFUL WHO YOU LET INTO YOUR LIFE

DO YOUR BEST

With introspection and awareness, your life will improve. Liberate yourself from toxic emotions. Don't be attached to the past. Let go of things and relationships that don't work. Practice gratitude for what you have rather than dwelling on Negative People. Forgiveness can heal the emotions.

HAVE A POSITIVE VIBE!

THE TAKEAWAY

Imagine a different world. Free yourself from negative thinking for a bright future you can embrace. As you build happiness from within, you don't need a reaction to every thought or emotion. When you are not constantly thinking, you can live intuitively.

INTUITION IS NOT AN EMOTION
YOUR INTUITION CAN BE SPOILED
BY YOUR EMOTIONS AND THINKING
LEARN TO TRUST YOUR INTUITION

All of us have uncontrollable thoughts, and we know negative thinking clutters our mind. So we learn to quiet our mind and detach from "fight, flight, or freeze" responses. We can drop habits and people that are holding us back.

YOU CAN CONTROL YOUR THINKING
BUT NOT THE OTHER PERSON'S BEHAVIOR
FINDING EMOTIONAL PEACE
IS A GOOD IDEA

If you are going to replay memories in your mind – play good memories. We need emotional responsibility to tell ourselves good things. To have an acceptance of change is part of a healthy life.

YOUR LIFE WILL CHANGE ON THE DAY
THE STRENGTH OF YOUR INNER WORLD
IS GREATER THAN THE INFLUENCES
FROM THE OUTSIDE WORLD

"In everything negative – there is something positive, and that's part of keeping a good mind."
Wilma Mankiller

<u>DANGER</u>

Chapter 21

It's important to realize that Anger is like a disease - a person can avoid it, and a person can get over it.

When I was first dating in the Single World, a woman told me, "<u>You are never going to have a great relationship until you get over your Anger Problem.</u>" I didn't even know I had an Anger Problem, but her words were the truth.

No one wants to chase away people or opportunities.

"HOW DID YOU RESPOND?
'NEVER IN ANGER' - MY MOTHER TAUGHT ME
THAT WOULD BE SELF-DEFEATING."
      Ruth Bader Ginsberg, Supreme Court Justice

AN INDIVIDUAL PROBLEM
Our Typical Guy is trying for a calm, patient, positive attitude. Anger is none of these things. It invokes the feeling to fight back against the stress, against the life situation, against a person.

"A soft answer turns away wrath but harsh words stir up anger."
      Proverbs 15:1

"Whosoever is slow to anger has great understanding, but he (she) *who has a hasty temper exalts folly."*
      Proverbs 14:29

These verses tell us to think before speaking. It's like I would tell my kids and now myself, "Brain in gear before mouth in motion."

Anger makes us lose self-control, and it makes everyone involved unhappy.

"Angry brains create angry bodies, which create angry brains, in a vicious circle that can trap us in an angry world. And worst of all, we might not even realize what's happening. Our angry brain has a way of convincing us that our angry thoughts, feelings, and actions are perfectly normal."
                    Ronald Potter-Efron, Healing the Angry Brain

ANGER WILL NOT JUST GO-AWAY
Understanding and healing anger is something each person has to do on their own. Slow down to evaluate your feelings and reactions. When in doubt, don't respond.

I have a friend who was sent to Anger Management Class. Pete hated going at first, but he got over his Anger Problem.

I asked, "What was the best thing you learned?"

Pete said, "TAKE TIME BEFORE I RESPOND, AND PRETEND MY RESPONSE IS A STICK OF DYNAMITE. I ASK MYSELF – DO I WANT THE CONSEQUENCES OF LIGHTING THIS STICK OF DYNAMITE?"

Pete is giving great advice. However, I can testify that someone can make us angry and we attack. I have ask myself the question and still said, "Yes, I want to light the stick of dynamite. I don't care what happens."

ERRRRRRRRRR! This is the Wrong Answer! If you ask yourself the question, the answer is "NO." Just asking the question should be enough of a Time-out to prevent explosions. The answer is always "NO." Find another answer: maybe compromise, maybe find a new friend, maybe it is your fault, maybe anger is the wrong emotion.

HAVE EMOTIONAL MATURITY
LET ANGER GO

CALM DOWN

Cooling off or a Time-out seems to be the 1st Step to defeat angry outbursts. Even a few seconds to ask about the Stick of Dynamite can be the necessary cooling off.

As in sports, make good use of your Time-outs. When you feel the game (relationship) is going against you, or a very important play (response) is required – call "Time-out!" Cool off and ask yourself: What will I gain by saying what I want to say? What do I have to lose? Do I want to ruin this relationship? What would be a wise response? Do I need to respond? Do I want to continue seeing them?

Don't let anger prevail when intelligence is what's required (brains not emotions). When we react from negative emotions, we make bad decisions.

People can also make up inner rationalizations or wrong assumptions and react negatively.

"Rationalize: to give a reasonable explanation without seeming to know that it is not the real one."

Webster's Dictionary

A person might not even realize they are making it up (tripping) until the dynamite explodes and they get the bad results and negative emotions like guilt, shame, or she is gone.

"When you get angry, you lose more than your temper."
Brahma Kumaris, Thought for Today

Our Typical Guy will be so happy when he didn't respond in anger that not responding will feel like real progress or even a victory. He will have the relief of not sabotaging his relationship. The relationship might need a re-evaluation, but it is better to not ruin it before the re-evaluation (especially since Our Typical Guy might need to re-evaluate and correct his own attitude or behavior).

Maybe the relationship needs level-headed conversation to see if it will continue. Relationships can be complicated, and anger doesn't help.

BRAIN WAVES

"Neuroplasticity" is the brain's <u>proven ability</u> to re-wire and heal itself. You can re-wire your brain to not suffer from anxiety, anger, worry, depression, or jealousy. You can learn to face new challenges with peace and calm.

"NEURONS THAT FIRE TOGETHER
WIRE TOGETHER"

Saying

It is proven that your brain is moldable and trainable. This fact is a Blessing. You have billions of cells and trillions of neurons (connections) in your brain that communicate with each other. What you think about and what you do will be re-enforced.

When you are concerned with _____, that is what gets caught in the fabric of your brain. Obviously, positive (helpful) thinking or not thinking is a way to "re-wire" your brain.

Your efforts to help this miraculous process will improve your life. You learn to experience a pause, see a lesson, or gain an insight. It's helpful to take things in stride – to go with the flow.

OUR MIND NEEDS TO UNWIND

TRAIN YOUR BRAIN

Just like we know right from wrong, we know (or have been told) if we have an Anger Problem. The good news is that we can rescue ourselves from anger and stress by training our brain, so it would be a good idea to get help from Experts. The Healing Mind was a PBS fundraiser show, while Healing the Angry Brain is a book by Ronald Potter-Efron.

"Doctors see the results of the toxic ways people deal with stress and anxiety: alcohol, smoking, drugs, pills, overeating and overreacting.

Most stress is more a consequence of how we respond to what happens, and we can change the way we respond. We learn to support what helps our body to heal and do more of that.

<u>It is not difficult to develop a Healing Mind with the right instruction, and giving yourself time to experiment and learn. You will have greater health, happiness and well-being. Put a plan into action to see how effective Mind-Body Healing Techniques can be.</u>"

Martin Rossman MD, The Healing Mind

If Our Typical Guy has ruined a potentially good relationship, he knows what to change, and that is to overcome his Anger Problem. If a person can't let go of anger or other negative emotional problems – they are stuck.

TRUST THAT LIFE IS HERE TO SUPPORT YOU WHEN YOU LET GO OF ANGER & RESENTMENT

SUPPRESSION DOESN'T WORK

Anger can be a real problem, and trying to just forget about it is not healthy. However, it is healthy to that know suppression will not work.

We speak of being positive, but that doesn't work if you are angry. If someone or something makes you angry, you are angry. It doesn't work to try to keep it back, or try to block it out of your awareness (suppress) - <u>because it's still there.</u>

It is said that emotions come in like waves. If a person is not able to ride their wave of angry emotion, then more pain is on the way. You can't deny your anger, so what can you do? Well, you can do all kinds of things including the angry response, act out, try to suppress, or runaway, but you can't deny that you are angry. Therefore, you are left with your feelings.

A person with an anger problem could examine the whole relationship to determine if they are justified in being angry. Of course, people can justify anything, especially their own behavior or logic. Ask yourself, "How much of my anger is tied to jealousy?"

WHEN ANGER COMES IN LIKE A WAVE
WE CAN'T DENY ANGRY EMOTIONS
OR TRUST OUR ANGRY THOUGHTS
LEARN TO RIDE THE WAVE OF EMOTION

REALIZE WHAT YOU ARE UP AGAINST

When Our Typical Guy finds himself angry over some incident with his love interest, he is confronting a lot more than his anger.

He might be highly attracted to her, his Big Brain could be troubling him, and he might think about the competition from other men (jealousy). Also, his mind might have expectations or hopes for a future with her. He also has his beliefs, points of view, judgments, grievances, and attachments for her. He makes assumptions about how she should, or should not be. With all these forces in his mind, it is no wonder that anger can light some dynamite. He can create justification for his angry reaction.

"Our angry brain has a way of convincing us that our angry thoughts, feelings, and actions are perfectly normal."
Ronald Potter-Efron, Healing the Angry Brain

When you realize that suppression doesn't work, you learn to not be attached to the outcome, to practice patience, and there are probably things you do not know. Look for peace, conciliation, and stability where you can find it. Learn to lower your compulsion to respond. You can lower anxiety and reactivity so that you don't have angry outbursts.

When uncomfortable things would happen, my Grandfather would tell me, "Be the bigger person." I think this means to not lower ourselves to the other person's level when they are being negative, antagonistic, or disappointing.

We need to see reality instead of our expectations. We know anger pushes people away - it is better to push anger away. Everyone is constantly making choices – choose peace for yourself.

END THE ANGRY OUTBURST

If a person is prone to anger, how can they end the angry response?

In the first place, <u>know that anger leads to bad decisions. Angry outbursts are sure to make matters worse.</u> Learn to not make serious or critical decisions at a time you are angry. These will be the moments you need to get past - you need to get through. Then you can engage in a process that is thoughtful and calming. You don't want to ruin your relationship. You might end it, but you don't want to ruin it with anger.

Rather than getting caught up in anger - take a Time-out. And it is good to talk to other people. But when someone is angry, these things are easier said than done. However, there are enjoyable Healing Exercises you can do that help you to stay calm and to end angry responses. You can come up with a proper response.

HEALING EXERCISES

Any or all of the following exercises can be used to reduce Anger, Anxiety, Jealousy, Worrying, Fear, Constant Thinking, Stress, or to adapt to Modern Living.

SOME PEOPLE RESIST CHANGE
BUT CHANGE CAN BE HEALING
IMAGINE BEING
HEALTHY AND CONTENT

Following are sample techniques summarized for you. Apps provide additional versions. Help is all around, but you might need to keep trying new things until you find ones you enjoy.

- **THE RELAXATION RESPONSE**

It seems that every calming exercise or athletic event requires us to practice deep breathing. These 3 Steps form a Relaxation Response:

1. **Belly breathing: Practice breathing with your diaphragm, not the chest. To locate your diaphragm, it is the triangle running down the inside of your rib cage and across your belly button. Breathe through your nose using your diaphragm. Test your breathing by placing one hand on your belly and one on your chest to feel which one goes out first – use belly breathing to calm your mind.**
2. **Relax your muscles: Keep breathing deep, relaxing, and letting things go while relaxing your body one part at a time.**
3. **Guided Imagery: Use your imagination to relax from your pleasant place. Imagine you are at the pleasant place, and keep relaxing more and more.**

   My pleasant place is Frenchman's Cove in Jamaica, or under my favorite oak trees at home in Oklahoma.

Take time for self-care. You want peace of mind, not just problem solving all the time.

- **LEARN TO OBSERVE YOUR THOUGHTS**

Our Typical Guy has developed a willingness to look at himself as the possible source of any relationship problems. He is learning to observe his mind (it's usually thinking). With self-reflection, he can notice ways to grow in relationships.

"THE MIND IS A WONDERFUL SERVANT
OR A TERRIBLE TASKMASTER"

Saying

At times, we blame the other person when we need to forgive ourselves for the choices (mistakes) we have made. If someone keeps making you angry, do you really want to keep seeing them? We are trying for relationships that are comforting, loving, supportive, and emotionally connected.

- **GET WORRIES OUT OF YOUR HEAD**

You can't solve any problems with worrying.

"Worry turns into a habitual bad habit. Studies have shown that 85% of worries never come true. Learning to <u>worry less</u> is the key to shifting from a Worried Mind to a Healing Mind.

Imagination is the most powerful force in this world except for Nature and the Creation of Life itself. Everything in the world comes from imagination. But if we let our imaginations run wild, it can come up with infinite things to worry about. We want to learn how to use <u>skillful imagination to solve problems</u> rather than create them unnecessarily – that's what the Healing Mind does for us."

Martin Rossman MD, The Healing Mind

Take charge to find solutions for what you can change, and recognize circumstances or people that will not change. It could be time to keep looking.

- **DO THESE THINGS TO IMPROVE YOUR LIFE**

"Look for the good in people.
Be quick to praise and slow to criticize.
Keep problems in perspective.
Take time before saying anything when you are upset.
Practice empathic listening to better understand people.
Give people the benefit of the doubt.

Share your thoughts and feelings.
Wait until you have all the facts before making a decision.
Let Go of grudges and practice Forgiveness.
Talk through your conflicts – Have a perspective of equality.
Face your problems directly."
Ronald Potter-Efron, Healing the Angry Brain

- **ADOPT THE *"CREATIVE PRINCIPLES OF LIFE"***
  "A Change of Attitude Brings a Change of Experience"

1. *"The Power of Gratitude: Being thankful helps you to believe. Life delivers if you believe………. Don't plant weeds in your vegetable garden.*
2. *The Infinite Power is always available and ready. Maintain an attitude of positive faith………..You are dealing with Natural Law.*
3. *Maintain a positive state of mind and move forward steadily.*
4. *Trust Life. Trust the power that brought you here that operates through you."*
Dan Custer, The Miracle of Mind Power

- **NON-RESPONSE**

In combating Anger, we make <u>major</u> improvements when we realize that Non-response is also a Response. When uncertain, take a step back to lower reactivity (not react). Eliminate the Angry Response. We can't control circumstances, but we can control the way we respond.

<u>The irony of not responding is that you are not doing anything</u>! You will be so happy that you didn't say, or do, anything negative. It will be easier to not react the next time, and you will gradually cease reacting as before.

I can testify that even after knowing not to give an angry response, and even after seeing I was always glad when I didn't respond - it can still be difficult to not respond.

By not responding, I could deal with what happened without an angry response and damage to the relationship. There are times we need to move on.

Of course, sometimes you <u>must</u> respond when you have justifiably been wronged (like when anyone would be angry – cheating, lying, stealing, etc). At times, you need to say something when you see how things really are, but you can be firm with nonaggression. Otherwise, non-response might be your best response.

- **DO YOU HAVE LOCK JAW (TEETH CLENCHING)?**

I do not have any Clinical Studies on a correlation between Lock Jaw (teeth clenching) and anger. However, I did have an Anger Problem, and I have to try to not clench my teeth (and jaw). Teeth clenching is related to stress, worry, or thinking. It can ruin your teeth and cause headaches (I have done both).

Thinking and trying to figure things out can create more stress. For peace of mind, live without clenching your teeth. Catch the problem – <u>gently</u> move the jaw side to side several times each day to avoid teeth/jaw clenching. We don't clench our teeth when we are having fun, smiling, or laughing.

THESE HEALING TECHNIQUES WORK!
You can find techniques that work for you. You don't have to live with an Angry Brain. It takes effort, will power, the ability to relax, and patience with yourself and others.

The Healing Exercises help you to live in the present. They are calming, reduce stress, recharge the body, and the brain itself. They all work, so learn the message that each has to offer.

"LET NOT YOUR HEART BE TROUBLED,"
Jesus, John 14:1

MAKE THE CHANGE

I realized no one would change because I got angry with them, or judged them in some way. Maybe a good talk would help, but not in anger.

It was only after many years that I learned to let Anger go. I saw that people are usually not going to change. I could accept them like they are, or move on. I saw my anger was often an assumption of how a relationship <u>should be</u>. Facing reality made me see my need for patience.

The fact an angry person is called a "hot-head" made me see that anger comes from the mind, and that angry thoughts are bad thoughts. I don't need to take things personal.

PATIENCE PREVENTS OVERREACTING
PATIENCE CHANGED MY LIFE

In retrospect, <u>it was what I expected to happen in a relationship which didn't happen that would result in frustration and resentment. I started looking for the cause of my resentment,</u>

rather than getting angry. I could let relationships unfold without trying for a certain outcome (learning detachment).

I ask myself, "Is it really worth it to say what I want to say?" or "Do I want to ruin this relationship?" I found it's a lot better to live life without lighting dynamite. Patience doesn't make me a pansy or a pushover- it keeps me from blowing up relationships.

LET ANGER GO

Stress makes us more impulsive. The Healing Exercises help you to relax and to realize that anger has almost no place in your life. (Anger won't solve any of your problems.) Find healthy ways to let go of stress. Be active, and take charge of your life.

You will never have great relationships, including with yourself, until you calm your nerves and are rid of anger. Take good care of yourself, respect yourself, and respect others. Take care of your brain. Exercise and feed your body healthy food. A simple plan:

Be Thankful
Practice Healing Exercises
Get out there and take on new challenges
Be cheerful and good things will happen

ENJOY YOUR RELATIONSHIPS
OR MOVE ON!

THE GREEN-EYED MONSTER

Chapter 22

Jealousy is the only emotion with its own name: *"O, beware my lord, of Jealousy; It is The Green-Eyed Monster which doth mock the meat it feeds on."*

Lago, Othello, William Shakespeare

Shakespeare called it *"The Green-Eyed Monster"* **knowing a person can act in monstrous ways, and it can eat you alive.**

There is also the expression *"Green with envy."* **I don't know if that was said during Shakespeare's time, but jealousy and envy are closely related frustrations and insecurities that raise the feeling to attack (like a Monster).**

"Jealous: 1. Worried or afraid that someone else is taking the love or attention that one has or wants 2. Unhappy because another has something we would like 3. Inclined to suspicions or fears of rivalry, unfaithfulness, etc 4. Watchful in guarding something 5. Intolerance of unfaithfulness or rivalry 6. Resentful and envious."

Webster's Dictionary

A Jealous Person will act like a fool, ruin their relationships, and/or drive themselves crazy. Jealousy is going down a road of fear, insecurity, and unhappiness. Our Typical Guy is <u>never</u> going to be in a great relationship if he is overly jealous.

Experts say jealousy often comes from a deep-rooted insecurity. Each of us must determine our insecurities by being

aware they exist and how they interfere in our life. Maybe it is a lack of confidence, or an inability to trust. Jealousy can stem from a feeling of ownership, fear of losing someone, or fear of being alone.

We have seen that Attachment leads to jealousy. Alleviate jealousy by not being Too Attached - Too Soon. If you have no attachment - you have no jealousy.

There must be Trust (not jealousy) for a relationship to succeed. Some people have a problem with trust because they trusted someone in the past and felt betrayed. It will take great communications to trust each other.

HOPE

In the real world with a real lover and real feelings, jealousy can be a struggle. Hope for a relationship to be seriously romantic is not an excuse for jealousy. Hope is inspiration to try harder. Control your mind and emotions so you do not do things you regret.

Accept that there is going to be competition for a nice woman, and learn to give her space. Women (and men) hate it when someone is possessive or controlling.

"Life is like a drama. If I understand the plot, there is great happiness".

Brahma Kumaris, Thought For Today

At times, relationships can be improved, or saved, because of what a person <u>doesn't do or doesn't say</u>. Maybe she is very attractive, and you are a man she goes out with that <u>doesn't get jealous or possessive</u>. That trait alone won't win her heart, but it could help. Relationships are a million little

things. Learn how to stay calm, to relax, and enjoy her company. Save yourself from <u>self-torture</u> with a non-jealous mindset.

KNOW THESE THINGS

These are things I have learned about jealousy from my past 22 years in the Single World. Maybe most people struggle at some time with jealousy, and they make a fool of themselves on occasion, but we want to keep it to a minimum.

- Being jealous or possessive will ruin your relationships.
- Unless you are married, you <u>don't know</u> if your current prospective lover friend is truly serious or not. Don't try to force a relationship.
- Jealousy starts with suspicions or being concerned with what they are doing when they are <u>not</u> with you. <u>Concentrate on what you are doing</u>. If they are a Cheater or Liar, they will be exposed over time.
- Unless you are married, you see the attitude "This is the One" could be out of whack or unrealistic. Accept that you might never find The One, but don't worry about it, and don't settle.
- You are going to let them prove They are the One rather than making that assumption. Sometimes it is hard to be patient, but relationship building takes time. Time to learn about the other is a good thing – time can keep you both from making mistakes. Accept that they have to also feel "You are the One."
- Every time you can resist the jealous impulse, you will be so glad. Jealous thinking and jealous acts are easier to resist the next time.
- You can enjoy their company and the relationship if your mind is free from jealousy,

Many people would like to find their Ideal Partner. Mutual chemistry (love and affection) and trust are the issues - not jealousy.

CREEPY IS BAD

"Don't be jealous" is easier said than done when there is a high level of attraction. Be careful to not make assumptions about what they are doing. Assumptions can be self-torture that lead to accusations (tripping). It is much better to go with the flow and keep quiet.

Let's look again at the definition of Jealous: *"3. Inclined to suspicions or fears of rivalry, unfaithfulness, etc 4. Watchful in guarding something 5. Intolerance of unfaithfulness or rivalry 6. Resentful and envious."*

This suspicious, watchful, intolerant, and resentful behavior can result in spying of some sort. People who are jealous are often called "creepy." A Creep is someone who sneaks around to spy on someone for unsavory purposes because of jealousy.

"Creep: a person thought of as annoying or disgusting."
Webster's Dictionary

It is good to stay far away from being creepy. It's not a good idea to be driving by their house, or any other type of spying, including Facebook. Know that spying/creeping will give emotional stress to everyone involved, and the Creep will get caught sooner or later.

When people act out of jealousy, they can do some crazy stuff: make harassing phone calls or texts, spying, stalking, social media pest, damage a car, and/or light a fire on

another's front porch! It is a Bad Idea to be out driving by or sneaking around someone. It is Creepy.

Yes, remember that going by their place because of jealousy is a really Bad Idea. A common story in the news is of a Jealous Person getting killed back at the ex-lovers place.

It can also be risky going back for other reasons, including to get your belongings. It's easy for incidents to Blow Up! That's what happened to a friend.

My friend was a super nice guy who had been living with a woman for a few years, but he had recently moved out. However, he still had his grill at her house. He had told her he was coming to pick it up, but on the morning of his arrival, she would not answer his calls or texts.

When he knocked on her door, no one answered, so he used his key to go in. Upon reaching the bedroom, he discovered her in bed with another man. They were naked and the man had a bag at the end of the bed. My friend thought the bag could have a gun, so he took out his gun. The woman was upset (crocodile tears) and got out of the bed to talk when all of a sudden her new man pushed her into my friend. The two men got into a big fight for the gun.

Thankfully, my friend was able to get the gun, and kick her new lover out into the snow. Being a super nice guy, he threw the man his underwear.

My friend left, but the police came from all around. This type of incident in the "old days" would have been labeled "domestic." I found out the results when I got back home from Colombia. With an unscrupulous District Attorney and ex-DA Judge, the charges were blown up to my friend (with no record) sentenced to 3 years in prison.

My friend did not have a jealousy problem. He was just there to get his stuff. (We know he would like a Do Over - we would all like some Do-Overs in life.)

The woman was obviously trying to make him jealous and trying to get caught. I guess the Moral of the story is:

"When you go – take your stuff" or

"If you get too close to an Old Flame – you could get burned."

ACCUSATIONS

It is not good to make suspicious accusations. The mind can make things up. If someone accuses the other of things they didn't do, the jealous accusation can ruin a relationship. There is no guarantee they will forgive you, so don't risk your relationship.

Accusations are like "shooting yourself in the foot." The other will always say they didn't do it (whatever accused of), and you will appear distrustful and jealous (you are, even if correct).

Yes, it can be difficult to be patient enough to wait out the truth of a relationship, but it is better to let it evolve without making accusations. You can do this by freeing yourself from making assumptions.

It can be difficult to not be jealous when a man dates an attractive woman. It's a challenge, but relationships have a chance to last if jealousy does not interfere. Try for peace of mind without jealousy. After all, you can't know what someone does all the time, and you sure can't control anyone.

Maybe you can talk to a Player friend. Obviously, they have no problem with jealousy. You will need to explain your problem because they don't see jealousy as a problem.

There are times a person can't do anything about them having others, but they still want to see them. Each must answer for themselves. In a non-monogamous Single World, Our Typical Guy will need to let relationships unfold.

Why make a fool out of yourself? You can figure out what is going on in your relationships if you are honest with yourself, communicate, listen, use common sense, and confide in friends. Whoever you are dating will need some space, and so will you.

Realize that jealousy (assumptions or accusations) will get you nowhere. You have to trust to give a relationship a chance, but stay on guard of your heart and health. Don't ignore friends, the Warning Signs, or your intuition.

"<u>We are very good at denying or avoiding the reality that suffering exists. Fear, jealousy, and desire are also forms of suffering</u> that at the very least, disturb our mind and can cause unhappiness as a more subtle form in basic anxiety or dissatisfaction with the imperfect nature of life. Regardless of the happiness we may experience, the reality never lives up to our expectations.

Wisdom is an antidote to ignorance. The path of developing wisdom leads to peace and freedom from both suffering and unhappiness."

Venerable Thubten Lhundrup
Meditation with Buddhist Principles

ENJOY YOUR RELATIONSHIPS
NOT SUFFER FROM YOUR RELATIONSHIPS

JEALOUS OUTBURSTS

There could be times when jealous emotions surface. This jealousy is accompanied by a strong desire to say something accusatory. It's like a person temporarily loses their mind to jealousy and then make calls or sends texts. Try to not do that.

How can you tell when it's happening? When you feel "worked up" or upset over something which includes her/him. Calm down with Healing Exercises when you get that worked up feeling because it is sure to have a bad result.

*"Our angry brain has a way of convincing us that our angry (*jealous*) thoughts, feelings, and actions are perfectly normal."*
                                    Ronald Potter-Efron, Healing the Angry Brain

Give yourself some time to regroup and calm down until the 'worked up' feeling has passed. Know that it could take until the next day or two. You will be glad you kept quiet even if you decide to quit seeing them.

Another clue of going off the tracks is when you feel like you are going to "straighten him/her up" or "recommend" a correction in their behavior. They will probably not like your recommendation, so it would be better to keep quiet. If they are accused of cheating or lying, it will be denied. It can be difficult to know for sure what is going on in another person's life (or mind).

Another clue is if you are upset about something she didn't do that involves your Big Brain. If she was not in the mood for you, or missing in action, it will not do any good to say something about it after the time has passed. Sometimes we wish we could change the way things are, but we can't. Try to be patient with yourself.

GIVE UP JUDGMENT
GIVE UP JEALOUSY

If you don't like their behavior, you can look for someone new, or continue to see them without being jealous. If this sounds harsh, it is probably just reality.

LET GO OF JEALOUSY

We have seen that it is not good to have unrealistic expectations or to make up imaginary suspicions. Learn to relax in your relationship to see where it goes. Dating is a process to get to know someone, and that will take time. Your relationship will reveal itself, which is a reason you don't need to pressure it.

If Our Typical Guy has unresolved issues or doubt, he can work on those without having jealous outbursts. If you find a person untrustworthy, it is up to you to move on. Sometimes we make bad choices. People reveal themselves over time. It might be sad when they are gone, but the sadness (hurt) will be temporary.

Some amount of surrender is required to adjust to life and to be in a relationship. Surrender would mean letting go of trying to control. Surrender could mean giving up on keeping jealousy as an emotion to find a different release, to get some help, or to get a different girlfriend/boyfriend. Behaviors seldom change, and there can be times you need to move on, but you can minimize jealousy. We all need healthy ways to let go of stress – find what works for you.

"Life is a magical experience that continues to unfold. When you have no fear (jealousy)*, you have no resistance... Remind yourself that every problem carries the seeds of opportunity to learn, to love, to grow in awareness, and simply to be happy to be alive."*
Don Miguel Ruiz, The Four Agreements Companion Book

DO THINGS CHEERFULLY AND NATURALLY
WITHOUT WORRY ABOUT THE OUTCOME
YOU MUST DEFEAT *"THE GREEN-EYED MONSTER"*
TO LIVE WITH JOY IN YOUR HEART

LYING

Chapter 23

If you are only out to have a good time, you might not care if someone is lying. But when someone feels they are "in love", it matters if the significant other is lying. We are not discussing little lies, but when the potential partner is not a real partner because they are lying to you.

IS THIS A SPECIAL RELATIONSHIP?

A person might think it is a special relationship, but the Thinker might be the only one serious. If they tell you, "I love you" or "You are my only one", you might want to believe them. Maybe it is true, maybe you had a wonderful night, or maybe they are leading you on.

People reveal things about themselves in dating. It can be easy for the love interest to fill in the blanks in the way you want (desire) to hear. You want to believe them, so they might lie to make you think it's all true, or they simply let you go on believing your projection (hope) for a special love relationship. Time will tell.

"HONESTY MAY BE THE BEST POLICY, BUT DECEPTION AND DISHONESTY ARE PART OF BEING HUMAN."
Yudhijit Bhattacharjee, Why We Lie, National Geographic

DON'T LIE TO YOURSELF

Our Typical Guy will be better off to not learn his lessons by being the victim in his own story.

Of course, we have all lied about things at times, and sometimes it is necessary. Circumstances might dictate a need to lie for the betterment of all, and children can be involved. At times, we lie to be kind. Lies are often harmless, but lying has the potential to turn into heartbreak. However, it would be a good start to not lie to yourself.

HOW COULD YOU LIE TO YOURSELF?

- **You can unconsciously put unwanted sights or thoughts out of your awareness.** *"Love is blind"* and deaf
- **You can suppress the truth within. 'Suppression' is when you try to forget, or to not think about painful unwanted thoughts, or you might <u>pretend</u> a situation is not causing you negative feelings – anger, jealousy, resentment.**
  This can be tricky because you <u>do</u> want to forget jealous or angry thoughts, but there might be a day when you know they were lying about not having others.
- **You tell yourself things about the relationship that are wishful thinking rather than reality. You might believe what you <u>want</u> to be true rather than what you should feel (see) is actually true.**
- **All of us have beliefs about relationships, the opposite sex, and ourselves that are simply not true. To discover your misconceptions, you can take time to recollect your interactions with others, and search your gut feelings for answers.**

"So much happens beneath the surface unconsciously. So how do you spot misperceptions if they happen unconsciously?
You find them is by paying attention and following the signs. Your consciousness will always send you clues that you can follow back to the source. This means that any mental or physical

issue in our external life can be mined for the corresponding issue inside us."

Habib Sadeghi, The Clarity Concept

When feelings come up, they are asking you to address them. You will create a lot of stress within if you lie to yourself.

ONCE YOU KNOW
YOU CANNOT UNKNOW

HOW CAN YOU SPOT A LIE?
NOTE: Men and Women lie equally, so anything said about women lying is also true for men. "<u>Liars and Manipulators are out there</u>" is a warning to the unwary.

Research says it is impossible to have a reliable method for telling when someone is lying. Evaluations of Lie Detector Machines show they have 90% - 51% accuracy depending on the skill of the Examiner, and if the subject is a skillful or habitual liar. And you can't give your romantic interest a Lie Detector Test even if you wanted to. That leaves you with gut feelings, friends, the totality of the circumstances, being honest with yourself, listening, and paying attention to what is said and done.

TV shows and books about lying were helpful. A good point was the *"tell"* from the game of poker where some people will do a particular body gesture when lying. In theory, you could spot the "tell" and spot a lie. The problem is that different people have totally different tells to go with their lie. They might touch or toss their hair, or do anything. It could be any body gesture, so the gestures are as unique as the people.

Poker books gave the most tips, but none say of a way to tell for sure when someone is lying. Body language and facial expressions are a clue, but that is difficult to rely on, especially if they are a Good Liar (and when you want to believe them).

You would need real proof, know their "tell", or have proper insight. It is difficult to know when emotions are involved. Also, we know that no one is totally truthful all the time, and it is OK for someone to not say everything they know every time.

Our Typical Guy is back to gut feelings, talking to friends, common sense, paying attention, and facing reality.

TRUE OR NOT?

Some people are excellent Liars as they work around emotions and the truth. Statements could be placed into categories showing a fundamental problem of Truth. It could be:

True
Mostly True
Half Truth
Mostly False
False
Pants on Fire

Yes, Pants on Fire as some are shameless Liars. It is their way of moving through life, and some are skillful. They will even lie when the truth would do just as good.

Obviously, Mostly True is not true.

With a Half Truth, the missing part covers the lie. It is "Lying by Omission." We make the mistake of filling in the blank with what we want to believe. If confronted, they might say, "I didn't lie. I just didn't tell you" or "You didn't ask about that." You are lead in the direction of believing the Half Truth is the Truth.

I had a woman tell me she hated Liars, but she was a Liar. I feel the least reliable fact is, "They looked me straight in the eye." A Liar probably knows they <u>need</u> to look us in the eye for us to believe their story. That factor will not be a clue.

"Trust your gut feeling" can be difficult if you are highly attracted and want to believe what they are telling you. Pay attention. You can observe reality if you have the courage to face the totality of the circumstances.

To what extent is money involved? If it's about money, a Liar will keep lying until Our Typical Guy's money is gone. He might miss them for awhile, but there are honest people in the world.

We need understanding to distinguish between the true and the false.

"Understanding: 1. the ability to think, learn, judge, etc; intelligence 2. having sympathy and good judgment 3.the fact of knowing what is meant."

Webster's Dictionary

WHAT'S OUR TYPICAL GUY TO DO?

<u>**It is better to look for the Warning Signs than trying to determine if someone is lying.**</u> **Remember that lying is an intentional act. The lie is told to fool or trick you. You do not want to be fooled or tricked. It can be difficult to know when dating in a busy, fast-paced world.**

Our Typical Guy is trying to live by the *Law of Detachment* **when not accusing his love interest of lying. He could let his relationships unfold naturally. Relationships are not a game.**

It's not a good attitude to look at people as a Liar, so hope it is true without being naive. Rather than being suspicious, Our Typical Guy could use Objective Thinking based on facts, instead of Subjective Thinking based on feelings, emotions, or illusion.

Why would they lie? There could be many reasons, but with lying they know your situation and might want to see what you have to give.

LOOKING FOR LOVE
CAN RESULT IN BELIEVING LIES

THE WAYS PEOPLE LIE

A Liar often uses one or more of *"The 4 D's"* when confronted: "DIVERT, DEFLECT, DECEIVE, and/or DENY." A "Good Liar" will use all 4 D's at various times. Lying becomes natural to them. Men and women can do the same things.

1. DIVERTS – Diverts by changing the topic (and in a hurry). If you are on to something, they will quickly change the conversation or do something distracting - initiating intimacy, have a headache, crying (crocodile tears) etc.

2. DEFLECTS – You ask something and they lie, but the story has plausibility.

"Plausible: seemingly true, acceptable, honest, etc, but thought of with some doubt or disbelief."
Webster's Dictionary

If you were honest with yourself, you probably wouldn't believe it. But when they explain the situation, there is a possibility it is true.

I have found from experience that Our Typical Guy should know he cannot find out more "truth" by continuing to quiz a woman, so don't even try. She will feel like she is being interrogated, and he won't get more information. It's not a Good Vibe in the relationship to continually quiz someone after they have given their answer. A person can believe it or not.

Our Typical Guy better be listening close and trust his feelings if doubt or disbelief. If you have doubt, it is probably for good reason. However, make sure it is not jealousy that you feel. Trust your intuition to feel the difference. (If you still don't know - be patient.)

Deflection can be to for them to blame someone or something else. Deflection can also be, "I don't know what you are talking about", or there is always an excuse. Liars are Masters of Excuses. They come up with excuses so fast that it sounds true.

3. **DECEIVES – A deceiver smoothly makes things <u>sound possible</u> about the relationship – <u>things that don't and won't happen</u>! They might tell you they love you and give sex, but it could be a lie about the love (and love has varying degrees). They let you believe the relationship is serious when they are not. The Deceiver might accuse you of something they are doing. For example, when they are cheating, they might accuse you of cheating by questioning you. With this tactic, it appears they are not cheating by making the first suspicion or accusation.**

Some people even deceive <u>themselves</u> by rationalizing there is more than the reality of the relationship.

"Rationalization: excuses, or the deceptive thinking that arises out of feelings not based on truth or understanding."
                                                                Roy Masters

I wish I had listened to friends. I had a married co-worker tell me about the woman I was dating, "She is not your friend, but I am." It was the Truth, but I kept seeing the one I was dating before finally admitting she was a Liar.

A Deceiver is <u>not</u> your friend. A Deceiver lies and denies when they have others. They have a Hidden Agenda. When your money is gone, they are gone. You were the only one serious.

PEOPLE CAN RATIONALIZE ANYTHING
BE A GREAT LISTENER

4. **DENIAL – A Liar can simply deny whatever it is. For some, lying is their** *"modus operandi"* **(way of operating) so it is seamless.**

A Liar denies with a straight face. Our Typical Guy might be young and naïve, but now he is aware that "Liars are out there." They can even rise to prominent positions in society, including District Attorney or President.

This could be THE LIAR'S CREED: ADMIT NOTHING – DENY EVERYTHING – MAKE COUNTER ACCUSATIONS – HAVE EXCUSES READY.

THE DILEMMA

Love or Imagined Love, makes a person vulnerable to lies. When discovered, a Liar will most likely do one of these things:

Reaction #1: Laugh It Off, change the subject, or the 4 D's
Reaction #2: Say, "I didn't want to hurt you" or "I didn't want to upset you" (If admitting it, which is unlikely)
Reaction #3: Say, "It is my business" or "It is none of your business"
Reaction #4: Not say anything. They don't want to talk about it

They can have one of these reactions, or walk away because:
- They know there is nothing you can do about it, but to leave. (To go ahead and leave would be a good idea.)
- They want you to overlook it as not serious that they have other boyfriends/girlfriends. (However, they might continue to deny they have other relationships even after you know.) You can hang around, that's up to you, but don't think it will ever be a serious relationship.
- They think you should have known, and/or accuse you of doing the same things. ("This is how it works nowadays.")
- People can do what they want. (You were not right for each other as long as lying is involved.)
- They are having sex with someone else, so sex is no problem for them.
- They are not hurt or heartbroken; they have been having fun. You are the only one hurt.

LYING IN THE MODERN WORLD

Lying has taken on more meanings with social media, fake news, dating apps, and new terms like Trump advisor Kelleyanne Conway's *"Alternative Facts."*

If Our Typical Guy finds a woman attractive, she has the advantage of being an exciting lie, and an Exciting Liar makes it more convincing. When she is exciting, he is more likely to believe it. An advertisement can give an exciting lie: "If you get this car - you get this woman."

Anyone can be deceived by a great Liar, but sometimes we have wishful thinking. The truth will eventually come out, but it is best to figure out the real situation as soon as possible.

Is the saying true? *"A leopard never changes his/her spots."* Some people will change their habits, but most will probably not. In other words, a person who gets around by telling lies will keep lying. <u>A Liar will continue to lie so don't lie to yourself.</u> However, if it is not about cheating or deceit, it could be best to overlook small lies and let the matter go. (We all lie about something sometimes. It's human nature.)

> *"There is no innocent explanation."*
> Bernie Madoff, Ponzi Scheme Fraudster

Maybe Our Typical Guy should be having a good time and not be concerned about finding his Ideal Woman. However, he has asked for help to find one.

LOOKING FOR LOVE

<u>The Bullsheet</u> can only tell Our Typical Guy to be strong, and be aware: Habitual Liars exist! They are often the

same person as a Manipulator. It is better to learn about Liars from this chapter than from an Imagined Ideal Partner. That can be a painful process.

A lot of people get fooled. <u>If you should fall for a Liar, the relationship will fall through so don't bother to send texts, calls, etc telling them how hurt or heartbroken you are.</u> Yes, it is going to hurt if you believed a Liar when you thought it was a monogamous loving relationship, and then find out otherwise.

You are on your own to figure out if someone is trustworthy. You can possibly avoid a Liar by following your intuition, by being a great listener, and not believing all you hear. See if you enjoy each other's company for extended times. See if they always want something and then are quickly gone. Some people don't want to know how deep the truth goes, but you can use your reasoning abilities and sensible thinking to properly evaluate the relationship.

Many men tend to go with Big Brain thinking while forgetting reason, common sense, or values. What are your values? What are the values of the person you are dating?

KNOWING EACH OTHER'S VALUES
MIGHT BE THE MOST IMPORTANT PART
OF KNOWING SOMEONE
OF TRUSTING SOMEONE

Be honest with others, and be honest with yourself. When you discover a Liar, it might be time to keep looking.

"REMOVE FAR FROM ME VANITY AND LIES"
Proverbs 30:8

IT'S OVER

Chapter 24

"It's never too late to become who you want to be. I hope you have a life that you're proud of, and if you find that you're not, I hope you have the strength to start over."
F. Scott Fitzgerald

Some lessons in life people must learn for themselves. That is when they will move on and not before. Even when a person realizes a relationship is over, the end tends to drag out.

If you know it's over - the sooner you act - the better. You might have come close, but it didn't work out.

THE BREAK-UP

Unless a person is hit by an unsuspected dump, there is a withering of hope and seeing reality before the break-up. Maybe it was a lack of sincerity or kindness, maybe the chemistry wasn't there, or you were not on the same wavelength. A breakdown in communications is often the problem, and it does take time to get to know someone.

Near the time of the break-up, a person arrives at the realization that there is a lack of shared interests, chemistry, and respect. There has grown to be more pain (disharmony) than pleasure in the relationship, and this assumes both are still trying. (If one is not trying, a break-up is certain.)

No one wants to feel like they give and give while the other party is not there or not giving back. A person can keep giving for only so long until they get to a breaking point. Relationships can take only take so much stress. Even then, there is the saying, *"Breaking up is hard to do."* **The amount of respect you have for yourself will determine how you evolve or grow out of the situation.**

UNDERSTAND YOUR OWN ACTIONS AND BEHAVIORS TO NAVIGATE YOUR WAY THROUGH RELATIONSHIPS DEVELOP INTROSPECTION
"THE LOOKS-WITHIN PLACE"

THE END

If you see these signs, you might want to break up and make it final:

- **Your intuition tells you they are the Wrong Person. It is certainly better to stay single than to be with the Wrong Person, even if there is sex (a Comfort Zone).**
- **If you have known them to lie on important matters, a break-up seems only a matter of time. In reality, was the lie about an important matter? Everyone lies some. Relationships can be tricky, so "How important is the matter?"**
- **Couples need shared activities and interests. Find out from the start if interests are shared. These are the things you do together to build a bond.**
- **If you cannot work as a team with money, the relationship will end - sooner or later.**
- **You don't laugh together anymore.**
- **If you know the romantic part is over, a break-up would be good for both. It's Romance and Affection that make relationships work.**

When it's over, the important thing for Our Typical Guy is he cared, he was honest, he did his best, and he learned something.

**AT THE TIME OF THE BREAK-UP
YOU MIGHT NOT FEEL IMPROVEMENT IS COMING
BUT YOU WILL COME OUT STRONGER
YOU WILL DO BETTER NEXT TIME**

A HIDDEN AGENDA

I learned this lesson from my English friends in the horse insurance business:

**SOME PEOPLE HAVE
A HIDDEN AGENDA**

A Hidden Agenda can be hard to detect, but it could be a possibility. A Hidden Agenda will damage/destroy a relationship.

How do you tell? What do they do? For example, they tell you something will happen <u>with you</u>, but it never happens. They are planning and doing something else. They might want to see what you have to give. You need awareness and to be discerning.

*"Discerning:1. having good judgment or understanding 2. To see or make out clearly; recognize / Are you able to **discern** right from wrong?"*

THE BREAK-UP WITH MY IMAGINED IDEAL WOMAN

I have learned the hard way (experience) from several women over the past 22 years. Single World relationships often don't last long, and it is difficult to find an Ideal Partner. I didn't feel like I met my Ideal Woman until the last one. However, there is finally that moment when you admit the relationship is over. (Most of us probably know way before we admit it.)

One day, I had to admit that who I thought was my Ideal Woman was an Imagined Ideal Woman. If we do not think properly, if we get Too Attached – Too Soon, or if we do not pay attention to Warning Signs, then miscalculations will turn to pain. In retrospect, the things I believed sound laughable. Don't let this be you.

You can move in a new direction with lessons learned, and surround yourself with good friends.

BE GLAD YOU FOUND OUT
BEFORE IT WENT ANY FURTHER
WAKE UP TO WHAT YOU HAVE WITHOUT THEM

At least I am free from delusion, and she is not on my mind. "Get Over It" might sound harsh at first, but it is a Good Idea. There will be break-ups, so don't let a relationship break you. You will find someone better for you. Life goes on.

LESSONS LEARNED - SIGNS IGNORED

I complained to my Scout friend that I was played. She pointed out things I ignored, and said I went along when the signs were there, so I could not complain about being played. A person can take advantage of us as long as we let them.

IMAGINED LOVE
MAKES ALLOWANCES FOR EXCUSES
BREAK-UP WHEN YOU KNOW IT'S OVER

"When people show you who they are – believe them the first time."

Maya Angelo

Break up, stay calm, take the hurt, and have confidence in yourself. Examine your mistakes.

**YOU HAVE TO LEARN AND CHANGE
OR YOU WILL KEEP GETTING
THE SAME RESULTS**

There is plenty to work on until you meet someone new. Gain perspective on the best ways to stay involved and move forward.

"Most of us feel like race horses champing at the bit, hoping for someone to open the gate and let us run. But the only person who can free us is ourselves.

We have moments when we see the total beauty of another person, and we feel that they can see the beauty in us. The world sees the special relationship as the only valid context for such an experience. That is our primary neurosis, our most painful delusion. We keep looking to the body for love, but it is not there. We embark upon an endless search for what we cannot find-- one person that holds the key to Heaven, but Heaven is within us...... It is joy to which we are entitled. No one is saying it's easy; but it's our goal."

Marianne Williamson, A Return To Love

THERE WILL BE TIME TO HEAL
IT TAKES EFFORT AND ENERGY
TO GET STRONGER

Breaking up also involves forgiveness which is a conscious decision to live peacefully without bitterness. When we are free from anxiety and judgment, we are at peace.

Yes, there needs to be forgiveness after a break-up, but it is not good to use "forgiveness" to go back to a relationship that was **not** previously a great relationship. Over the years, I have seen a lot of people go back to a relationship that suffered a break-up. These people try to make it work, but it rarely does.

Besides being a witness, I have done it myself. The relationship might be better for a little while, but the same underlying problems come up again.

However, a few move-back-in relationships do succeed, but there would need to be maximum forgiveness with major changes in attitude by both (and probably better sex).

In the end, you will see the break-up was for your good so that you can look for someone with mutual chemistry, trust, friendship, and love.

RESILIENCE
Hardships strengthen us, but the concept is easier to accept after the hard times are over. Adversity is anything that sets us back, but resilience allows us to build strength.

"Resilience is the strength and speed of our response to adversity – and we can build it. Tragedy does not have to be pervasive, or permanent, but resilience can be. We can all find strength within ourselves and build strength together. We can build

resilience and carry it with us throughout our lives. There is a light within each of us that will not be extinguished."
                     Sheryl Sandberg and Adam Grant, *Option B*

RESILIENCE IS ABOUT
ENABLING NEW OPTIONS FOR YOURSELF
SELF-RELIANCE IS HAVING RESILIENCE

Resilience is a necessary skill you might not have considered, yet it is a key to happiness/contentment. You can tell yourself, "No one is going to have power over my life."
Learn to love and laugh again through friendships and self-confidence. Be resilient and live guilt free. We all make mistakes and get rebuffed.
IT IS NEVER TOO LATE
TO LEARN
OR TO CHANGE

THE BITTER AND THE SWEET

When we are disappointed, or life does not turn out as we thought, we can remember the words of my Great-Aunt Nellie:
"YOU HAVE TO TAKE THE BITTER
   WITH THE SWEET"
With Male Selective Hearing, I would ignore this saying as I did not like the bitter part. However, sayings get to be sayings for good reason, and we will get some bitter along the way. Our setbacks are only temporary if we can recover to make good decisions. The spirit will present you with more opportunities, and someone else will be better suited for you than the one before. That has happened to me every time. I try to remember the good times, and to always learn something.

Break-ups can be painful. I want to live in a Good Place, so I typed a page for Refrigerator Art:

HOW TO BE IN A GOOD PLACE
FEEL JOY & LOVE **IN MY HEART**-------**NO MATTER WHAT**
BE POSITIVE------------------*EMPTY OUT ALL THE NEGATIVE*
FAITH ---- *NOT DOUBT*--------------------**LIVE IN THE PRESENT**
FORGIVENESS----*OTHERS AND MYSELF*---**FOR ALL SAKE**
BE A FRIEND
NO SELF-PITY ------------------ *BE STRONG !!!*------**NO ANGER**
LEARN TO BE A GREAT LISTENER
SLOW DOWN -----*BE POLITE*-------*BE CALM*-------*LOVE LIFE*
ENJOY LIFE--*LIFE IS SHORT*
BE CHEERFUL .... *NOT ATTACHED TO OUTCOME*
DON'T THINK TOO MUCH -------------------- *INNER SILENCE*
SMILE !!!....................... **BE PATIENT** ....**& AWARE**
BE THANKFUL ----------*BE INDEPENDENT WITH RESPECT*
WATCH MY *TONE OF VOICE*
NO CURSING Low Class &Children Around
SEX ???????????   don't know, maybe Real Love someday
GET UP !!! *WE ALL FALL SOMETIME* ....Do Yoga & Exercise
MOVE FORWARD.......*MENTAL & OVERALL TOUGHNESS*
BE HAPPY WITH LIFE *NOT LOOKING IN REAR VIEW MIRROR*
BE A WARRIOR --------*NOT A WORRIER*-----and keep working
THE POWER OF LOVE------------- **WILL WIN MY BATTLES**
LET MY LIGHT SHINE ^^^^^^^^^^^^^^^^^^^^^^^^^^^^^^^

LETTING GO

Chapter 25

Letting Go can be difficult. You cared about someone, and thought it was a special romantic relationship. You probably still care to some degree, but now you might have hurt feelings and negative emotions.

Many people give up on having a relationship because of prior disappointments. Above all, don't give up.

After the break-up there could be hard times, but there is relief in not spending more emotion, time, and money going down a Dead End Road. You might have fallen for them, but it wasn't to be.

Letting go is an empowering moment. You learn to leave behind people or things that are not good for you. You have the courage to let go of what you cannot change. The pressure you felt is lifted.

MAKE A FRESH START
LET GO OF THE PAST
DON'T WORRY ABOUT WHERE YOU ARE GOING
GOOD THINGS WILL HAPPEN

LET GO OF TRYING TO CONTROL

Relationships can only take so much stress, and the end can be similar to a death. But rather than dead, they are still alive on the other side of town - and often with someone else! You have to let go, or you can drive yourself crazy with angry or jealous thinking.

Why do we stay in bad relationships, or relationships based on sex? We are weak. Maybe we were in a Comfort Zone, maybe a fear of loss, or fear of being alone. Maybe they were an Imagined Ideal Partner.

Letting go can be a challenge, but if we accept relationships will end, we see letting go is for our benefit. Master this skill knowing that freedom, peace of mind, and the opportunity to meet someone new is coming your way.

NO MATTER WHAT THE SITUATION
YOU WILL ALWAYS GET THROUGH IT
IT HAPPENED AND <u>IT'S DONE</u>
IT'S ALL BEHIND YOU NOW

You should want to be strong enough to see the truth of your relationship more than wanting to see a particular outcome. Let go in a healthy way to build new relationships. You can find someone new that will be better for you.

"I BELIEVE THAT EVERYTHING HAPPENS FOR A REASON.
PEOPLE CHANGE SO THAT YOU CAN LEARN TO <u>LET GO</u>.
THINGS GO WRONG SO THAT
YOU CAN APPRECIATE THEM WHEN THEY'RE RIGHT.
YOU BELIEVE LESS SO YOU EVENTUALLY LEARN TO TRUST NO ONE BUT YOURSELF,
AND SOMETIMES GOOD THINGS FALL APART
SO BETTER THINGS CAN FALL TOGETHER."

Marilyn Monroe

"HOW-TO" LET GO

Of course, it can be a disappointing time after the break-up. But we all go through disappointments and break-ups. Pick yourself up, dust yourself off, and start over again with little hesitation. Don't sit in a room and sulk about it. Don't have self-talk that is misinformation, blaming, or mind-shaming (what's wrong with me/guilt). In the end, you might be surprised your relationship lasted as long as it did rather than that it came to an end.

You can start letting go by practicing not thinking about them. <u>Believe</u> everything is going to work out better for you, even if it's hard to see at the moment. Otherwise, if you think of them – Stop! Let go to release needless mental chatter.

You know in life that letting go will be required of you because death is involved (our pets, families, and life teaches us that). There is a natural time (a few days) for mourning a romantic relationship because trying to hold onto the past will rob your energy.

A person does not want to be bitter about what might appear to be a defeat (the relationship was probably just a mistake or a mismatch). And letting go of the relationship is better than blaming them. Either way, admit it is over. You can still be friends, but realize this is rare in real life. It is probably better to block their number, delete social media viewing, cut the strings, and say to yourself, "This is over. I'm moving on."

YOU CAN USE YOUR HEALING EXERCISES TO HELP WITH LETTING GO

At first, it would probably be a good idea to reflect on analyzing the type of relationship you had (you don't want to keep making the same mistakes). You might discover some faults or weaknesses that you can correct. Whatever it was, it

didn't work out, and it came to an end. Move on for personal growth, right thinking, or not thinking. Examine your feelings and have creative ideas and projects for yourself.

LIFE GOES ON
BE MENTALLY STRONG
CONCENTRATE ON WHAT <u>YOU</u> ARE DOING

CONCENTRATION

I took a break from working on this chapter to rototill the garden. I had to get gas from the shed, but there was a little limb hanging in the way. Right before I snapped the limb, I was thinking about the things written above and thought, "I am really on to something with this 'concentrate on what you are doing'."

That thought made me remember, "I need to work on my posture", so I stood up straight to snap the limb. Just then, the little limb was part of a giant limb that broke off and fell from 12 feet in the air barely grazing my head. It was so close it made a big gash on my hand!!! CONCENTRATE ON WHAT <u>YOU</u> ARE DOING saved my life that day. It felt like a bullet whizzed right in front of my head when that limb flashed by.

Concentration, forgiveness, and humility can propel us to the next level, but we have to let go of the past. Anyway, we can't change the past even if we wanted to. Forget about what others are doing. You are responsible for your happiness, so concentrate on what <u>you</u> are doing.

Letting go might be difficult, but if it didn't work out with one, there will be more. Sometimes we need a break to learn the lessons from the last relationship so we can improve our inner direction. We must let go of the Wrong One to find the Right One.

We will let go of everything when our life is over. Appreciate what you have - not just things, but relationships, family, health, and everything for which to be Thankful.

HANKERING AND LAMENTING

The Vedic texts tell us to **not** go through life *"hankering and lamenting."* All of us do it some, but don't live your life that way.

"Hanker: to have a strong wish or longing; crave."
Webster's Dictionary
"Lament: to feel sorrow over something; mourn."
Webster's Dictionary

"People desire things and want to possess them. We desire that which we do not have, and we lament for that which we have lost."
Srila Prabhupada, The Path of Perfection

We all want something, but we will never enjoy our life *"hankering and lamenting."* If you learned something, your next relationship will be better than your last.

A TEST OF RESILIENCE

Resilience is our ability to bounce back from disappointments. We don't know what will happen, but something discouraging is sure to happen at some time. Stress is sure to come your way. Resilience is required to not be stuck in the past, resentful, or depressed.

Knowing that we will be forced to let go of relationships makes us choose to have a life of liberation and power. To be resilient, we are forced to expel negativity (hard feelings). Let go without dwelling on them, and without getting discouraged about relationships in general.

To have respect for yourself and to understand your self-worth, you need self-love. You still have time for great relationships, so take care of yourself.

DON'T LET ANYONE TAKE YOUR POWER
JUST KEEP GOING

"When there is faith and victory in the mind, success can be gained. If thoughts are weak, there is defeat."

"To taste the sweetness of life, you must have the power to forget the past."
Brahma Kumanis, Thought For Today

REDEMPTION

Letting go is difficult, but know you will <u>always</u> get a chance at redemption, even if it might take awhile. Redemption means that you will regain your focus and find a better life. You will be saved from an error. Life can provide you with opportunity at any moment, and often when you least expect it.

This story is not about lovers or relationships, but it shows redemption is certain. The redemption that applies my story to you is that a new lover, and/or a new way of loving will be in your future when you let go. The spirit works in life to deliver redemption.

I was working in the starting gate at the racetrack. It was a long time ago at La Mesa Park in Raton, New Mexico. As Assistant Starter, I would load and handle horses in the gate for the races.

The 1st day on the job I was told, "George, these horses have more muscles in their neck than you have in your whole body." I couldn't say anything because it was true. It was a dangerous job, but I loved it. Nowadays, the Gate Crew wears helmets and protective jackets, but we had only baseball caps.

In the starting gate, the horses are inside an enclosure from which it looks impossible to escape, but horses can be amazing athletes. The older guys told me a horse can flip backwards out of the gate. I was new (green), so I had to believe what looked impossible.

The 1st day of racing, I had a nervous filly flip before the start of a race. She started shaking then reared so high and fast that she landed on her back, and flipped over backwards. It was embarrassing to see my horse run off down the track; wait while horses were unloaded; and then reloaded with my horse being "scratched."

My co-workers had their fun, so after the flip they told me "How-to" keep a horse from flipping. They showed how to pull their head close to my body, and squeeze their ear if need be depending on how much they acted up (if you control the head, you control the rest of the horse). I didn't lose another horse for a long time.

A few months later, instead of flipping - my horse reared up and slid his back against the pad on the back of his starting gate stall while he was pawing forward with his hooves. I had lost my grip, and was in front of him with nowhere to go. I thought I could get pawed and possibly killed, so I climbed out the front of the gate. This must have looked comical to the fans in the stands as I was later informed they were laughing. I received a total ribbing from my co-workers.

There wasn't much I could do, but I wanted redemption. I wanted a horse to act up so I could prove myself. I couldn't see how that would happen for a long time, but the spirit can come through for us quicker than we think.

It was only 5 days later that it was Futurity Day. These are the days when 2-year-old Quarter Horses race for the big money. On Futurity Days, the Boss would remind us out of the side of his mouth while chewing tobacco, "They (trainers) will be trying today boys." "Trying" meant the horses were hopped up and ready to go. This was in 1975, so the Test Barn did not have sophisticated labs. I hated Futurity Days, but I wanted redemption for climbing out the front of the starting gate.

It was over 45 years ago, but I will never forget looking at the program and seeing the horse assigned to me for the next race. It was in the name, and I could feel he was the one I was looking for. His name was Phantom Streak. When he came within sight, I saw all the blood vessels in his neck were super bulging out, his nostrils were flared wide open, and he was prancing like he was fired up (hopped), and ready to go. I knew he was the one. When I got him in the gate, everything was OK, but then some of the other horses started to act up and make the whole starting gate rock. Instead of pulling his head up next to me like I had learned to do, I let Phantom Streak just stand there. He got nervous, and then he exploded!!!! He reared straight up and starting pawing the air over and over. I planted my right ear into his shoulder and held on to the rein close to his head. I said to myself, "I am not going to let go. He will have to kill me to make me let go." With my ear planted in his shoulder, I could feel his muscles powering and rolling over and over with constant pawing high in the air. Finally, he came down, the gate opened, he ran off and all the gate hands let out a giant cheer. That was Redemption!

This story of Redemption is also an example of the Spiritual World that overlaps the Material World. The Spiritual World operates by different laws that are imperceptible to us.

When you let go, you will get new opportunities. You will also get redemption, and find one better for you than the one before.

**LET GO
TO GROW**

"When one door of happiness closes, another opens; but often we look so long at the closed door that we do not see the one which has been opened for us."

Helen Keller

THE HOUSE PARTY

Chapter 26

Most grown-up people would like to have an enjoyable time that includes wonderful sex. Our Typical Guy is in this group.

**OPPORTUNITY CAN ARISE
AT A GOOD HOUSE PARTY**

Even if you have been married awhile, the House Party is a special time to keep romance alive.

Our Typical Guy has made arrangements, and she is coming over. It's time for a House Party For 2!! (It could be a Car Party, but a House Party has more options.) The work is done, and it's time to have fun. Relax to have a good time.

If Our Typical Guy is inexperienced, he might think the House Party is the difficult part. But if he doesn't talk too much, and he goes with the flow, both should have a good time. Don't have sky high expectations because that could leave you frustrated. Make plans that will bring you closer together no matter what happens. Set the mood, imagine how the evening will go, and light up the party with a happy tone - keep it going.

**BUILDING THE FIRE TAKES TWO
SETTING THE MOOD IS UP TO YOU**

START THE PARTY
It is not luck that she is showing up.

"Success is not luck – I don't believe in pure luck. You have to create your own luck. You have to be aware of the opportunities around you and take advantage of them."

Bruce Lee, Striking Thoughts

A lot of work goes into a good House Party, but it can be worth it. It's about having a good Vibe, interesting conversation, and making a connection.

It's finally time!!! Have your place super clean and a nice candle burning. Play good music. (Remember that liking the same type of music is important for a great relationship. Don't ask "Why?" It just is.) The music is a little faster at the start to get the party moving, but be able to slow it down when the Vibe is right. Be sure to ask ahead what she likes to drink, or whatever, and have it for her. Create a great atmosphere.

**GET HER TO RELAX, TO TALK, TO DRINK, TO DANCE
SHE IS AT THE HOUSE FOR A PARTY
THERE IS NO PRESSURE
LET IT HAPPEN!!!**

Our Typical Guy is not acting (showing some emotion that does not really exist), but he is immersing himself (deeply absorbed or getting into) the party. He is having a good time!

These are some suggested mindsets for Our Typical Guy, or you:

From my horse insurance sales experience, I go with what Sales books call "assumed acceptance." Whether it's true or not, at least it is positive and hopeful. I tell myself, "She wants to have fun too."

Remember to not goof it up with too much talking. There is time at the start for her to relax, so don't bring up needless conversation. Look at her face to see if she is interested. Don't ramble on about something when you should be engaging her in conversation, dancing, or doing what she wants to do. However, she is probably not going to come over and start out with dancing.

Maybe you already took her to dinner, or did an activity together. The conversation could be light-hearted, including flirting or compliments. Flirting is for fun, and compliments are to show appreciation. (If her being there does not have you complimenting her, she is not your type.) See what she brings up to discuss or to do. You might watch a movie, or whatever she wants. The candle helps set the mood along with good music. Let them work for you.

Visualize ahead how the party will unfold, and see if you can make it happen. Make up a story in your mind about how the party will ideally happen. See if the party can be like a play you both act out. The visualization might help you relax, and make your parties more fun. You certainly have a role to play. Think ahead what you will talk about so you don't raise issues, and that will help you remember to keep quiet. Think up some exciting fun so you both have a great time.

It's amazing how the visualization technique actually works. For example, you can imagine the entire party with every line for each to say, and see how close your party goes to the script. It will surprise you!

Concentrate on the sensations happening. Not so fast - slow the pace to make it last. Relax and enjoy. Maybe pretend you are in charge, and see if she will go along. She might enjoy a massage. Use your imagination, but be spontaneous.

SHE IS WITH YOU
THERE ARE NO LISTS OF WHAT TO DO
THE ACTION IS TOO FAST FOR A LIST
REACTIONS CAN BE SPONTANEOUS LOVE

Some women like to smoke at the House Party. A poem from Ardmore might have made my romantic life more enjoyable if I had remembered it earlier. It was much later that I realized the importance of poetry in romance.

"She smokes, She fucks."

Unknown

Maybe she doesn't smoke, but let her unwind. Make the party fun to her. It's about her getting in the mood.

If the party is winding down and you can't think of anything else to say, then say what one told me, "LET'S DO SOMETHING!!!" She is the one actually in control, so she will do what she wants.

"Life is like a movie – write your own ending. Keep believing and keep pretending."

Jim Henson, Muppets creator

THE BIG BRAIN
To meet her and get her to your house has <u>not</u> been effortless. You had fortitude and discipline (personal growth) to make it happen. Now is the time for the Little Brain to carry

out your visualization. However, the Big Brain could finally get a chance to take over, but it is very important that the Big Brain does not talk or appear too soon.

Some people don't think the Big Brain can talk, but I can testify that it can. If you are at the House Party and you blurt out something rude, crude or presumptuous - that is the Big Brain talking!

After saying it, Our Typical Guy might feel like, "Why did I say that?" Then he realizes his Big Brain took over, and IT was talking.

Examples are difficult because it just happens, maybe "Could you go ahead and take off some of those clothes?" IT can blurt out rude stuff like, "I would love to see you naked!" or "I really do want to fuck you" or anything that makes her feel rushed or pressured. Don't let the Big Brain talk!

PARTY ON!!!

There was a show where two young women were talking, and one was planning to "do it" with her boyfriend that night. It was her 1st time, and she was asking her experienced girlfriend about her anxiety. Her friend said, "Don't worry. He will know what to do. You won't have to do anything." This is also how a man needs to be. You will know what to do. It's natural, so let nature work. She will help if there is to be success.

"Success – means doing something sincerely and whole heartedly. And you usually have to have the help of other people to achieve it."

Bruce Lee, Striking Thoughts

Let the music, candle, refreshments carry the party. The keep your mouth shut strategy has been proven mathematically:

"IF (A = SUCCESS), THEN THE FORMULA IS:
A = X + Y + Z
X BEING WORK
Y BEING PLAY
Z BEING KEEPING YOUR MOUTH SHUT"

Albert Einstein

Everyone wants to enjoy life and to be happy/content. Our Typical Guy realizes happiness comes from within, but being in a relationship with a nice woman can be wonderful and healing.

LIVE, LAUGH, LOVE
IS ALL YOU NEED TO KNOW
ENJOY WHAT IS COMFORTABLE FOR BOTH

A great relationship with great sex can change the way you look at the world. A Great House Party should have you both feeling recharged and full of life. However, some persuasion might be required along the way.

PERSUASION

Most men wish that wanting to would be good enough. Especially after several dates, he develops hopes. I was like that when I first joined the Single World.

After dating one I liked, I remember trying to convince her because "I wanted to."

She replied, "If I did it with everyone that wanted to, I would be busy all the time."

A man has to come up with more to be with an attractive woman. It is not a problem for her to have sex, but men need skills.

**BE PATIENT
BUT DON'T LET THINGS DRAG OUT TOO LONG
YOU CAN ASK HER TO SHARE IT WITH YOU
AT THE HOUSE PARTY!!!**

The 1944 song *"Baby, Its Cold Outside"* **was targeted to go off the airwaves as a man "forcing" himself on a woman.** The Wall Street Journal, 12/13/2018, **printed the lyrics below, and Jim Carlton wrote about the modern contention with split opinions.**

The song has only friendly lyrics (a lot less suggestive than the songs of today). The morals were far different in 1944, and this woman lived at home with her parents. However, the song does show that a little persuasion might be required.

"BABY, IT'S COLD OUTSIDE"   Frank Loesser

HER	HIM
"I really can't stay	*But baby it's cold outside*
I got to go away	*But baby it's cold outside*
This evening has been	*Been hoping that you would drop in*
So very nice	*I'll hold your hands, they're just like ice*
My mother will start to worry	*Beautiful what's your hurry?*
My father will be pacing the floor	*Listen to the fireplace roar*
So really I better scurry	*Beautiful please don't hurry*
But maybe just a half a drink more	*Put some records on while I pour*
The neighbors might think	*Baby it's bad out there*

I wish I knew how   *Your eyes are like stars right now*
To break this spell   *I'll take your hat, your hair looks swell*
I ought to say "No, no, no sir"   *Mind if I move in closer?*
At least I'm just saying that I tried.
[Chorus]
I really can't stay   *Oh, baby don't hold out*
Baby it's cold outside………"

He simply tries to persuade her to stay. She is last to say *"Baby it's cold outside"*, **and** *"At least I'm just saying that I tried."* **The song leaves us guessing, but enjoying the banter. Many women today are more aggressive than in the 1940s, but some persuasion might be required to allow her to relax. Dating and relationships are always a matter of Respect and Consent.**

PERSUASION IS <u>NOT</u> COERCION
NOT IMPOSING
BUT PROPOSING

A MOMENT IN TIME

At the House Party, there could be a Moment in Time, or only an Instant for Opportunity.

I was having a House Party and giving her a massage when a song played, *"I'm going to give you everything I've got."* She rolled over and said, "I'm going to give you everything I've got." It seemed like an open invitation, but it wasn't. She fell asleep and didn't wake up in the same mood. When she said she was giving it, I should have captured that moment in time and told her "It's ON." (She could have still said "No.")

There was another time she came over after being at a party with her friends. She was in her best mood when she first arrived. I should have taken that instant to propose having fun at the start - not thinking there should always be a relaxation time. Instead, she was having fun for awhile, then threw up, and her good mood was gone.

I learned when she says she is "going to do something", to say "<u>OK let's do that NOW</u>!" Otherwise, it might not happen.

She might be ready when she gives you THAT dance. A man needs to be able to feel the Vibe – it can be just a moment in time.

CAPTURE THE MOOD

THE PARTY IS OVER

What if your House Party does not have as big a climax as you would like? That's OK. You tried, and you didn't put pressure on her. Maybe she needs more time; maybe you are still getting to know each other; you could be a Saver; maybe it will take a little more persuasion, or maybe you are not right for each other.

You can try again for Magic at your next House Party.

SHOULD YOU GET MARRIED, AND WHEN?

Chapter 27

It feels like people have a natural inclination to want to get married. Whether the feeling is totally natural, or if indoctrination induced, most people seem to have an urge or a dream for marriage. Maybe people subconsciously know the advantages and benefits outweigh the disadvantages, <u>if</u> you are able to find a true friend and lover. But there will still be bumps along the way.

Helen Fisher, Biological Anthropologist, answers the question, *"What are Singles looking for?*

1. Respect

2. Physical Attraction

3. Laughing Together

4. Making Time for Each Other

Data shows the best relationships are where there is a balance of power and each respects the other."

To get married or not is a question that each must answer for themselves. In today's world, it feels like it would be a small miracle to get it right.

"Miracle: an amazing or remarkable event: it is usually thought of as caused by God."

Webster's Dictionary

THE CHANGE OF LIFE

When a person is serious about marriage, they are often <u>thinking only about the benefits</u>, or what they will gain. But a person should also consider ahead of time <u>what they will lose</u>,

including some freedoms. A person needs to realize that marriage will be their biggest Change of Life.

There could be a deep psychological reluctance to accept the facts that have changed - you will be moving from the Single World to the Married World.

It took me over a year to adjust to Marriage, and I had the advantage of living away from relatives and single friends in a New Mexico town of 550 people. There was little distraction or temptation, and that is good for marriage. But years later, the marriage fell apart because of few mutual interests.

After 24 years of marriage, my brother told me, "She loves you, but she doesn't like you."

Later she told me, "You have your fans." I knew she was not one of them. It was over.

My Dad's obituary read, "He survived two marriages."

Some people have to try marriage more than once. My neighbor said, "I finally got it right on my 3rd try." Maybe I should talk more to him.

All I can say is "Good Luck", and you need shared interests and activities with mutual enjoyment. Also, practice patience. Believe in Love.

"By all means marry. If you get a good wife, you will become happy. If you get a bad one, you will become a philosopher."

Socrates, Greek philosopher

Marriage is a situation beyond an individual's control because marriage is based on cooperation, mutual commitment, compromise, <u>and</u> chemistry. Consider all the things we have talked about: friendship, shared activities,

trust, communications, affection, great sex, kindness. And don't make assumptions about a relationship based on early performance (infatuation, lust, fun to be with, great stuff) but that would be a good start.

A HAPPY MARRIAGE REQUIRES A STRONG FOUNDATION

BEING "IN LOVE"

People who think they are in love tend to see the world through rose-colored glasses. Your life can be rosy if you choose the Right One and show proper respect.

Some people get tired of "looking", so they marry someone shortly thereafter. Please don't settle for less than the Right One for you. And be patient in dating because it might seem like a long wait. However, a few months after marriage, you will realize it was a short wait.

Some people in love are actually "in lust", and this won't work over the long-term – there is a lot more to marriage than sex.

Know that your world will certainly be different after marriage. Talk to married friends, and maybe a marriage counselor to get an idea of what is involved. Observe the people you know that appear to have a Happy Marriage, and talk to them.

IF YOU ASK THE RIGHT QUESTIONS YOU MIGHT FIND THE RIGHT ANSWERS

ASK YOURSELF

Examine your heart for your true feelings, and be honest with yourself. Don't let anyone talk you into anything, or rely on information from your Big Brain or Short-Term Mood. Remember that marriage is a lifelong commitment. Ask yourself:

- **Do you think you really want to try to live the rest of your life with this one person?**
- **Do they want the same with you?**
- **Do you no longer want to go on dates with other people?**

I remember an attractive woman telling me, "My husband knows he is getting divorced if I catch him sitting at a table making Goo Goo Eyes at another woman."

I thought that sounded harsh, but I discovered she knew making Goo Goo Eyes leads to more. Yes, a married man can enjoy lunch or some things with another woman, but be careful with the Goo Goo Eyes if you want to stay married or keep your girlfriend.

- **What is the level of commitment to each other, and to marriage?**

In retrospect, I think I would have benefited from taking a Maturity Test (if there was/is such a thing). It would have helped me see if I was really ready for marriage, or to understand that I was not.

- **How "needy" is each of you? Needy is someone who emotionally exhausts their partner – insecure or clingy.**
- **Do you have activities you enjoy doing together (not including movies, eating, sex, or routines).**
- **Are you able to settle disputes without drama or causing resentment? We can all be aware to keep improving in this area.**

- **Do you both want children, or not? Both should express their feelings regarding children and pets.**

Of course, you can't foresee all possible issues, but these things I can say: I signed-up our son for tackle football without her permission. (I don't have an answer for this, but I don't think she ever got over resenting this.) On piano lessons, she would nag at him to practice until it disrupted the family vibe, (I don't believe in nagging as a way to get things done.) Also, I know a woman who would love to get a dog, but her husband bitches and says, "No." (I would get a dog anyway, but I guess that's why I'm not married anymore,)

- **Do you think you like their parents?**

Of course, your future spouse will probably be a lot like one or both of their parents. I never really liked either one of my ex-wife's parents, and my marriage "bit the dust." In retrospect, this is a good clue to examine..

- **What are your values? What are their values?**

If you disregard these questions, it will be at your own risk because <u>these issues will arise in marriage</u>. Do not deny facing factors that should be obvious.

Only the Test of Time, and the performance of each will answer these questions, but marriage could be a good idea if you find a great match.

FAULTY IMAGINATION

Some people marry who hardly know each other. This sounds ridiculous, but we have all seen it happen. Before considering marriage, a person needs to dissolve faulty imagination. It usually takes at least 2 years to know someone, and the better you know them, the better your chances.

We have all known people who decide someday, "I'm ready to get married" (wish to get married), and they get married shortly thereafter. These "it's time" marriages rarely result in a Happy Marriage.

Many people who think they want to marry might be just lonely, or going back to a Comfort Zone. These marriages won't be happy, so go with the flow to find the Right One.

If you do marry, it won't be long until *"the honeymoon is over."* **Yes, the euphoria will wear off, and it will get down to day-to-day living.**

CONSIDER REALITY FACTORS <u>BEFORE</u> MARRIGE

In 1999, a woman told me why some women don't want marriage:

"If a man cannot change a woman's life for the better, there is no reason for her to marry. A woman can sit at the table broke by herself. She would still have the chance to find a man that can change her life, or she can live her life without having to deal with a man, unless on her terms."

Her statement might sound cold, but the story is about the practical aspects of marriage because being broke for long will make marriage <u>very difficult (stressful)</u>. Some things don't change.

In regards to finances, if a couple starts with only love and friendship, the money situation will work out if both are dedicated to ALL-IN TEAMBUILDING. In other words, <u>current</u> finances might not be a determining factor for marriage. However, the money situation and agreeing on your budget is important.

RESPONSE ABILITY

This play on words involves your ability to have a proper response in marriage, <u>and</u> that marriage brings a lot more responsibility to each. Marriage is about trust, and being dependable to the one you love. (If you are Single and make a mistake, it harms only you.)

"Responsible: 1. able to be trusted or depended upon; reliable 2. having to do with important duties 3. supposed or expected to take care of something or do something."
Webster's Dictionary

The man should not think of housework, grocery shopping, or anything else as "women's work." If he does, then he has major problems that will carry over to other parts of married life.

It is very important to Think <u>before</u> responding to your partner (or anyone).

"Keep your words soft and sweet because they are the ones you will have to eat."
Saying

It's not only about what you say, but what you write. Whether it be in a card, note, email, or text message - things you write can come back to bite.

I remember when I was a teenager with a water gun, and spelled FUCK really big on the side of the horse. It was hot weather, and I thought it would soak in real fast, but it didn't. I was horrified when my Grandfather showed up and asked, "Who did that?"

I said, "David (my brother) did it."

My Grandfather said, "He sure does have a dirty mind."

I knew he knew who did it. I learned that words we write (or say) might not go away as fast as we think.

MARRIAGE IS A BIG STEP

If you are serious about getting married, read the book 101 Questions To Ask *Before* You Get Engaged by H. Norman Wright. **(Notice he said *Before Engaged* not Married.)**

Ask and answer the questions with your prospective partner. Make your own questions to go with Mr. Wright's. You must work together as a team to prosper. What's important to each of you? *"I have heard many people say, "The person I married was not the same one I honeymooned with. What happened? The answer is simple. They married a stranger. There was either courtship deception, naïveté or not enough questions were asked.*

Most people discovered the answers to the questions after they were married. They were shocked, dismayed, and felt deceived. Many of the questions are direct and blunt. You may think, "I couldn't ask that!" You may be hesitant, but why? You may think you're going to offend your partner, or you may be thinking these seem so unromantic - or you may not want to hear their answer (ignorance is not bliss) - or you may be worrying, "What if they ask me the same questions?" Well, your partner should ask you the same questions!

You can ask the questions and discover the answer now, or not ask them and discover the answers later. It's better for you to be in charge of when you find out (you will find out). As you read the questions, <u>they may sound like warnings. They are!</u>"

H. Norman Wright

RED FLAGS

H. Norman Wright calls his warnings signs *"Red Flags."* They are <u>common sense</u> (keep your eyes and ears open). Don't live in denial of what you see and hear.

Besides trying to help you find the Right Person, <u>The Bullsheet</u> is also trying to help you avoid marrying the Wrong Person. Consider all the little things from our Warning Signs, Mr. Wright's *"Red Flags"* and the annoying traits each of you has as they will be amplified in marriage. Ask and answer each other's questions. Your Ideal Partner might turn into an Imagined Ideal Partner when you find out more. And don't expect someone to change unless they are already in the process.

"Continue to interview them right up to the last moments before marriage. If that inner voice tells you that you are making a mistake, at least stop and listen to it and be willing to put things on hold until issues can be clarified in the relationship."

H. Norman Wright

VALUES

<u>The Bullsheet</u> defines Values: 1. one's judgment of what is important in life 2. a person's principles, or approved standard of behavior 3. the way a person evaluates people, actions, things or situations 4. chosen beliefs (maybe current indoctrination) 5. the way one feels, thinks, performs, and makes choices about the things they care about.

It would be good to examine values, including how you each feel and act regarding commitment, accountability, respect, openness, affection, empathy, loyalty, finances, sex and love.

Our Typical Guy might not have considered the importance of values in relationships. He might think she is cute, has a great personality, and She's the One he wants to marry. But he should be aware that he could have some Blind Spots (areas in which he is uninformed, or lacks understanding, including of the other's true feelings or motives).

Before marriage (or even getting serious), you will need to take time for introspection. Think about, and <u>write down</u>, what you value. If you don't know yourself, you will not have the ability to know someone else.

KNOWING AND RESPECTING
EACH OTHER'S VALUES
THAT'S A REAL CONNECTION

WHEN IS THE RIGHT TIME FOR MARRIAGE?
If Our Typical Guy wants to get married, the answer is: When he has found his Ideal Woman; she feels he is her Ideal Man; both have asked and answered all of each other's questions <u>together</u>; and both are still ALL IN. Don't slack off by not asking the questions, or you could *"marry a stranger."*

Think of all the responsibilities that marriage brings. A person might realize they don't want to get married anymore! There is no hurry.

BE THANKFUL FOR WHAT YOU HAVE
MARRIAGE IS GUESS WORK AND INTUITION
ASK QUESTIONS AND MAKE GOOD CHOICES
IT'S ONE OF THE BIGGEST DECISIONS OF YOUR LIFE

MARRIAGE WITHOUT A MARRIAGE

It's also possible for Our Typical Guy to be in a relationship with his Ideal Woman, but there is no marriage. Some women do not want to marry - period. She could have rationale against marriage even if the relationship is close to a perfect match.

Before her performance at the Super Bowl, Shakira was on 60 Minutes, CBS showing her living as a couple for the past 10 years with Barcelona soccer star Gerard Pique. They have 2 boys 5 & 7 at the time.

Interviewer to Shakira: "For all intensive purposes you 2 are married, but not officially married."

Shakira: "To tell you the truth, marriage scares the ____ out of me. I don't want him to see me as 'The Wife.' I like him seeing me as 'His Girlfriend'; exactly, 'Lover'; 'His Girlfriend' - like 'Forbidden Fruit.' I want to keep him on his toes. I want him to think that, 'Anything is possible depending on behavior'."

The Boyfriend rolls his eyes and smiles. It looked like he had heard the story 1000 times, so he will be happy/content without being married.

Some people will never get married (for various reasons), even though they might have lived together for years. People can be unpredictable as fewer follow society norms.

HOW DO YOU KNOW?

The Right One would be someone who wants to share Life together (ALL-IN Teammate/Lover/Friend); you have mutual attraction <u>and</u> mutual interests; you both strive for deep bonds of trust; you unite to build a great friendship; you agree on finances; you both feel they are The Love of your Life; you agree on children; there is romance and great chemistry - then it could be the time that you should get married.

MARRIAGE IS AN AGREEMENT TO COMPROMISE FOR LOVE

You also need to recognize that even if everything is in place and the sex is great for both, you can still ruin the relationship with selfish words, attitudes, and desires. Our Typical Guy will need to move from self-focused to union-focused, and know that selfishness causes deep resentment in marriage. It is important to not do things that cause resentment in your spouse. If married, you will know what these things are.

TONE OF VOICE IS ALWAYS IMPORTANT ESPECIALLY IN MARRIAGE

Our discussion confirms the conviction: **Do not settle for less than your Ideal Partner**. Marriage is a partnership of love, faith, chemistry, friendship, trust, and courage. You are going to need all the help you can get to find the Right One and to make it work for both. Ask your friends, family, and God/The Creator for guidance. Patience will help you.

It's a question of if your current partner is the Right One for you, **and** if both are ready for marriage. The stars can align for love.

YES!!!

Most people probably have to overcome their reservations about Marriage. However, it might be right for you if you feel like this Lady when she asked herself if she should marry:

"Will you marry me?" He asked.

"He was the one person who made me feel seen and cared for and uplifted. Still, I was reluctant to commit.

My parents went through a dramatic and corrosive divorce when I was 13. Most of the pain in my life has come from marriage – and its ending. Marriage is the one thing that has made me mostly likely to run, and least likely to trust.

I reminded myself where I was, who I was with – and most important, who I am now.

In that moment of "Yes!" my world expanded. In that moment, instead of fear, I chose gratitude. I was exactly where I needed to be. I still had my dark corners – I may always – but I could learn to live with them and still claim the life I wanted and deserve. I could live in the present and not in the past."

Gina Tomaine, Learning to Be Loved in Tulum
Yoga Journal

MEDITATION

Chapter 28

**MAYBE IT SHOULD NOT BE CALLED MEDITATION
BECAUSE FEW KNOW WHAT THAT IS
MAYBE IT SHOULD BE CALLED OBSERVATION
WE CAN OBSERVE OUR THOUGHTS & FEELINGS**

      To be accepting of life and the things you can't change will make your life more peaceful. Meditation helps you identify distracting thoughts, anxieties, and emotions that interfere with your life. To not be caught up in your thoughts would help to clear the clutter from your mind.

      With observing, you could sense what is real and what is important. We are usually looking to the outside world, but we could benefit by looking to our inner world.

**WE CAN GO ON AN INWARD JOURNEY
TO DISCOVER INNER PEACE
DON'T GIVE UP BEFORE YOU START!**

MAKE THE SWITCH

      Most people will never meditate as a result of hearing about its virtues or reading books and articles about it. Most people seem to be overwhelmed by the topic and tune it out as "impossible", "it's not for me", "I don't understand it", or "I don't have time." But once you are convinced of its importance, you can find a way.

**SWITCH YOUR MIND
FROM THINKING ALL THE TIME
TO OBSERVING SOME OF THE TIME**

WHAT'S AT STAKE?

Everyone's mind dwells on something. Why not make it healthy and healing?

"By your own thoughts you make or mar your life. As you build within by the power of thought, so will your outward life and circumstances shape themselves accordingly.

The intelligent practice of self-control quickly leads to knowledge of one's interior thought-forces. In the measure you master yourself, that you control your mental forces instead of being controlled by them, will you master your affairs and outward circumstances."

James Allen, As A Man Thinketh

In 1901, James Allen told us what is at stake through our thoughts - OUR LIFE! Direction must come from within, but one problem is our constant thinking.

We want to relax and make wise decisions. We know to not tell ourselves negative things. We do not want to be controlled by outside influences. Meditation can provide us with the power to achieve these things. We can be grateful, enjoy inner contentment, and sense the spiritual.

"Our life will follow our thoughts."

Saying

CONSTANT THINKING

What about the internal dialogue we all engage? The *"Default Mode Network"* **is what Neuroscientists call our mind's habitual, repetitive, often negative, emotion-based thinking. This repetitive thinking is called by Buddhists,** *"the Monkey*

Mind" **with thoughts that are,** *"unsettled, restless, fanciful, inconsistent, confused, indecisive, or uncontrollable."*

We would be better off if our *"Default Mode Network"* **included observing rather than thinking all the time. We could live in the present. We could live in peace.**

**A PEACEFUL MIND IS THE ONLY WAY
TO BUILD A PEACEFUL LIFE**

"Be free from the Virtual Reality of your thinking."

"You are the Thinker – not the thinking."

Roy Masters

**WHY ARE WE RELUCTANT TO MEDITATE?
Starting out is the most difficult part of any project, and most don't know what Meditation is. It sounds too difficult and abstract:**

"For the mind is restless, turbulent, obstinate, and very strong, and to subdue it is, it seems to me, more difficult than controlling the wind."

Arjuna, Bhagavad-Gita, 6.34

It also sounds like a waste of time to quit thinking. Why would you want your brain to do nothing? If you try, you quickly find that you are probably not going to stop your thinking mind for very long.

**IF YOU WATCH YOUR THOUGHTS
YOU CAN CALMLY OBSERVE THEM**

"I've had many troubles in my life, the most of which never happened."

Mark Twain

Most of us are constantly distracted by cell phones, other people, talk programs, television, computers, social media, or our own runaway mind that wants to control everything. Daily effort to observe your thoughts and actions will bring great rewards.

MINDFULNESS & MEDITATION
Mindfulness - What's that?

"MINDFULNESS IS A STATE OF MIND. IT IS A MENTAL STATE OF LIVING IN THE PRESENT TENSE IN A NON-JUDGMENTAL WAY."

"Mindfulness will enable you to live younger and live longer. You learn to live in the 'present.' Mindfulness carves out new pathways for relieving stress, anxiety, depression, and offers tools for managing pain. It enhances your focus for improved performance.

In a chaotic world with more stress, you gain a few seconds to be free from worry and regret. <u>You learn to stretch these few seconds into more and more of your life to be free from worry, or whatever your problems.</u>"

What is its relationship to Meditation?

"MEDITATION IS THE DAILY PRACTICE THAT GETS YOU FOCUSED, LIKE EXERCISE GETS YOU INTO SHAPE."

Mindfulness Goes Mainstream, PBS

The goal is to live in the Present - the Ever Present - the Now. When we live in the present, we won't be concerned about looking into the past, or be anxious about the future. When some old memory comes back - let it flow by. See what you are meant to see, or to unwind from your mind, and move into the present. It's a good thing (healing) to let go of some old memories. With meditation and forgiveness for all, including yourself, you will be free from anything holding you back.

"If someone does not forgive you – forgive their unforgivenss."

Roy Masters

LIVING IN THE PRESENT

Most people tend to think about what they don't have, instead of being thankful for what they do have. When you remember to be thankful, you become even more thankful.

**TO APPRECIATE YOUR BLESSINGS
IS AT THE ROOT OF LIFE CHANGE
FOR YOUR HEART AND MIND**

- **Enjoy everyday living**
- **Be calm, patient, and positive**
- **Live a healthy lifestyle**
- **Don't let resentment into your life**
- **Be an Observer of your thoughts, actions, and feelings**
- **It would be nice to enjoy a romantic relationship**
- **Adopt a meditation (observation) daily practice**

"You have to protect your 'secret place', your inner sanctuary. Do not let things get on the inside, and don't worry. Guard your heart, your place of peace and faith. Have no negative thinking, and let God go to work."

Joel Osteen

YOUR CIRCUMSTANCES ARE NOT YOU

Neuroscientists have proven the brain's ability to create new neurons and pathways (neuroplasticity). You should want your new brain cells and pathways to be positive, or else you will be creating negative neuron pathways! (That sounds like Victim Mentality.)

New neuron pathways remind us <u>our brain has the power to change</u>. This sounds wonderful, so self-discipline is the test.

*"For he who has conquered the mind,
The mind is the best of friends;
But for one who has failed to do so,
His* (Her) *very mind will be the greatest enemy."*

Bhagavad-Gita 6.6

Meditation will help to calm a restless mind. Outside influences (advertising, peer pressure, propaganda, social media, etc) seek to control you while you have limited outer knowledge on which to rely. But if you meditate, be still, and listen - you might perceive what is true.

You can meditate and observe to see if the pieces of the puzzle (your relationships, thinking, or life) need to be put together in a different way. Gradually, you realize stress is not constant, and that you can be successful and happy regardless of your current situation.

MEDITATION DEDICATION

Why is it so difficult to actually meditate (to do what seems like nothing)? Why do we not get started and practice for a little each day? We all need Meditation Dedication.

Actually trying meditation started for me upon returning from Colombia in February of 2020. My excuse for not meditating had always been that I didn't want to sit. When I had a sitting job, I sure didn't want to sit anymore – forget it. We can make a lot of excuses to not do what is good for us. We can meditate lying down, reclining, walking, or while being in nature. It's all therapeutic!

<u>I feel that something of life changing importance has to happen to persuade or encourage most people to actually try to practice meditation.</u> Meditation could help a person facing stress, high anxiety, or maybe a lack of faith. For me, it was to discover why I had done all the stupid things I had done. I wanted to change. I started learning about patience, and how meditation helps me to enjoy life and make better choices.

You can find a meditation or observation practice that will work for you. My choice has been the Observation Exercise from the recording by Roy Masters. There are also many breathing exercises to enjoy, and many other ways to relax your mind.

"If I make THIS MOMENT happy, it will increase my chances of having the next moment happy also."
Brahma Kumaris, Thought For Today

BE RENEWED FROM WITHIN

Meditation is almost impossible to describe which might be a reason it sounds impossible to do. Some topics are beyond words.

In 2021+, it feels like "Everybody's Busy" with their concerns, interests, frustrations, phones, and things to do. In such a Busy World, it's obvious that calming the mind would be helpful.

You can raise your awareness by practicing meditation for just a few seconds or minutes each day or night.

"You learn to stretch these few seconds into more and more of your life to be free from worry, or whatever your problems."
Mindfulness Goes Mainstream, PBS

- **You make progress just by trying**
- **When you decide it is important to calm your restless mind, you will find techniques to enjoy**
- **Meditation needs to become a daily habit (self-discipline is a good thing)**
- **If one practice doesn't work for you - find another**
- **Keep doing your daily practice - it's worth the effort**

You will gradually move from thinking all the time to observing some of the time. Meditation will improve your life, and you can find time to do it.

THE DEEPER YOUR CALM
THE DEEPER THE SATISFACTION
IT'S A NATURAL THING TO DO

SUGGESTIONS

Realize that there are many different types of mediation, and variations are as different as the people involved. Healing practices and calming techniques come to us from around the world. There are books and online resources to help you relax your mind.

A friend said he meditated every day, so I asked what he did, "I breathe in to the count of 4 and out to the count of 4. I breathe in calm, and breathe out stress." That sounds easy, so deep breathing could be your choice. Smooth, calm breathing encourages your nervous system to relax.

A mantra and/or chanting can be a form of meditation. You can choose your mantra. Never pay for a mantra. *OM* is a simple mantra.

Martial Arts can be a way to meditation. Martial Arts are the development of mind, body, and spirit. *Tai Chi* is described as *"meditation in motion."* It promotes serenity through gentle movements connecting the mind and body.

Singing, dancing, walking, running, swimming, cycling, music, or journaling could be used for meditation.

As early as 6th Century India, Caitanya Mahaprabhu informed us about our material world, *"In this Age of Quarrel and Hypocrisy, the means of deliverance is chanting the Great Mantra: 'Hare Krsna, Hare Krsna, Krsna Krsna, Hare Hara/ Hare Rama, Hare Rama, Rama Rama, Hare Hare'."* The Great Mantra is said to allow our mind to transcend the Material World to connect us to the Spiritual World - to be a *"transcendentalist."*

Yoga practices include meditation. Yoga is good for unity of mind, body, and spirit. Yoga is good for everyone.

Remember that your mind can be *"the best of friends, or your greatest enemy."* (A person's mind as their own enemy might explain a depression, anxiety, or a Malcontent.)

The internal dialogue is often that voice in our head telling us something negative, or what we can't achieve ("I can't find a girlfriend", "I'm can't do that", "I'm ugly", "It's too hard"). We should realize that we have the power to improve our life by observing and controlling our internal dialogue. For now, most of us can only imagine our life without a constant internal dialogue, but with mediation, we can create our lives in a new way.

"WE OURSELVES MUST CHANGE IN ORDER TO MASTER CHANGE."

Robert F. Kennedy

Don't have expectations for your meditation practice. Just keep practicing until it becomes a daily habit. Meditation can expand your mind, expand your awareness, and expand your horizons. New ideas and insights will be coming to you.

Meditation (observation) will also improve your mental health. It might take time, but you will become more proactive and less reactive. That will help your relationships. You will see that relationships are never constant, but always in flow.

DAILY EFFORT IS THE KEY
IN TRYING TO CALM YOUR MIND
BUILD SELF-DISCIPLINE FROM WITHIN

WHAT IS YOUR MEDITATION PRACTICE?
Whatever works for you. It feels like the 1st Step is to convince yourself of the important benefits from the

meditation of your choice. How can something that seems like doing nothing be important?

"Mind-power shows man the way to inner happiness, which gives him or her immunity to outer inconveniences."

Paramhansa Yogananda, How To Be Happy All The Time

We know that *"Introspection – the Looks-within Place"* **is one of the Four Directions we must visit in becoming a** *"Total Being or Whole Person."* **Apps, videos, classes, and CDs are available for guidance. You can find something to enjoy.**

LEARN TO BREATHE DEEP AND RELAX
LEARN TO LIVE IN THE HERE AND NOW
LIKE WITH ANY PRACTICE
YOU GET BETTER OVER TIME

"Turn off your mind, relax, and float downstream."
John Lennon

KEEP PRACTICING

Meditation is a powerful life changing tool. A daily practice will contribute to your happiness. Don't feel like nothing is happening.

In 2021+, it feels like few know what mediation really is. <u>It must be that meditation is to be experienced – not described</u>. However, even if we don't understand it, practicing mediation every day will help us to discover more about life, more about ourselves, and to be more peaceful.

IT IS ALWAYS THE RIGHT TIME
TO RESOLVE ISSUES WITH YOURSELF

"Normally, we aren't aware of the intensity of our inner dialogue. Our attention is focused on what is going on around us, so the wild crazy scenarios running through the mind generally escape our notice. But when we meditate – ah, then we see them.

Meditation allows the buried feelings, obstructive ideas, and painful emotions to float to the top of our Consciousness, where they can be recognized and removed. The inner witness can become a platform from which you can begin to heal these buried feelings."

Sally Kempton, Meditation for the Love of It, Yoga Journal

Besides the concept of mindfulness (living in the now), meditation allows you to see *"buried feelings, obstructive ideas, and painful emotions."* **Yes, it is not pleasant to be reminded of the stupid or disrespectful things we have done; or mistakes we have made; or suppressed resentments we hold; or people we need to forgive (including ourselves), but these thoughts and feelings** *"float to the top of our Consciousness where they can be recognized, removed, and you can heal these buried feelings."* **These are some of the ways that meditation brings healing.**

By practicing meditation, you go through life relaxing more, breathing deeper, observing instead of thinking, being more aware, and feeling less attached to stressful situations or future outcomes. You show more empathy, compassion, and kindness. You live in the "now." You go from Me, Me, Me to We. You feel the joy in living.

LOVE HAS A VIBRATION
RAISE YOUR VIBRATION

A HAPPY MARRIAGE

Chapter 29

"We must be our own before we can be there for another."
                                        Ralph Waldo Emerson

Some people believe it is impossible to have a Happy Marriage, or that the phrase is an oxymoron. I hope they are wrong. We know it won't be All Happy, but with the Right One it should be Overall Happy, and Sometimes Wonderful as long as both keep trying.

After years of marriage, many people fall back into thinking about what they don't have instead of being thankful for what they do have. In a Happy Marriage, both of you are thankful for each other and what you have together.

"I remember when I was a kid, my Dad telling me what he thought it took for a man to be happy. Simple things really: a wife he loves; a decent job; friends and neighbors who like and respect him; and there for awhile, I had all that. Without even realizing it, I had all that. <u>I was a happy man.</u>"
                                        A Simple Plan, Paramount Pictures

This Happy Man Formula reminds us it is a Blessing to have a spouse with mutual love.

Helen Fisher, Biological Anthropologist, studied brain scans of couples to reveal the secrets of long-term Happy Marriages:

"There are 3 regions of the brain in action in a Happy Marriage:
1. *a brain with empathy*
2. *a brain linked with handling your own emotions*
3. *a brain linked with positive illusions – the ability to overlook what you don't like - to focus on what you do like.*

So empathy, self-control, and the ability to overlook your partner's weaknesses are the keys to a Happy Marriage."

If you have the chemistry she describes and that leads to love and marriage - keep that going. Trust in what you have, and do your part. The more you take care of your marriage, the more it gives back.

"Lust is temporary, romance can be nice, but love is the most important thing of all. Because without love - lust and romance will always be short-lived."

Danielle Steel

LEARN ABOUT LOVE

Doing things together you both enjoy is key to a Happy Marriage. A marriage will not work if both do not enjoy activities together. Make time for fun, share your thoughts and feelings, believe in your spouse and show it!

Couples must keep the romance alive by showing passion (strong love and enthusiasm). Share in the making of a home for a happy/content marriage.

I asked a friend who appears to have a Happy Marriage what he thought to recommend about marriage.

He said, "<u>You better know what you are getting into</u>."

Eric Fromm describes people who <u>don't know</u> what they are getting into with marriage:

"If two people who have been strangers feel one, this moment of oneness is one of the most exciting experiences in life. It is all the more wonderful for persons who have been shut off, isolated, without love. This miracle of sudden intimacy is often combined with sexual attraction and consummation. However, this type of love is by its very nature not lasting.

The two persons become well acquainted, their intimacy loses more and more its miraculous character, until their antagonism, their disappointments, their mutual boredom kills whatever is left of the initial excitement.

Yet, in the beginning they do not know all this: in fact, they take the intensity of the infatuation, this being crazy about each other, for proof of the intensity of their love, while it may only prove the degree of their preceding loneliness.....

To have a happy marriage, we must include recognition of love as an informed practice rather than an unmerited grace."

Eric Fromm, The Art of Loving

Yes, the newness of the Infatuation Period and physical appearance dwindles over time. We need to learn "How-to" love: *"Master this supreme human skill."* **Eric Fromm says,** *"Love is an art."*

We have seen that people should be very careful to not fall into a Comfort Zone, or marry the Wrong One. Take your time to choose the Right One for you. If you find the Right One – do the things that keep it together. That would be showing love.

Trust, Loyalty, and Love are all important, so don't say or do stupid stuff. Always be happy to see your spouse when they show up.

STAND STRONG

If you are reflecting on marriage, be sure to ask yourself this question: "Will he/she stand strong beside me?" Contemplate this last sentence from a great book:

"The scouts had reported that the soldiers were starting against the Indians and now the great camp had to break up. But there was a sadness even among the strong-talking ones when the first camp, the Cheyenne, started away. Here and there a man watched too, and a few of the young ones hurried to their horses and rode after the Cheyenne, some of the best warriors of the Oglalas. It was hard for Crazy Horse to see them go, but the Cheyenne women were very good - not so beautiful as some of the Oglalas, but they stood strong beside a man, very strong beside a man."

Crazy Horse by Mari Sandoz

You should value someone who will stand strong beside you. In that manner, you will be stronger together. You will be a good partner if you stand strong beside them.

- Make sure you are being supportive - not divisive.
- If there is a problem – talk it over.
- For you both to be happy - build each other up with encouraging words, good deeds, friendship, and love.

**EACH DAY IN MARRIAGE
YOU WILL GROW
CLOSER TOGETHER
OR FURTHER APART**

NEW RULES IN MARRIAGE

To have a Happy Marriage, Our Typical Guy should know there are often Different Rules for the man than for the woman.

For example, women are often late getting back home. She does not want to be quizzed about why she was late. <u>The Bullsheet</u> is letting you know she will often be late, and it doesn't mean she was having sex with someone else. An amazing thing about a woman being late is that to her it is never a big deal. She didn't need to call, and she wasn't late in her mind. However, if the man is late, he has some explaining to do if he did not call. The man should not be back late without calling or texting ahead.

In the days before email, there was faxing. I remember a fax called *"THE RULES"*. I don't have a copy, but from what I can remember:

1. *THE RULES are set by the woman.*
2. *THE RULES are subject to change without notice at any time.*
3. *The man is supposed to automatically know THE RULES and the changes.*
4. *The woman has the right to be angry or upset at any time.*
5. *The man must remain calm at all times unless the woman wants him to be angry or upset.*
6. *The woman is never wrong.*
7. *The man should immediately apologize for any violation of THE RULES.*

As with all jokes, the truth in it is what makes it funny.

COMPROMISE IS REQUIRED

A Happy Marriage involves willingness to compromise. For example, if you have children - find ways to balance family and romance. And we know there will be compromise in sex life. It will still be happy/content if both are All-In to make it fun and satisfying. Make each other feel that nothing can come between your love for each other.

"There is nothing wrong with sometimes being intimate just to please your partner, or vice versa. In successful long-term relationships, people accommodate each other. You might sit through an action movie when you'd rather see a drama. Your partner may want steak but join you for sushi. We do this for each other out of love - the joy of making someone you care for happy. Why should sex be any different?"

Marta Meana, Professor of Psychology, UNLV

Couples with love do nice things for each other to keep the fire alive. One does something for the other, whether it be a honey-do project, or something nicer.

A person might need to ask for what they want (few are mind readers). However, if the sex is usually frustrating, the marriage will be usually frustrating. But you can communicate hopes, new things you would like to try, make plans together, or be spontaneous together.

SHARE STEADFAST COMMITMENT
TO SHARE STEADFAST LOVE

Our Typical Guy will need to be patient in marriage. He will not be out chasing around anymore, but he can keep romance alive at home, and do a good job for her. Express your appreciation.

Life is the Greatest! There are so many things we can do for a happy home, whether married or not.

COMMUNICATIONS

The ability to have great communications is possibly the most important part of a Happy Marriage. Communications are not only oral, but includes body language, affection, and deeds.

With good conversation, you discover problems or gain a proper understanding while trying for agreement. Don't keep things that are bothering you inside. A couple can't fix a problem if you they don't know what it is, and a lot of knowledge can come out of a good conversation. A lot of healing can come out of great sex.

**WITHOUT GREAT COMMUNICATIONS
THERE IS NOT GOING TO BE A HAPPY MARRIAGE**

We know money can trigger people emotionally. It is well known that financial matters are a major cause of dispute and possible divorce. Communications about money are very important, so learn how each of you feels about spending and a budget (this should be done <u>before</u> marriage, but the Reader might already be married – it's never too late to talk).

However, don't be obsessed about money, or you won't enjoy each other, yourself, or your marriage. Work together on your budget. Know that the money part will work out if both keep trying.

*"THERE'S NO PEACE TO BE FOUND
IN ALWAYS WANTING MORE"*

Ken Honda, Happy Money

Arguing skills are also an important form of communication. The idea is to avoid drama, and develop arguing skills (conflict resolution) that does not hurt each other. The Reader might need more on developing these skills than what <u>The Bullsheet</u> can provide.

FACE THE REALITY OF TENSIONS
DON'T ALLOW RESENTMENT INTO YOUR MARRIAGE

BE A GREAT LISTENER

Listening is also an important part of communications. Know that learning to listen is not the same as being silenced.

Men should know that women often want to talk about things without trying to find a solution. The man is supposed to listen. Men are Problem Solvers so "just listening" can be difficult, but it appears to be a necessary skill. Listening has something to do with patience, respect, and trying to understand (empathy).

I am still working to be a better listener. At least, I have learned to not interrupt as that is rude. Also, I want to slow down and be polite.

HAPPILY EVER AFTER

If you get married, try for Happily Ever After, but realize we all have flaws and there will be stressful times. We all have a Bad Day sometimes. Be able to recognize when you are having a Bad Day to prevent blow-ups from happening.

Remember to control your emotions and to let small things go (overlooking).

Good communications will solve every problem except lying and cheating. If you want a Happy Marriage - don't lie, go out with others, be dishonest with money, or do anything that will destroy the trust.

"A happy wife makes for a happy life." **This saying might be all you need to know. If you picked the Right One and there is love - the keys to harmony are within you.**

SEX IN MARRIAGE

If a couple can't work the sex out, it won't be a Happy Marriage.

Couples get along for the long run when they on the same wavelength as to the importance and fulfillment of sex. Sex should be discussed openly both before and during marriage.

A friend who appears to have a Happy Marriage told me it takes 3 things:
1. Good Communication
2. Good Conflict Resolution
3. A Bond of a Spiritual Dimension.

I asked where sex figured in this Happy Marriage. He said sex is chemistry, and you have it or you don't. If you do have the chemistry, both should know to <u>Keep the Fire Alive</u>.

We know that everyone has a different sex drive and different sexual preferences, so communication of desire is an important part of marriage. Sex is always about the mood and going with the flow. Sex (and life) is about Respect. There is no love without respect.

But even in a marriage where sex was good (often great) for many years, a person might think sex is getting boring. However, it has been argued that boring is an excuse, and the real problem is that one, or both, have anger or resentment which results in no sex or holding-back.

Be realistic - one will find out early if the other is a "cold fish" or a "dead fuck" i.e. Bad in Bed. If cold fish is the case, the marriage is probably already over, unless both have a low sex drive. Otherwise, if one gets cut off, or the sex is labeled "boring", it is probably because of unresolved anger or resentment. And frustration by itself can create more anger and resentment. Of course, these problems can erupt even in long-time married couples as it often takes time for resentments to build. Each should be open to revealing resentments and traumas so these feelings don't build up to ruin sex life and the marriage.

Even if not caused by anger or resentment, the boring excuse is said to still not be legitimate because dedicated couples have a duty to not let boredom take over. Sex life does not get boring in marriage if there is great communications, creative romance, and both keep trying.

BOREDOM IS A CHOICE - TRY ROMANCE
AND HAVE A GOOD TALK
<u>ROMANCE IS CREATED</u>
GIVING A LOVING EFFORT IS WHAT COUNTS

Our Typical Guy will need the awareness to put her first by showing her respect, attention, and affection (we not me).

My best tip for sex in marriage is to encourage you to build a real friendship above all. (The lack of real friendship is why *"She loves you, but she doesn't like you"* results in divorce or an unhappy marriage.)

Another tip about sex for a Happy Marriage is to have creativity – not the Same Time, Same Place, Same Position. However, after I was dismissing same-o same-o, a friend told me, "I like to have a regular Tee Time." People's different preferences and sex drive is why it's difficult to generalize about sex.

Be adventuresome and excited to be with each other. Plan and go on Date Nights to keep romance alive. It doesn't have to be expensive to be fun.

Variety does make sex more exciting. Tell each other what you would like to try. Remember that you can work together to make it fun and exciting for both by keeping communication lines open. We keep learning as we go - it's on-the-job training.

MORE TO DO FOR A HAPPY MARRIAGE

Allowing each other freedom to do things they enjoy is part of a Happy Marriage. Yes, both need separate activities and time alone. Give each other space by making time for free time. Don't react negatively to your partner spending time on their interests and activities, or being with their friends. You will also need Activity Time or Friend Time for yourself. This concept of being alone in marriage is reflected in this poem.

Marriage
"...Sing and dance together and be joyous,
but let each of you be alone,
Even as the strings of the lute are alone though
they quiver with the same music.
Give your hearts, but not into each other's keeping.

For only the hand of Life can contain your hearts.
And stand together yet not too near together:
For the pillars of the temple stand apart,
And the oak tree and the cypress grow
not in each other's shadow."
                              The Prophet by Kahlil Gibran

    One of my best tips for a Happy Marriage is to enjoy shared interests and activities. This time <u>together</u> that is fun for both will sustain you both along with great sex. To keep activities happening, it is up to <u>both</u> to communicate things you would enjoy doing together, and how each likes to go about it.

    Massages are healing, and fun for the receiver and the giver if you do a good job. Touch can be a wonderful thing.

    There are so many outdoor activities or sports to enjoy together. Find out what perks up your Partner. Hopefully, you will find out about mutual interests and <u>enthusiasm for participation</u> **before** marriage. You can work together to find a new activity you both to enjoy – keep trying new things.

    It is healthy for your marriage to go on dates and have romantic activities. Take some time out for a romantic getaway. A vacation can be a lot less expensive than a divorce.

    A person does not usually want to think about what could go wrong in their marriage. However, it might be a good idea to anticipate possible problems, because sooner or later, something disturbing is certain to happen.

    A Tip for Preventing Problems is to not let resentment (ill feelings towards others) build-up inside of you. If something is bothering you – get it out, and talk about it with your Partner. No problem is off-limits or too small if it is

bothering one of you on the inside. Encourage your partner to speak up. Otherwise, the problem or disgruntled feeling will continue to build until there is anger or resentment which can result in a blow-up. Modern marriages cannot endure a lot of blow-ups, and the more resentment builds up, the bigger the blow-up.

Get things straight before marriage, and keep things straight during marriage. In this way, you can continue to enjoy each other as you solve problems together along the way.

A tip especially for Our Typical Guy is to not get his wife anything practical for a gift, unless she specifically asked for it. One Christmas, I gave my wife a broom as a "stocking stuffer" gift. This gift was not well received, and she probably remembers it over all the nice gifts from 24 years of marriage. Later, I heard a guy say he gave his wife a vacuum, and he had a similar unforgettable result.

Another tip for Our Typical Guy is to do things for his wife without wanting or expecting something in return. By wanting something, a person will not be giving a good vibe to the marriage and they will be frustrated most of the time. Show affection without expectation. Do things cheerfully.

Once again, I must remind you that marriage will not be happy all the time. Therefore, it appears to me that the happiness of a marriage often depends on how skillful at conflict resolution a couple is. A couple that is able to keep disagreements from escalating will have a much greater chance to enjoy a Happy Marriage.

Another tip is to nurture your own and your spouse's spiritual efforts and feelings. We know that Spiritual Life is ¼ of being a Complete Person. To have a spiritual bond would elevate your marriage.

To maintain harmony in your marriage, it would be good to keep learning all you can about marriage. In *The Miracle of Mind Power,* Dan Custer tells us, *"Marriage is the greatest adventure in human relations. No marriage can be successful unless each partner loves the other as themselves.*

It is unfortunate but true many people marry for money or because of sex drive or to get away from domineering parents or because of loneliness...

*When two people get married for the right motive – to be partners through life in their **work, play, love, and worship** – they get the good they hope for. Plans must be made which satisfy both and to which both agree. As healthy partners, they work it out together, and plan what each will do.*

If you desire a happy marriage, you must want to give as well as receive. Remember, you don't want to get a husband; you don't want to have a wife; you want to be a good partner. If that is your motive, you have the right to a happy marriage."

MARRIAGE IS LIKE A FLOWER GARDEN

When the ground (marriage) is good - get the weeds out and plant the seeds.
You will get flowers and butterflies will come.
Yes, some weeds will pop back up, but you can pull them out, and bring in the flowers to remind you of your happy home.
Use keen observation and kindness when pruning your garden so as to not cut good growth.
You will need to water (love) and fertilize (contribute to) your garden.
Each day enjoy and recognize its beauty.

Your garden is a world of give and take, responsibility, and joy.
When the flower pops open, the feeling is indescribable.
Send good vibes to your garden.

TRUSTED FRIENDS AND LOVERS

A warm heart and a trustworthy companion are part of what we are looking for. Stand very strong beside each other. Know there will be Give and Take, and every relationship has difficult moments. Keep in mind that your relationship should be bigger than yourself.

"The thing I miss most is having a trusted friend I could talk to any time about anything. I cherish that because we had to go through a lot of things together. And the second thing I miss most is having his arms around me. He was very expressive, loving and I miss that. I miss that a lot."
Rachael Robinson, wife of Jackie Robinson

A HAPPY MARRIGE IS ABOUT TRUST AND LOVE
THE TRUST IS A HEAVENLY PROMISE - EVEN SACRED
A HAPPY MARRIGE IS A JOY TO YOUR HEART
APPRECIATE YOUR LIFE TOGETHER

The quality of a relationship depends on the underlying friendship. For a Happy/Content Marriage, you have found a Best Friend in each other – a Confidant.

MAKE IT HAPPY

Of course, not everyone will experience a Happy Marriage. Many will choose the Wrong One; many will never marry; many will goof-up a good thing; and many will not re-marry. However, a person can still enjoy great relationships even if they never have a happy marriage.

It is proven that a Happy Marriage brings health, happiness, financial benefits, emotional growth, and security. Keep your relationship fresh and exciting. This means having spontaneity, excitement, and new experiences for each other. Men need to do a good job for her. Neither will need to find someone new because marriage and sex gets better and better over time if both stay All-In.

In marriage, the fruit of your dedicated efforts is to create a bond that improves your lives, creates a pleasant vibe at home, meets the desires of both, and you enjoy your time together. Always be reaching out for better ways to communicate. Be sure to take time for date nights and going on getaways (without the kids). Be thankful for what you have together.

A Happy Marriage is made up of Friendship, Respect, Affection, Caring, Appreciation, Empathy, Laughing Together, Mutual Interests and Love. Each of these is required to keep a marriage growing in love. Of course, no one remembers these all the time, but keep them in mind to have the Vibe that will give you a Happy Marriage.

"True fortune is a wonderful spouse – I think when a couple marry, they either go into heaven or live in hell. They may have a fairy-tale-like life, or they may suffer a lot. I am a fortunate man. I am a fortunate not because my films have broken box office records, but because I have a good wife, Linda. She is unsurpassed. Why do I say this? First, I believe a couple should develop a kind of friendship. Linda and I have this kind of friendship. We understand each other, like a pair of good friends. We thus can spend our time together happily. My wife is the luckiest thing that ever happened to me – not The Big Boss.*"*

Bruce Lee, Striking Thoughts

TODAY AND TOMORROW

Chapter 30

TODAY YOU ARE ____
TOMORROW YOU ARE 70
LIFE IS SHORT
I CAN TESTIFY - TODAY I AM 73

"Life is like a voyage through time. You have been given so many years to gather the treasures of love, courage, and wisdom. In the matrix of enduring patience, everything grows as a matter of course, without struggle. So do not be in a hurry for results."

Roy Masters

This Final Chapter was planned to end on my return from Colombia, but it has taken longer to finish and a pandemic arrived.

When things are going good (a relationship or Pre-Corornavirus) a person might want life to go on like this forever. But that's not reality. Real Life is times change, things change, and change keeps coming to us all.

Go with the flow of life by strengthening your ability to adjust to change. Prepare yourself for bold action. You will need courage and wisdom to build strength in the New Age.

Coronavirus has accelerated change, and brought many things to light. Jobs have been lost, and the entire economic system is in question. Today is December 21, 2020.

THE POST-PANDEMIC WORLD

It is clear that the Pandemic has had a negative impact on people's overall mental health, much less social life, and so-called social norms. In this complex world, we wonder how

Post-Pandemic Life is going to be different for you and Our Typical Guy? What about the Relationship Between the Sexes for 2021+? What about the fact that the rate of dating, the marriage rate, and the birth rate are all falling?

The Pandemic has given many people a pause with time to reflect. After staying at home thinking for 2 years, people might be having more conversations about intimacy and the details of their relationships. People can build better a understanding.

In general, it feels like people will be more reserved, more protective, and more standoffish after their Pandemic Experience. This could make relationship building more difficult. But a Post-Pandemic Lonelier World won't have to happen for you.

In these times of facing increased reservations, Our Typical Guy will need to be more willing to step up and say something to the ones he would like to date.

Rather than looking at stepping up as daunting, it is better to view it as challenging.

> *"Challenge: to call for skill, effort, or imagination."*
> Webster's Dictionary

Of course, if you are making connections online, you avoid the need to step up to approach someone. Dating websites make it look easy to meet. This is why online is the preferred method for meeting people in 2021+, but there will be times when opportunity appears in person.

The Bullsheet hopes you have discovered good tips for gaining confidence in your relationships. However, as with dancing, flirting, and conversation, you are on your own to make improvements. A great relationship with romance is possible if you try.

YOUR POWER TO IMPROVE YOUR LIFE
IS IN THE SEEDS YOU SOW EACH DAY
NEVER GIVE UP
IN LIFE AND IN LOVE

THINGS TO COME

<u>The Bullsheet</u> has tried to stay on topic and answer the 3 Questions from Chapter One. We have not had discussions on economics, politics, religion, inequality, racism, health care, continuous war, pollution, or waste. These areas affect our lives, but you can read other books for details.

"The last thing we want to be is well adjusted to injustice."
Cornell West

We have seen from history that one person <u>can</u> make a difference: Brother Martin Luther King, Jr., Bob Marley, Noam Chomsky, Ralph Nader, Freddie Mercury, Edward Snowden, Rev. William Barber II, and many more. If one person can make a difference, then a generation of people can surely make a difference.

People can change. The Ostrich Generation became the Plaid Shirt/Free Thinker Generation. With the Courageous/Millennial and the Creative Generations, we know there is hope. The younger generations can unite with Native People for mission-driven action to fight injustice, chemicals, and climate destruction.

**"*MORDOR*" IS HERE
IN THE ALBERTA TAR SANDS**

We need to reform the System (the way Government does business). "Reform" simply means to highly restrict lobbying, campaign finance reform, end insider trading and stock buy-backs, decrease Military and Surveillance spending while increasing funding for Real Communities (schools, hospitals, children). In the New Age, we need programs and policies that help Real People.

"IT'S UNREAL TO THINK THE PEOPLE WHO CREATED THE PROBLEMS WILL SOLVE THE PROBLEMS."

Saying

**THESE YOUNG PEOPLE CAN GET TOGETHER
AND GET THINGS DONE
SOME OF THE SMART ONES WILL SEE A BETTER WAY
UNLIKE TODAY - IT WILL FEATURE COMMON SENSE**

Common sense will include good intelligence, back to the basics to find good solutions, and to do what is fair.

"PEOPLE WHO SAY IT CAN'T BE DONE ARE TAKING A BACK SEAT TO THOSE WHO ARE DOING SOMETHING."

Naomi Klien

It is going to take all those willing to speak up, write up, and vote up to preserve justice for the protection of Real People and Mother Earth. New paths will emerge.

"Activists created the freedoms we enjoy today. There are new ways of political action. People can win victories."

Noam Chomsky

SOLUTIONS

This is not an economics book, but we have our Financial Life as 1/4 of being a Complete Person. All of us need enough money to survive while these are looking like troubling economic times for many people.

"Not everything that is faced can be changed. But nothing can be changed until it is faced."

James Baldwin

We need Real Leaders for the New Age. This country has had Real Leaders: Abraham Lincoln, Brother Martin Luther King Jr., Robert Kennedy, John Kennedy, but they were all assassinated. <u>If just 1 of them had lived, it would be a Different World today</u>. Franklin Roosevelt was a Real Leader who survived, so it can be done. FDR cared about people, and along with Francis Perkins, created the New Deal. Many of the programs have been dismantled, but they can be revived and improved upon. The New Deal Programs have been <u>proven to be successful at reviving an economy</u>. People want what is fair, and to have hope for a brighter future for themselves and their children.

NO ONE IS TAKING RICH PEOPLE'S MONEY
THEY GET BAILOUTS AND TAX BREAKS
REAL PEOPLE NEED GOOD PAYING JOBS
WITH MEANINGFUL WORK FOR THE NEW AGE

We know things are not changing fast enough. Very little is being done to regulate and tax multi-national corporations, to slow pollution, fight corruption, and to protect the Earth's climate systems. Hopefully, a New Consciousness is arriving for the New Age.

> *"WE DON'T OWN THE EARTH*
> *THE EARTH OWNS US*
> *WE ARE IT'S CARETAKERS*
> *AND IT IS HOLY"*
>
> Leonard Crow Dog

REALITY HAS MANDATES

Outdated and polluting ideas are burning out (slowly, because they are still in power and making money). These rich people and corporations are very protective of their power and money while the young people are on the outside. But these younger generations will not back down. There is a shift in the willingness to combat greed and to make changes based on new and better ideas. *"Fridays For Future"* and Allies battle against *"The Megamachine"* and *"Military Madness."* New movements are on the rise. People are helping each other.

> *"TO PROTECTORS EVERYWHERE*
> *CONTINUE TO RISE LIKE A MIGHTY WAVE."*
>
> Hawaiian Natives

If humankind and politicians do not deal with reality, there will be consequences. Billionaire funded groups (ALEC, etc) have set out to dismantle government, privatize public services, and discredit society's legitimate needs by making little social investment.

They divide the country while disguising themselves as "freedom" or "prosperity" - freedom and prosperity for them to not pay taxes or to not have a duty to help protect the Earth's water, air and disadvantaged people (young, old, disabled). Realistic integrity realizes (or implies) that everything is built on the backs of others, and every business uses the highways, airports, internet and other public facilities.

As you watch life unfold, speak up when given a chance, and do what you can. You might not have the money, but you have a voice.

"What matters is the countless small deeds of unknown people who lay the basis for the significant events that enter history. They are the ones who did it in the past, and they will be the ones that do it in the future,"
Howard Zinn, A People's History of the United States

LIFE GOES ON

I started 2021 at 8200 feet in the Andes Mountains outside Santa Elena, Colombia. For New Year's Eve, the locals were burning a dummy that symbolized burning your Old Self to become a New Person. After returning to Oklahoma, I lit a bonfire and burned Old George, so New George has arrived. You can also become your own New Person.

As your situation and relationships evolve - stay calm, patient, and positive while putting your tips and skills into practice. How do you know what to do? You experiment to find what works for you. Trust yourself and trust in God.

"VISION WITHOUT EXECUTION IS HALLUCINATION."
Thomas Edison

HOPES AND DREAMS

We all have Hopes and Dreams along with Vision and Imagination. Some Readers are married, while some search for their Ideal Partner, and others prefer being single.

LOVE IS YOUR GREATEST STRENGTH
GRATITUDE, PATIENCE, AND HUMILITY
GIVE YOU MORE STRENGTH
YOU MUST BE STRONG

You won't fail if you have the courage to hold on to your dreams and develop yourself.

> *"COURAGE IS MORE EXHILERATING THAN FEAR AND IN THE LONG RUN – IT IS EASIER."*
> Eleanor Roosevelt

Your Dreams can come true, but you have to believe and work for them.

"I guess you might say my fantastic transformations sound like some yoga fairy tale – and it is. It's a fairy tale I brought to life with the power of positive thoughts and perseverance. You can do the same thing with your fairy tales if you believe."
Ebony Smith, Yoga Transformed Me

MAKE CHANGE HAPPEN

In the 1970s, I kept horses while living in New Mexico. I will never forget being at the Feed Store and a Lady Cashier telling me, "<u>If you don't slow down - life is going to pass you by</u>."

Her statement doesn't sound like much, but whatever it is that awakens you to "slow down to enjoy your life" will change you forever. When you rush around, you are not enjoying your time. When you shift to slowing down and calming your thoughts - then inspirations and insights will come to you.

Slow down to go with the flow of life. If you feel stuck in a particular situation or relationship, you can reflect on ways to make it better, or a need to let go.

Relax to lower anxiety and to shift your perspective. Learn to <u>not</u> listen to that voice in your head when you have emotion-based thinking. Learn to live intuitively.

"Everyone is born with certain gifts. Some people find them when they are young, others may need time to search. Uncovering your talents, and finding what brings you joy, is one of the most important things in life.

If you are no longer burdened by the past, you will be surprised at how quickly your talents will be revealed to you. When you take an inventory of your life, all the dots begin to connect. Getting into a state of flow will become second nature. Difficulty and struggles will transform into fun and adventure right before your eyes."

Ken Honda, Happy Money

How do you plan to make change happen? Whether with dating, relationships, career, life, or any challenge, your answer could be similar to this:

"My motivation has to come from love. Whether love of the people in my life, love for future generations, or love of the planet. I was taught by Native Elders, 'There it is. What are you going to do?'

Rather than being depressed, angry, or "it's too late"- I changed my life. Taking action has completely changed me from the inside out, just by taking action. Greta Thunberg said, 'Action is the antidote to despair.'

We have to let go of the results. It keeps coming back to – What's the Right Action? What's the Right Action?"

Dahr Jamril, The End of Ice

*"ACTS OF COURAGE
BRING MORE ACTS OF COURAGE'*

Saying

MOVING INTO THE FUTURE

Feel worthy of love. You can work on personal growth to enjoy life, to be thankful, and to be a Complete Person. Support yourself, your family, and society while safeguarding the Earth. When you are considering "What is the right thing to do?"

"IT IS THE DIFFERENCE BETWEEN WHAT YOU 'COULD DO', AND WHAT YOU 'SHOULD DO'."

Edward Snowden

We will discover aspects of our understanding where we need to raise our awareness (like when dealing with members of the opposite sex). When a lack of awareness is revealed, we learn what we need to do.

Believe in yourself to make your dreams come true. Learn to let go of excuses, self-imposed negative thinking, any destructive habits or limiting beliefs that hold you back (I can't do it, I'm ugly, old, tired, etc).

Free yourself up by not being overzealous about opinions – your own or other peoples. An opinion is not worth

losing a friend. It is good to be knowledgeable, but don't let opinions keep you from enjoying other people. It could be time to change the topic.

We know we can't turn back the clock, and that a part of life is our own internal education, our internal healing. We have learned through meditation (observation) that we can change our thinking. Our mind can heal our little traumas of self-judgment or distorted beliefs about relationships, the world, or ourselves.

To be a Great Listener would improve our life. That might prove to be too difficult, but we can keep getting better at listening, at guarding against resentment, and being careful what we say and text.

Life is about having and showing respect. Be happy with life by having peace of mind. When socializing, you will know what to do or how to adjust.

RESTORE YOUR HEALTH
CONNECT TO NATURE
AND THE PEOPLE YOU LOVE

There is a risk to making changes, but there is a risk to remain the same. When you want to make something happen, move into your discomfort and do something. Then keep going, or try and try again. Possibilities will open up.

Remember the Spiritual nature of life. However, it is inconceivable to our minds how Spirit works, just as it is inconceivable to our mind that we are traveling through space at 514,000 miles per hour. Yes, that is the speed the Earth <u>and</u> Sun travel as we orbit the Milky Way Galaxy. Also, the Earth spins at 800 miles per hour as we orbit the Sun - yet it feels like we are standing still.

OUR MINDS ARE LIMITED
"EVERY DAY IS A BLESSING" **- IS <u>NOT</u> JUST A SAYING**
ENJOY EVERY SECOND
ENJOY YOUR RIDE ON SPACESHIP EARTH

STRONG HEARTS NEEDED

At age 73, and near the end……. of this book, it feels like it would be amiss to not say anything about death. I hear people say they are afraid of death, but death is a natural part of life. I see no reason to be afraid. Death shows us to appreciate Life, and to be wise with our time.

Sometimes I try to feel what it would be like to experience death, but I only get a small lift-off feeling. I do know there will be a day when my spirit leaves this body, but I'm not trying to rush the matter. However, I do remember the words of Chief Seattle:

"Dead, did I say? There is no death, only a change of worlds."

In parting words to my friend, Our Typical Guy and you, I say don't be ashamed of your frustrations or desires or loneliness, but have hope with forward looking thoughts. Be spontaneous, but avoid compulsive actions and reactions. You can go through life with character building – strengthening your good qualities while realizing that self-discipline and self-confidence are good things. My #1 Tip is for you is to have Patience with your life.

We know that relationships and families can be complicated, so remember that patient non-response is a response.

When emotions take over – logic is forgotten, and emotional reactions often accelerate problems.

Whether in relationships or overall, encourage and enable others to show your love for life. Enjoy today, whether single or married, and be more playful. People are meant to be playful, to have fun, to explore, and to enjoy adventure – together

If you feel you have a Special Relationship, go beyond standard expectations and show them every day that you care.

"There are many ways you can add value to your relationships: Inspire someone to take action, lend a helping hand, be interested in someone, be interesting yourself, give without expectation, provide a new perspective, lead by example, listen more, give compliments and appreciation freely, express gratitude for people in your life by the actions you take to show it, Love someone."

Jacqueline Wales

HAPPY TRAILS TO YOU

I hope you have enjoyed this book. Thank you for reading. I hope you feel like you have made a New Friend. I hope all your relationships keep improving, and you experience wonderful romance. Know that I am always wishing you the Best of Life!!!!

To pursue inner peace has become more important than ever. Keep trying to bring a positive vibration. We have seen that our thoughts, words, and actions create our lives moment by moment, and if there is no action - there is no hope.

"WHAT GOOD IS MY VISION IF I DO NOT FOLLOW IT?"

Crazy Horse

In the seven years it has taken to write this book, we have traveled Full Circle from Oklahoma in 2014, to New Year's Day in Jamaica 2015, to New Year's Day in Columbia 2020, and back home to Oklahoma for 2021+. When I had to leave early from my planned retirement in Colombia, Brenda my hostess told me, "God must have an important Mission for you to call you back so soon." I hope this book is part of that Mission.

When can people accept the message of peace? If you want, you can choose at any moment to be happy, content, patient, and peaceful. We know that love comes from within, and we can cultivate that love.

At a time I was discouraged, my 83 year old Auntie asked me, "Has there ever been a time that God has let you down?"

I had to answer "No."

Besides wishing Blessings for you, I hope you have great relationships with heart-to-heart connections. Be sure to appreciate and enjoy the time you have. Of course, I am wishing you romance, and that this book brings sparkle to your relationships.

"Sparkle: to shine brightly with flashes of light; to be vivacious and witty; a glimmering flash of light; to be lively"

In closing, I have a New Message for you and for all your New Years that follow:

IT'S A TAKE IT EASY ATMOSPHERE
TO HAVE A HAPPY YEAR
DON'T BE LAZY
AND DON'T PROCRASTINATE

WORKS CITED

A Simple Plan. Dir. Sam Raimi. Paramount Pictures, 1993
"Akhenaten." National Geographic, May, 2017
Allen, James. As A Man Thinketh. Penguin Group, 1903
Arguelles, Jose. The Mayan Factor: Path Beyond Technology.
  Bear & Company, 1987
_ _ _. Time in the Technosphere: The Law of Time in Human
  Affairs. Bear & Company, 2002
Barn Burner Inc. barnburnerproducts.com
Bhattacharjee, Yudhijit. "Why We Lie."National Geographic, 2017
Body Heat. Dir. Lawrence Kasdan. Ladd, 1981
Brown, Dee. Bury My Heart at Wounded Knee: An Indian History
  of the American West. Sterling, 1970
Carson, Rachel. "Rachel Carson." American Experience.
  PBS, OETA, 2017
Castaneda, Carlos. The Active Side of Infinity. Harper, 1998
Chopra Deepak. The Seven Spiritual Laws of Success
  Amber-Allen, 1994
_ _ _. The Path of Love, Harmony, 1996
Chun, Wayne. Breath of Life. Link TV, 2017
Consumed, a documentary. Dir: Richard Heap, Slackjaw, 2011
Custer, Dan. The Miracle of Mind Power. Prentice Hall, 1960
Franz, Philomena. DW Focus on Europe, Link TV
Fromm, Eric. The Art of Loving. Harper, 1956
Furman, Joel. Dr. Furman's Immunity Solution. PBS OETA, 2017
Gibran, Kahlil. The Prophet. New York: Knopf, 1945
Global 3000. Link TV, 2018

Grant, Adam and Sheryl Sandberg. Option B: Facing Adversity, Building New York: Knopf, 2017

Hanscom, David. Back In Control: A Surgeon's Roadmap Out of Chronic Pain. Vertis, 2012

Harley, Jr. William F. His Needs, Her Needs. Revell, 1986

Hedges, Chris. On Contact. RTTV, 2018

Hendrix, Jimi. "Jimi Hendrix; Hear My Train a Comin'." American Masters, PBS OETA, 2013

Honda, Ken. Happy Money: The Japanese Art of Making Peace with Your Money. Simon, 2019

James, Jesse. In Depth with Graham Bensinger. ABC TV, 2015

Jamril, Dahr. The End of Ice. PirateTVSeattle. Link TV, 2019

Jenkins, John Major. The 2012 Story: The Myths, Fallacies, and Truth Behind the Most Intriging Date in History. TarcherPerigee, 2009

Kempton, Sally. "Meditation for the Love of It." Yoga Journal, 2018

King, Larry. Larry King NOW. RTTV, 2019

Kumaris, Brahma. Thought for Today. Brahma Kumaris Publications Lankard, Charlotte. The Daily Oklahoman, 2017

Lee, Bruce. Striking Thoughts: Wisdom for Daily Living. Tuttle, 2000

Little Big Man. Dir. Arthur Penn. Cinema Center Films, 1970

Lhundrup, Venerable Thubten. Practical Meditation with Buddhist Principles. Hinkler, 2006

Lennon, John and the Plastic Ono Band. "Give Peace A Chance." Live Peace in Toronto 1969. Apple, 1969

Linnell, Renee. The Burn Zone: A Memoir. Link TV, 2018

Loesser, Frank. "Baby, It's Cold Outside." Edwin H. Morris, 1944 and Jim Carlton. The Wall Street Journal, 12/13/2018

Love Fraud. True Crime Documentary Series. Showtime, 2020

Mankiller, Wilma. Mankiller. Red-Horse Native Productions, PBS, 2017

Marley, Bob. "Redemption Song." Uprising, Island Records, 1980

Marsalis, Wynton. "Dedicated to Chaos." On Jazz, PBS OETA, 2016

Masters, Roy. How Your Mind Can keep You Well: An Introduction to Stress Management. Foundation, 1976

Meana, Marta. Oprah Magazine, 2009

Mindfulness Goes Mainstream, WGBH. PBS OETA, 2017

Monroe, Marilyn. Marilyn: The Icon. British Film Institute, 2015

Nash, Graham. "Military Madness." Songs For Beginners, Atlantic, 1971

"Nicoya Peninsula, Costa Rica." Americas Now. Link TV, 2018

Osteen, Joel. CBS TV, 2018

Othello. By William Shakespeare

Patrick, Danica. Pretty Intense, Epix, 2017

Plutocracy V: Subterranean Fire. Link TV, 2019

Potter-Efron, Ronald. Healing the Angry Brain: How Understanding the Way Your Brain Works Can Help You Control Anger & Aggression. New York: MJF, 2012

Powerofpositivity.com. Self Help Community, Power of Positivity, 2009

Prabhupada, Srila. The Path of Perfection: Yoga for the Modern Age, Bhaktivedanta Book Trust, 1979

Presley, Elvis. Elvis in 1956. PBS OETA, 2017

Proverbs 1: 2-4. KJV. Zondervan, 1994 and Proverbs 14: 29. Proverbs 15: 1. NASV. Zondervan, 1995

Rizopoulos, Natasha. "Sutra 1.12, Patanjali. Practice Well, Embodying the Sutra." Yoga Journal, 2017

Robinson, Rachael. Jackie Robinson. PBS OETA, 2018

Rock, Chris. Good Hair. Dir. Jeff Stilson. HBO Films, 2009

Rossman, Martin. The Healing Mind. PBS OETA, 2018

Ruiz, Don Miguel and Janet Mills. The Four Agreements Companion Book: Using The Four Agreements To Master Your Life. Amber-Allen, 2000

Sadeghi, Habib. The Clarity Concept: 12 Steps to Finding Renewed Energy, Spiritual Fulfillment, and Emotional Healing. New York: Grand Central, 2017

Sandoz, Mari. Crazy Horse: the strange man of the Oglalas. New York: Knopf, 1942, reprinted 50th Anniversary Ed. Nebraska UP, 1992

Scheilder, Fabian. The End of the Megamachine: A Brief History of a Failing Civilization. Zero, 2020

Seattle, Chief of the Suquamish and Duwamish Tribes. Suquamish.nsn.us

Sheiner, Marcy, Sex for the Clueless: How to Enjoy a More Erotic and Exciting Life. Citadel, 2001

Smith, Ebony. "Yoga Transformed Me." Yoga Journal, 2019

Stella at 95. PBS OETA, 2012

Storm, Hyemeyohsts. Seven Arrows. New York: Ballantine, 1972

Thaden, Louise. Fly Girls: How Five Brave Women Defied All Odds and Made Aviation History, Keith O'Brien, Amazon, 2018

Thunberg, Greta. Fridays For Future: School Strike for Climate Change, Founded in Sweden, 2018
Thunder Hawk, Madonna. <u>Warrior Women</u>. PBS OETA, 2018
Tomaine, Gina. "Learning to Be Loved in Tulum." <u>Yoga Journal</u>, 2019
Underwood, Colton. <u>The Bachelor</u>. ABCTV, 2019
Webster's New World Basic Dictionary. New York: Houghton Mifflin, 1998
Williamson, Marianne. A Return to Love: Reflections on the Principles of A Course in Miracles. Harper, 1992
Wright, H. Norman. 101 Questions To Ask *Before* You Get Engaged, Harvest House, 2004
Yogananda. How To Be Happy All The Time, Crystal Clarity, 2006
Zinn, Howard. A People's History of the United States, Harper, 1980

Made in the USA
Middletown, DE
24 June 2023

33314417R00195